Gilmore Girls and the
Politics of Identity

Gilmore Girls and the Politics of Identity

Essays on Family and Feminism in the Television Series

Edited by
RITCH CALVIN

McFarland & Company, Inc., Publishers
Jefferson, North Carolina, and London

LIBRARY OF CONGRESS CATALOGUING-IN-PUBLICATION DATA

Gilmore girls and the politics of identity : essays on family and
feminism in the television series / Ritch Calvin.
p.   cm.
Includes bibliographical references and index.

ISBN 978-0-7864-3727-6
softcover : 50# alkaline paper ∞

1. Gilmore girls (Television program)   I. Calvin, Ritch, 1958–
PN1992.77.G54G55   2008
791.45'72 — dc22   2008012733

British Library cataloguing data are available

Cover photograph: Lauren Graham as Lorelai Gilmore, Alexis Bledel as
Rory Gilmore (Warner Bros./Photofest)

Manufactured in the United States of America

McFarland & Company, Inc., Publishers
Box 611, Jefferson, North Carolina 28640
www.mcfarlandpub.com

Acknowledgments

I would like to thank each and every contributor to this book. Without their essays, the book would not exist. The e-mail communications we have had have been enlivening and fruitful. Further, I appreciate that they have tolerated (with apparent patience and good grace) my endless stream of e-mails. Thank you, all.

I would like to thank Maureen Langdon-Shaiman and Mark Shaiman for their input in this volume. Our conversations have been enriching and enlightening. And their work on the manuscript has, without a doubt, made it better. Thank you, Maureen and Mark.

Finally, I would like to thank Saima Anjam for her lengthy conversations about this and other televisions shows and their relationship to feminism and for her comments on this manuscript. Thank you, Saima.

Table of Contents

Acknowledgments   v

Introduction — "Where You Lead": Gilmore Girls and the
  Politics of Identity
  Ritch Calvin   1

Welcome to Stars Hollow: *Gilmore Girls*, Utopia, and
  the Hyperreal
  Erin K. Johns and Kristin L. Smith   23

Rory Gilmore and Faux Feminism: An Ivy League Education
  and Intellectual Banter Does Not a Feminist Make
  Molly McCaffrey   35

Reinventing the Bitch: The Dynamicism of Paris Geller
  Angela Ridinger-Dotterman   50

Drats! Foiled Again: A Contrast in Definitions
  Anne K. Burke Erickson   63

Good Girls, Bad Girls, and Motorcycles: Negotiating Feminism
  Alicia Skipper   80

Got MILF? Losing Lorelai in Season Seven
  Tiffany Aldrich MacBain and Mita Mahato   96

Wheat Balls, Gravlax, Pop Tarts: Mothering and Power
  Melanie Haupt   114

Generation Gap? Mothers, Daughters, and Music
  Faye Woods   127

Like Mother-Daughter, Like Daughter-Mother: Constructs
  of Motherhood in Three Generations
  Stacia M. Fleegal   143

Gender Lies in Stars Hollow
    Brenda Boyle and Olivia Combe   159

Food Fights: Food and Its Consumption as a Narrative Device
    Lindsay Coleman   175

Still More Gilmore: How Internet Fan Communities
    Remediate *Gilmore Girls*
        Daniel Smith-Rowsey   193

Appendix: Episode Guide   205
Notes on Contributors   213
Character Index   217
General Index   219

Introduction —
"Where You Lead"
Gilmore Girls *and the Politics of Identity*

RITCH CALVIN

I begin this introduction in what has come to be an almost *de rigueur* manner: an autobiographical positioning or, if you prefer, a confessional. Nearly everyone who writes about television shows, or, more generally, popular culture, seems to feel the need to justify her or his analytical project and personal tastes. And, to be sure, I have often been questioned about, and felt the need to justify, my viewing of *Gilmore Girls*. But I am a fan of the show, though it wasn't always that way. I recall the promos leading into the first season of the series, and I recall thinking that it would be something worth investigating as a viewer and as a feminist scholar. When the "Pilot" (1.01) aired on 5 October, 2000, I was ready with my VCR and snacks. Oddly enough, though, I was not particularly overwhelmed by the first episode (even though I view it in retrospect as quite good). A few weeks passed, and I thought that, perhaps, I should give the series another chance, and from that moment I was hooked. It seemed to me that, as is so often the case with a television series, the writers and actors needed some time to get their legs, to find their way, and to hone their characters. In this, *Gilmore Girls* was fortunate that it wasn't yanked from the air before it had the time to develop as a series and to develop a fan base. The examples of shows that did not get such a chance are legion.[1]

But what did strike me in the very first episode was that it positioned itself, or more precisely, at least some of the characters positioned themselves, as feminist. In the "Pilot" (1.01), Rory explains to Dean that she is named Lorelai, the same as her mother, because "She named me after herself. She was lying in the hospital thinking about how men name boys after themselves all the time, you know, so why couldn't women? She says her feminism just kind of took over." To be sure, the f-word isn't used again until the seventh season, but it seemed so rare that a TV character would use the word "feminism" without derision or that a series premise would be so fundamentally feminist. So, despite being a fan, and despite the appeal of a series that has feminist potential, I try to remain a critical observer.

It has also struck me that so little attention has been paid to the show within academic circles. Other shows that have been posited as feminist (or progressive) in one way or another have garnered quite a lot of attention, from *Sex and the City*, to *Xena, the Warrior Princess*, to *Buffy the Vampire Slayer*. Indeed, cottage industries have grown up around them. In part, they have drawn more attention because they were more popular, drawing a larger audience and developing larger fan communities. Nevertheless, *Gilmore Girls* has drawn quite well over the seven years of its run, and has developed a devoted and diverse fan base. During its first season, it drew an average Nielsen rating of 3.56 (which means approximately 3.9 million viewers per episode), which increased to 4.4 during the second season. In the fourth year, when Lorelai and Luke were together as a couple, the figure rose to 4.8. While these pale in comparison to *American Idol* (which is often airing in the same time slot and registers a Nielsen rating of 30 or more), it has been sufficient to keep it on the air for seven seasons and to build a devoted following. As a sign of its appeal, as of this writing in 2007, the series has approximately 94 websites, including *Gilmore Girls* (www.gilmoregirls.org), Gilmore Guide (www.gilmoreguide.org), Luminary: An All Gilmore Guide, and Gilmore Girl Fan (in Dutch). And, as Daniel Smith-Rowsey examines in his essay, *Gilmore Girls*, like so many other series, has spawned an ever-growing body of fan-generated fiction. Finally, in response to the call for papers for the present volume, I received submissions from Australia, Brazil, England, Slovenia, and the U.S., an indicator of the show's transcultural appeal.[2]

Another reason for the lack of attention might be the fact that critics haven't quite known where to place the show, or how to respond to its own version of other-worldliness. Shows like *Xena* and *Buffy* both fell squarely, and comfortably, within the inherited parameters of a fantasy show. We as viewers are quite familiar with the conventions of the sword and sorcery tale, and although *Xena* does challenge and update some of those conventions, the inherited structure remains familiar. In addition, we also know the vampire narrative, and setting a series like *Buffy* in contemporary times in a high school serves to update the narrative, but does not render it unintelligible. But the other-worldliness of the *Gilmore Girls* is of a different kind. Ostensibly, the show is set in the small Connecticut town of Stars Hollow. Though the consistent spectacle of color and the festivities of excess serve to render the small town otherworldly, it does not fit easily into the traditional conventions of fantasy.

One of the first questions that generally has to be raised, and then answered, in a volume about a television series is: why should an academic volume be dedicated to this particular series? Although certain segments of academia, and certain academics, still contend that popular culture in general, and television in particular, is beneath scrutiny, I think that a significant portion of the academic world understands and believes that television is not only a worthy field of inquiry, but a necessary one at that. The arguments for television as an object of study have been rehearsed in countless books and articles, and I resist repeating them here. After all, television is the entertainment of the masses, just as storytellers, plays, and serialized fiction were in the past; it is not only in retrospect that it gets "elevated" to relevance.

But the argument for or against a particular television series is something of a different question. On the one hand, one can argue that literary or cultural analyses can be applied to any "text," including any television series, and reveal elements of narrative structure, social tendencies and values, gender norms, and so on. Do some series, however, have more depth and richness to them? Are some texts more worthy of analysis than others? And if they are, what are the criteria for such an evaluation? A survey of the shelves of a good local bookstore or a university library might reveal that a great deal of time and energy has been spent upon the analysis of certain television series such as *Buffy the Vampire Slayer*, *Angel*, and *Xena the Warrior Princess*. From that one might, quite erroneously, conclude that fantasy has moved into the forefront of both public and academic consciousness. But one does wonder what it is about those particular series that has rendered them amenable to analytical inquiry. However, other, more contemporaneously grounded and (perhaps) less fantastical series such as *Seinfeld*, *The West Wing*, and *Sex and the City* have also engendered a great deal of academic attention. And then there is *The Simpsons*.

For one, *Buffy*, *Angel*, and *Xena* all operate, as science fiction and fantasy does, by creating a discursive space apart from the familiar, in order to turn the lens back upon the quotidian. By confronting the strange, the Other, we as viewers are better able to see our own pre-conceptions and practices, and reevaluate and perhaps undermine them in the process. Such an argument is not far from Judith Butler's notion that masculinity is most made visible in drag. In other words, these three shows, even though they seem to be grounded in a different reality, actually have a great deal to say about gender norms and sexuality within our own everyday lived experience, and they say it in ways that resonate with viewers. *Seinfeld*, *West Wing*, and *Sex and the City*, on the other hand, also have a great deal to say about contemporary social and political norms, but they do so by representing them within a familiar, real-world narrative framework, and within this familiar framework, they examine, either directly or indirectly, our interpersonal relationships and the politics of identity. Jerry, George, Elaine, and Kramer frequently discuss the appropriate time to wait before breaking up with someone, whether or not someone fakes an orgasm, the proper amount of time to keep a greeting card, the responsibility (and preference) for birth control options, the propriety of discussing some-one's racial background, and so on. Similarly, Carrie, Samantha, Charlotte, and Miranda openly and freely question norms and practices, undermine (and rein-force) received notions of behavior, decorum, dress, sexuality, and language. And while these aspects of these series resonate with viewers, so too do they resonate with critics who tend to look for disruptions, disjunctions, and diver-gences. And I would suggest that that is why a series such as, say, *Friends*, which was also enormously popular, has not garnered the same critical attention as *Buffy* and *Sex*.

So, does commercial and popular success equate academic attention and critique-worthiness? If so, that would seem rather odd, since academia and academics so often seem to position themselves against, or as critical of, com-mercial trends. On the other hand, if one is arguing for the effects of a partic-ular series upon its viewers, then having a large viewership might suggest a larger effect, socially. Perhaps more significantly, as Jes Battis points out in his volume on *Buffy*, the line between critic and consumer has been erased (10). According to Battis, those academics who write about *Buffy* tend to be fans of the show. While I believe this to be true (and I know that it often holds true in the case of the present volume), I do not believe this to be an entirely new phenomenon. For example, I can readily recall my undergraduate days and my college professors and their excitement at teaching the texts and authors they love. Is a Joyce scholar a Joyce scholar because it constitutes a career move, because Joyce left behind a significant body of work, or because he or she loves reading Joyce? The decision is probably the result of some combination of all three elements; however, the decision arguably begins with the latter. As another example, in early 2007, a scholar appeared on NPR's *Talk of the Nation* argu-ing, in part out of his love for Shakespeare's language, that we all try to incor-porate examples of Shakespeare's work in our everyday speech ("Would Life Be Better"). And yes, *Buffy* scholars tend to consume the residua of the series: the DVDs, t-shirts, books and journals, and conferences, but so, too, do Joyce scholars. Just check the bookshelves in their offices.

Why, then, a volume on *Gilmore Girls*? What makes it critique-worthy? As Bonnie Dow suggests in her book, *Prime-Time Feminism*, texts or shows must always be read within the historical context of their production and recep-tion. According to her, if television is a product of a historical moment, if tel-evision responds to and reflects current cultural, political, and ideological beliefs and practices, if television is a negotiation between hegemonic and counter-discourses, it must then include and negotiate constantly shifting con-structions such as "woman," "femininity," "motherhood," and "family," among others (16–22). As several of the essays herein will attest, *Gilmore Girls* emerged at a particular historical moment and, as such, it reflects and illustrates many contemporary social developments — though it also avoids or elides a number of other significant contemporary social issues. As with so many other series within television history, *Gilmore Girls* has a particular take on interpersonal relationships as they function in the initial years of the 21st century, and it has a particular perspective on the formulation of personal identity. And while the relationships on *Gilmore Girls* do not represent every possibility, they do illustrate certain possibilities, some of which have not been much explored to date in prime-time television, including the possibilities of romantic, platonic, cross-cultural, cross-generational, and familial relationships and some of the configurations that have emerged in the 2000s. According to creator/writer/producer Amy Sherman-Palladino, she created the characters for the series for two primary reasons: to represent a mother and daughter that were more like friends than mother-daughter, and to represent a young female in contemporary society who was focused on her studies and career, a bit naïve, and not sexually active.

> What to me had not been done was a girl who wasn't fucking around at 14. A girl who was not interested in boys, not because of an aversion to boys, but who just was academically goal-oriented and really that's what made her tick. And a girl who was very comfortable in her skin. Didn't need to be popular, wasn't popular, and didn't care. Didn't look longingly at the group over by the soda fountain with the good shoes. Because she had her best friend, her mom, and she had her other friends, and she had her life [LaTempa].

And:

> I thought it would be fun to write about a mom and daughter who were pals instead of just a mother-daughter relationship.... I also wanted to put this style teen on TV. Sexually innocent teens are not represented. I thought it would be interesting, especially with a mother who was more sexually aware than she was at that age [Bird].

Both of these formulations exist within contemporary society, but neither can be found with any frequency within mainstream cultural representations.

Apart from the representation of (under)represented individuals, the television landscape has been littered with representations of the family, some of which have been idealized and perfectly functional and some of which have been demonized and completely dysfunctional: from the idyllic families of 1950s sitcoms, to the extended families of *The Waltons*, to the melded families of *The Brady Bunch* and *Reba*, to the non-genetic families of *Buffy* and *Girlfriends*. Like much of the television universe before it, *Gilmore Girls* takes the family as a central organizing focus. The central relationship of the series focuses on the relationship between Lorelai Gilmore (Lauren Graham) and Rory Gilmore (Alexis Bledel). The ads and the setup for the series lead us to believe that it is a relationship unlike any other mother-daughter relationship in TV history. In fact, they operate, at times, less like mother-daughter and more like sisters. Bonnie Dow, however, notes that the series *One Day at a Time* began this process of breaking down the mother-daughter divide, as Ann Romano often interacted with and talked to her daughters as though they were peers, and without playing the "mom" card, and that this strategy was consistent with a particular moment within feminism that sought to undermine traditional hierarchical structures, including familial relations (70). But as Faye Woods argues in this volume, the representation of the collapse of the generational divide in *Gilmore Girls* appears at a historical moment when mothers are, in fact, behaving more and more like friends or siblings. Sherman-Palladino asserts that the Lorelai-Rory relationship is at the heart of the series; however, that fact is quickly undermined. Although Lorelai and Rory believe that they have an openness and honesty between them, and while they believe that they can talk to each other about anything, including relationships and sex, we find that, from the very first episode, they are every bit as unable to talk about these issues as any other mother and daughter. Despite the fact that they are close, despite the fact that they share so many activities, despite the fact that they share so many tastes and proclivities, they are at times unable to bridge that gap. In this sense, *Gilmore Girls* illustrates, in both Lorelai and Rory, the ways in which identity is formulated and established both with and against that which is around us.

But while the Lorelai-Rory relationship is central to the series, it is not the only family and not the only familial model. As several of the essays in this volume argue, the Gilmore family offers several models including the matriarch (in the form of the original Lorelai, Richard's mother), the traditional patriarch and his faithful wife (Richard and Emily), and the mother and daughter as companions. But *Gilmore Girls* offers a number of other possible familial arrangements, including the fairly "traditional" Sookie St. James–Jackson Belleville relationship. Although Sookie originally pursues the relationship, she is a brilliant chef, which raises her work and status. In addition, Jackson works out of doors and, at one point, serves a head town politician. Nevertheless, despite all these very traditional arrangements, they also offer a model wherein both parents are dedicated and committed to their work, and both appear to be equally involved in domestic labors and raising the children. The Kim household, on the other hand, offers still another model, one in which the father is entirely absent. Whereas the "absent" character often fulfills a comic function, such as the absent Vera on *Cheers* or Maris on *Frasier*, the absent father in the Kim household illustrates a strong matriarch who has no (apparent) need for male support despite Mrs. Kim's otherwise very traditional religious-based mores. On the other hand, Luke Danes becomes a single "father" after his sister, Liz, dumps her son, Jess, in his lap, and then becomes a father when he discovers his twelve-year-old daughter, April, after she tracks him down while completing a science experiment. While Luke initially functions as a male loner figure, over the last six seasons, he undergoes a transformation and becomes a dedicated father and a model for the possibilities of male single-parenthood and an argument surrounding male parental rights. Through his experiences with Rory, Jess, and April, Luke offers an example of, and reflects the shifting social attitudes surrounding, men and their investment in nurturing and parenting.

As a Women's Studies professor and a feminist, I find one of the most remarkable aspects about *Gilmore Girls* is the fact that it focuses on female characters. Of course, throughout the history of broadcast television within the U.S., many shows have either featured a primary female character or, even closer to the case at hand, been constructed around an ensemble of women. Historically, female-lead series have included: *Ally McBeal* (1997–2002), *Alice* (1976–1985), *Blossom* (1990–1995), *The Bonnie Hunt Show* (1995–1996), *Buffy, the Vampire Slayer* (1997–2003), *Cagney and Lacey* (1982–1988), *The Carol Burnett Show* (1960; 1967–1978; 1991), *Caroline in the City* (1995–1999), *Cybill* (1995–1998), *The Debbie Reynolds Show* (1969–1970), *The Donna Reed Show* (1958–1966), *The Doris Day Show* (1968–1973), *Dr. Quinn, Medicine Woman* (1993–1998), *Ellen* (1994–1998), *Eve* (2003–2006), *Fay* (1975–1976), *Felicity* (1998–2002), *Frannie's Turn* (1992), *The Geena Davis Show* (2000–2001), *Gidget* (1965–1966), *Hazel* (1961–1966), *Hope and Faith* (2003–2006), *I Love Lucy* (1951–1957) *Jenny* (1997), *The Julie Andrews Hour* (1972–1973), *Laverne and Shirley* (1976–1983), *The Leslie Uggams Show* (1969), *The Lucy Show* (1962–1968), *Mary Tyler Moore* (1970–1977), *Maude* (1972–1978), *Moesha* (1996–2001), *Murphy Brown* (1988–1998), *The New Adventures of Old Christine* (2006–), *The Patty Duke Show* (1963–1966), *The Paula Poundstone Show* (1993), *Phyllis* (1975–1977), *Reba* (2001–2007), *Rhoda* (1974–1978), *Roseanne* (1988–1997), *Sabrina, the Teenage Witch* (1996–2003), *The Sandy Duncan Show* (1972), *Suddenly Susan* (1996–2000), *The Tracey Ullman Show* (1987–1990), *Veronica Mars* (2004–2007), and *Xena, Warrior Princess* (1995–2001).

Many of these have been variety shows that tell us less about the representation of women, the relationships among women, and the social and political issues of everyday lived experiences than do scripted sitcoms, dramas, and dramedies. Nevertheless, in looking back through the history of broadcast television in the U.S., we see that the heyday of female-lead series was in the 50s and 60s. From the titles alone, it would appear that nearly half the shows being broadcast in any one given year were female-lead, but the number of female-lead shows dropped markedly in the 1980s. Although some shows with strong, female lead characters (*Roseanne* and *Murphy Brown*, for example), emerged from the 1980s, the number of women featured dropped, a reflection of the broader cultural politics of the 80s, including the backlash against gains made by women in the economic, political, and cultural arenas. And to be sure, shows that have not featured a lead female character have had a great deal to say about women's everyday lived experience and the shifts in social, political, and cultural practices. But the fact that so few shows, as of this writing in 2007, center upon a titular female character represents a significant cultural shift.[3] Aniko Bodroghkozy, in an essay lamenting the decline of feminism and feminists in prime-time TV, suggests that "for the past 30 years, successful TV programs that grappled with gender issues had to, at some level, acknowledge the existence of a feminist revolution in gender relations. In our post–9/11 world of anxiety over terrorism and threats from out there, are we turning homeward for the imagined safety and stability of a domestic realm characterized by rigidly defined gender roles?"

None of this is to suggest that only programs that have a female title character or are female-led can have anything to say about women and women's lives. Certainly, a television show such as *Everybody Loves Raymond*, which ran concurrently with *Gilmore Girls*, has a great deal to say about women, their lives, and, in particular, their relations with men. Marie and Debra Barone represent two generations of women who are full-time, stay-at-home wives and mothers. And while the stay-at-home mother was once a staple in mainstream television, that figure is something of a rarity by the year 2000. Both Marie and Debra live with men who operate within traditional gender models, and *Everybody* often examines, and sometimes, challenges, those received norms. Nevertheless, these women's lives are examined through the lens of the men around them. Dramas such as *Law & Order* and *CSI:* are filled with female characters, and they offer viewers examples of women who are intelligent and successful, though they nearly always conform to cultural standards of beauty and are highly sexualized. While these shows offer representations of women who have careers, they focus on the case at hand and tend to avoid both personal relationships and examinations of the effects of gender in the workplace. On the other hand, a program such as *Ugly Betty*, centered upon a female character, represents not only her relations with men, but also her constant negotiations of gender, sexuality, and particularly, standards of beauty.

Apart from those programs that have featured female title characters, a smaller number have been built around a female cast and, to varying degrees, lived in the world of women: *Designing Women* (1986–1993), *Desperate Housewives* (2004–), *Girlfriends* (2000–), *Golden Girls* (1985–1992), *Sex and the City* (1998–2004), and *Sisters* (1991–1996).[4] These shows are built around a female cast, and although men do appear in them, they are always outnumbered. *Designing Women* and *Girlfriends*, for example, both feature one male character in the opening credits. While male characters do appear, the shows are set in the world of women and focus on women's issues. And in the absence of men, the women in these series are able to deal with issues that might not be possible in other heterogeneous settings. Furthermore, these female ensembles multiply the appeal for female viewers. As Dow suggests, a female cast — rather than single, feminist figures such as Mary Richards or Maude — makes it more likely that women will identify with the ideological meaning of the show because they have "multiple opportunities for character identification" (118). In the case of *Gilmore Girls*, then, presenting three primary female leads (Emily, Lorelai, and Rory) and a number of secondary female characters (Sookie, Lane, and

Paris), of different social backgrounds, of different educational backgrounds, of different ages, allows for greater viewer identification and greater viewer participation in the negotiation of ideological differences.[5]

Apart from the narrative conceits and the characterizations, one of the elements that renders *Gilmore Girls* as a rich text for analysis is its intertextuality. For example, *The Simpsons* has been popular, with both viewers and critics, for a number of reasons, and one of those reasons is the intertexuality of the episodes. The writers of *The Simpsons* weave into their dialogues and plotlines as many references and allusions as possible. The interplay of other television shows, politics, current events, history, and other forms of cultural production make for a rich, multi-layered text that lends itself to literary or textual analysis. Although the number of references and allusions in any one episode of *Gilmore Girls* may not equal that of any one episode of *The Simpsons*, it is, nevertheless, richly multi-layered, or "polyvalent" (Condit qtd. in Dow). Amy Sherman-Palladino and the cast of other writers work numerous overt and oblique references into the characters' dialogue and plot lines. And, indeed, one of the popular appeals of the series is to trace the references and "Gilmorisms." As with *The Simpsons*, fans actively participate in unraveling these allusions, and it is one of the ways in which such an interactive viewing experience captivates an audience. But the allusions are not gratuitous. Indeed, as Erin Johns and Kristin Smith demonstrate, these references, the kinds of references, their sources, and their strategic deployment all contribute to the development of character and the furtherance of a particular worldview. They help signify and separate characters (and perhaps affect viewer identification) by class, by educational background, and by age.

Perhaps even more important to the show's appeal than the intertextuality is the way in which it focuses on two women who are more focused on careers than on relationships with men.[6] Granted, as the show progressed, one of the complaints from viewers and critics was that it had begun to focus too much on relationships. In other words, it had gotten away from its original focus. But one of the advantages of writing about a complete series is that we can see the grand arc of the narrative, the final outcome, and see who is left standing on the stage at the end of the play. From the series' conclusion, one might argue that it returns to that original theme and demonstrates that these two women, especially Rory, remain committed to their visions of life and career. In addition, I would argue (contrary to MacBain and Mahato) that the ambiguity in the finale also signals a return to the series' original premise for Lorelai, as well. While viewers have strong opinions on whether or not Lorelai and Luke are reunited romantically, the textual evidence remains ambiguous. Despite the fact that Lorelai and Luke kiss romantically, despite the fact that Lorelai is wearing the necklace that Luke bought for her, in the final scene, he remains waiting in the background. In this scene Lorelai's relationship with Luke is secondary to the primacy of Lorelai's relationship with Rory.

Furthermore, very few shows in history, and indeed, very few characters within shows, have ever posited themselves as openly, overtly feminist. As Bonnie Dow argues in *Prime-Time Feminism*, some shows have functioned as feminist by opening doors for women, by subverting traditional paradigms, and so on. According to her, *The Mary Tyler Moore Show* operated as the first explicitly feminist show, with Mary Richards as the first prime-time feminist. But one of the interesting aspects of that show, according to Dow, was the way in which the character of Mary Richards served to mediate and soften the cultural discourse of the time. The late 1960s and early 1970s in the U.S. was a moment in time when, although feminists were transforming political and social practices, they were often perceived as threats. While "moderate" feminists such as Gloria Steinem were palatable, more "radical" feminists such as Ti-Grace Atkinson were not. So, while Mary Richards did serve to represent feminist concerns about marriage, relationships, work-place politics, and women's earning potential among others, Richards was able to do so in a non-threatening manner. And it is for this reason that Dow argues that more overtly feminist shows such as *Maude* were less successful. Maude was, in many ways, the anti–Mary Richards, who was able to personify many of the contemporaneous feminist issues and render them less threatening to a mainstream audience (24–61).

What defines a feminist show, for Dow and for me, is rooted in the history of the expression, "the personal is political." Although the sociologist C. Wright Mills articulated the ideas behind the expression, namely that personal conditions and political conditions intersect, he did not employ the exact phrase. The origin of the expression is commonly attributed to Carol Hanisch, who used it in an essay in 1969, entitled "The Personal Is Political." For her, and for the civil rights and women's rights activists who used the expression in the 60s and 70s, it meant that an individual's oppression and marginalization were not necessarily the result of individual choices or circumstances, but rather, effects of social and political institutions that create and perpetuate inequalities. In other words, "the experiences, feelings, and possibilities of our personal lives were not just a matter of personal preferences and choices but were limited, molded, and defined by the broader political and social setting" (Z Staff).

So, apart from being one of the first working women on television who did not see work as a prelude to marriage, apart from being one of the first single, independent women in prime time, Mary Richards is (arguably) a feminist character because she rejects the traditional feminine role as doctor's wife and enters a work space that is clearly coded as masculine. Whenever Mary Richards encounters obstacles and inequalities—and she frequently does— these inequalities are not functions of her own character flaws or because of her own choices; they are clearly a consequence of "broader political and social" conditions. For example, she is paid less money as a producer than are her male counterparts, and this inequality becomes the storyline.

After *The Mary Tyler Moore Show*, Dow argues that *One Day at a Time* was the most overtly feminist show on prime-time TV. She argues that it raises complex feminist issues, as did *The Mary Tyler Moore Show*, but it usually dissolves them by reducing them to the individual psychology of one of the characters instead of being the effects of social injustice. In this, *One Day at a Time* reflects a shift in broader cultural attitudes and in the usage of the expression "the personal is political." Over time, the accepted meaning and usage of the expression shifted to an argument that "the choices we make personally have political implications" and that "all the choices we make, even the ones that seem totally apolitical and personal, have political implications. The choice to wear make-up or not, to watch TV or not, to eat this or that or not, to wear this or that item of clothing, to use a bank or not...is personal, but it is also political" (Z Staff). The end effect of this is that, while the original usage of the expression meant that, in order to effect change, we had to examine and transform political institutions and practices, in the latter usage, it means we need to examine our own personal choices in order to effect any change.

In *One Day at a Time*, Ann Romano sets out on her own for reasons similar to Mary Richards'; she feels as though she's being controlled, limited, and infantilized by her husband. Just as Mary Richards pushes the boundaries of what kinds of women could be represented in prime time, so, too, does Ann Romano, because, prior to her, representing a (unrepentant) divorcée was taboo. Furthermore, Ann Romano is more liberated and independent than Mary Richards; she takes back her maiden name and uses "Ms." as her title (Dow 61). But, while Ann is often overtly feminist in her stance, and while she often raises complex feminist issues, they are just as often reduced to personal issues. For example, the fact that her husband wants to cut back on child support payments so that his new wife, whom he supports in lavish style, will not leave him is "resolved" by getting him to talk to his new wife, because she will understand and stay with him. In other words, the broader social issues of husbands turning to younger women, of divorced women (and their children) living in near-poverty, of the numbers of husbands and fathers who do not pay adequate support to their children are all unexamined; instead, it is a personal matter between two individuals.

However, the history and use of the term "postfeminism" is both complex and contested. As Lisa Yaszek traces in her online essay, "I'll Be Postfeminist in a Postpatriarchy," the "origin stories" for the term are varied, placing its initial use anywhere from 1920 to the mid–1970s. Furthermore, the ways in which the term gets used varies, as well. While the very first use was to suggest that, following the ratification of the 19th Amendment, the work of feminism was finished and we had entered a postfeminist era. According to Yaszek, later uses tried to reconcile "the binary between equality-based or 'liberal' feminism and difference-based or 'radical' feminism." In the field of feminist media studies, however, Yaszek notes that conservative, media-generated visions of postfeminism are guided by the implicit (and sometimes explicit) assumption that women *can't* have it all, that they must chose between: feminism and femininity (Moseley and Read 231); workplace and family (Probyn 147); protest against patriarchy and participation in romance and marriage (Samuelian 46); "crazy" collective political action and "more balanced" individual solutions (Press 11). In essence, then, conservative media postfeminism offers its viewers a depoliticized notion of choice that ultimately reinforces a patri-archal and capitalist status quo.

According to Dow, since *The Mary Tyler Moore Show* and *One Day at a Time*, a number of postfeminist series or characters have appeared on the small screen. Dow examines *Designing Women, Murphy Brown*, and *Dr. Quinn, Medicine Woman* in detail, but she concludes that they all, in differing ways, reflect a "depoliticized" postfeminist ideology that begins with the shift in "the personal is political" as evidenced through *One Day at a Time*. More recently, shows such as *Buffy* and *Commander in Chief* openly espouse a feminist politics (though, in the case of *Commander in Chief*, that fact probably led to the defeat of Mac in the election and the end of the very brief run for the series). Other shows, such as *Everwood*, have featured a feminist (or Women's Studies major), though this political consciousness emerges more fully near the end of the series, and it is not an integral aspect of the series.

Gilmore Girls, on the other hand, positions itself from the very first episode as feminist. When Rory Gilmore meets the new boy in town, Dean Forester, and introduces herself, she explains that her mother named her daughter after herself, just as men often do, because her feminism "took over" (1.01, "Pilot"). Furthermore, from the show's inception, Lorelai is more interested in running the Independence Inn (the site of her personal independence and escape from her parents' house) than she is in romantic relationships. But, working at the Independence Inn for someone else does not satisfy Lorelai; she seeks further independence and autonomy through establishing her own business, the Dragonfly Inn. Similarly, Rory has always been a studious individual, focused, from a very young age, on getting into Harvard and becoming a world-traveling journalist like Christiane Amanpour, whom she finally meets in the series finale (7.22, "Bon Voyage"). But while the show sets itself up as feminist, whether or not it succeeds on those grounds—or what kind of feminism it espouses—is open to debate, as the essays by Molly McCaffrey and Alicia Skipper demonstrate. Nevertheless, Lorelai's ability to succeed, to become independent, to support herself and her child as a single mother are, in part, the legacy of second-wave feminism. To be certain, she had a surrogate family as a support system, and to be certain, she had a real family that she could, when circumstances dictate, turn to—two safety nets that most single mothers do not have. In this sense, the setting and plotlines are removed from the "real world." In addition, Lorelai's predicament is the consequence of her own personal actions and choices (to have the baby, to not get married, to reject the financial support of her parents, to work in the service industry) and not the consequences of larger social and political inequalities. Certainly, many of her frustrations stem from her parents, who, in many ways, signify the old, patriarchal order. Furthermore, Rory's educational opportunities, her career aspirations, and her ability to pursue both professional and romantic interests are also legacies of feminism, but these are once again personal choices that are never challenged or thwarted by any forces outside her own foibles. Read in this manner, then, and considering the history of the way in which television shows reflect and mediate (some of) the dominant ideologies, *Gilmore Girls* fits within the model of "postfeminist" shows such as *One Day at a Time* and *Murphy Brown*.

Gilmore Girls

The series opening, which premiered on October 5, 2000, ostensibly features the two Gilmore Girls, Lorelai (32) and her daughter Rory (16). The cast that surrounds them, though, is large and important to the development of both the show and Lorelai and Rory. In the first episode (1.01, "Pilot"), we find Lorelai and Rory Gilmore living in the magical, other-worldly Connecticut town of Stars Hollow, population 9,973 (McLoone). Sherman-Palladino contends that she was inspired when she and her husband visited Washington Depot, Connecticut and found a "ridiculously Norman Rockwell" town in which people were asking "Where's the pumpkin patch?" (Pfefferman), and its quaintness and charm became the foundation for the fictional Stars Hollow. In this fictional Connecticut, Lorelai had grown up in nearby Hartford, where she was the rich, pampered, and unruly daughter of Richard and Emily Gilmore. Despite their plans for her future — her education, her grooming, and her training — she became pregnant at age sixteen. Instead of marrying, as her parents and her boyfriend, Christopher, wanted, she ran away, determined to raise her daughter on her own terms. In this sense, her actions mirror those of Mary Richards, who rejected a marriage proposal from a doctor, and Ann Romano, who walked out on a marriage because she felt she was being treated like a child and lacked the ability to stand on her own. But since *Gilmore Girls* appeared at a significantly different moment in time, their (the show's and the characters') possibilities are more varied.

As the series opens, Rory is now sixteen, the same age as her mother when she got pregnant. But Lorelai maintains that Rory has had a very different upbringing than did Lorelai, and she comments that Rory is a "good girl" (an assertion examined by Anne Burke Erickson herein). After a nearly sixteen-year estrangement from her parents, Lorelai finds herself compelled to return to her parents to ask for money when she discovers that she cannot afford to pay the tuition to the elite prep school into which Rory has been accepted. Since both Lorelai and Rory have been fixated on Rory's education and entrance into Harvard, they both believe that Chilton is her only hope of acceptance into Harvard. This, then, is the narrative conceit that brings Lorelai back into her parents' lives and sets up the conflicts between the elder and younger Gilmore families. The elder Gilmore family (in the persons of Richard, Emily, and the family matriarch, Lorelai) represents stability, decorum, civility, haute couture, old money, and conservative politics (both personal and political). The younger Gilmore family (in the persons of Lorelai and Rory) represents the personal freedoms available in the flight from the old, conservative cultural values, including irreverence, trendy clothing, popular culture, fast food, and liberal politics (personal and political). This, then, on the surface level, is the primary narrative strategy and the primary source of conflicting ideologies.[7] For Emily Gilmore, her identity resides in very traditional, received notions of both class and gender, and when both her daughter and her granddaughter overtly challenge those foundational beliefs, Emily either lashes out or, in rare human moments, sees the possibilities of alternative modes of being. But, in some ways, Lorelai Gilmore is every bit as rigid in her rejection of those very same foundational identities. She has rejected the class and gender identities of her mother, and is determined to keep her daughter from stepping into them, as well.

But this, I think, is how and why *Gilmore Girls* makes for such a rich text to examine. It offers overt and covert challenges to received cultural norms and practices; it aligns itself with contemporary cultural ideologies in all (or, some of) their heterogeneity; and it offers the ambiguity and ambivalence of living in and through such a moment in time. All of these characters, with the possible exception of the family matriarch, go through periods, or moments, of doubt and of transformation. While Lorelai has been so certain and so determined to reject all of the old-money, elitist practices of her parents, and she is so certain that her daughter would also willingly and unequivocally reject them, she is stunned when she finds that her daughter not only partakes of them, but enjoys them on some level. While Rory can, on the one hand, engage with her mother in a witty deconstruction of 1950s gender roles while watching an episode of *The Donna Reed Show*, she also finds pleasure in donning the Donna Reed uniform and catering to her boyfriend (1.14, "That Damn Donna Reed"). While Emily Gilmore seems so certain in the ways and customs of elite society, she is able, at times, to see the possibilities that her daughter has experienced and that she never will (7.15, "I'm a Kayak, Hear Me Roar").

While the trajectory of the series seems to be built around the idea of getting Rory through prep school, into Harvard, and out into the field next to Christiane Amanpour, what actually happens is more about the everyday lived experiences of the Gilmore Girls and their friends and family, and their struggles to define themselves—in relation to the elder Gilmores, to each other, and to the culture ("high" and "low") in which they find themselves immersed. And this, I would argue, is the secondary narrative strategy and the source of additional conflict. Because Lorelai had made a conscious decision to, largely, hold her romantic life in abeyance while she raised Rory, at the series opening, we find that task largely completed, and so Lorelai begins to delve more and more into her romantic life. We see her enter (and leave) a series of relationships, with Max Medina, Jason "Digger" Stiles, Luke Danes, and Christopher Hayden. And, of course, Rory is now at that same dangerous age when her own mother got pregnant, and Rory's interest in boys also emerges in the "Pilot" when Dean, the lonesome, dangerous, and attractive stranger appears in town. Rory also negotiates a series of boyfriends, including Dean Forester, Jess Mariano, and Logan Huntzberger. So while Emily, predictably, disagrees with both Lorelai and Rory's choices of romantic partners (with exceptions), and schemes to make her own wishes come true, Lorelai and Rory themselves struggle with resolving the apparent conflicts between their ideological perspectives and their romantic inclinations (see essays by Brenda Boyle and Olivia Combe and by Tiffany Aldrich MacBain and Mita Mahato).

But after a series of relationships (personal, romantic, and professional), after her experiences as editor of the *Yale Daily News*, Rory discovers that, although the foundation of her identity has been laid, and although she has experienced the allure and benefits of an upper-middle-class lifestyle, she rejects the marriage proposal by her wealthy suitor, Logan Huntzberger, because she has now, at the series' finale, discovered her sense of self and her purpose. As she prepares to leave the comfort of her mother's home, of Stars Hollow, and of the safety net that her extended family has created, she tells her mother, "Mom, you've already given me everything I need" (7.22, "Bon Voyage").

Criticism(s)

The criticisms raised against the show are several. One of the primary concerns is that the show, the storylines, and the characters are too precious; critics do not accept that people like this exist, and because of this apparent disconnect, they cannot engage in a willful suspension of their disbelief. I would argue that this criticism stems directly from the question of verisimilitude and realism. And, for me, this question always takes me directly back to George Eliot. In the 17th chapter of her novel *Adam Bede*, entitled "In Which the Story Pauses a Little," Eliot considers the notion of realism and the relation of the text to some real, external world: "Certainly I could, if I held it the highest vocation of the novelist to represent things as they never have been and never will be. Then, of course, I might refashion life and character entirely after my own liking... . But it happens, on the contrary, that my strongest effort is to avoid any such arbitrary picture, and to give a faithful account of men and things as they have mirrored themselves in my mind" (165).

Here, we see Eliot making the argument that fiction, fictional worlds, should be perfect reflections of the world around them (or around the author). The notion, of course, has been roundly and repeatedly dismissed (and, it must be said, persistently championed). Nevertheless, we see today in television and film a desire to "keep it real," to represent a gritty reality, to represent the possible horrors of life in the city, life on the streets. Television shows like *Oz*, *The West Wing*, *Law & Order* (all three), *CSI:* (all three), and *The Sopranos* are lauded for their "realistic" portrayals of contemporary life. However, when critics and viewers talk about "realistic," these assertions seem to stand in for "vulgar," or "brutal," or "violent." The problem, of course, is that, while some of contemporary life is brutal and vulgar, not all of it is. There are other modes of being, and some of them are found, for example, in the small New England towns visited by Amy Sherman-Palladino and Daniel Palladino. Secondly, these television series no more hold a mirror up to the world than does *The Wizard of Oz* or *Matlock*. The narrative contrivances in any one episode of *Law & Order* are as scripted, and as false, as any Romance. By comparing the closing arguments made in a capital case in real life with the closing arguments made by Jack McCoy on *Law & Order*, it becomes readily apparent that these shows do not hold a mirror up to the world. The narrative and visual contrivances on *CSI:* are just as obvious, and just as false: DNA tests are processed in seconds, minute bits of evidence appear as large as small rocks. While a toxicology report on *CSI:* takes minutes, in real life, those same results often take weeks. Furthermore, the visual contrivances are just as obvious: the high contrast panoramas of *CSI: Miami* appear no more real than the extravagant panoramas of Stars Hollow during one of the many, many town festivals. In fact, they appear just as other-worldly as the scenes in *Gilmore Girls*.

Scripted television shows (sitcoms, dramas, and dramedies), like novels, are not true or absolute reflections of the "real world," but are selective reflections and representations of some world. And as with novels, television narratives are constructed within historical and aesthetic traditions and conventions. When the realist novel was in vogue, a great many novels employed those conventions; when the gritty "reality" of crime dramas is in vogue, a great many programs fall in line and replicate the conventions. Because this is the current dominant representation style in prime-time television, both viewers' and critics' expectations are shaped by it. Nevertheless, a small number of programs do resist the dominant mode, and they do so for varying reasons. *Seventh Heaven*, for example, rejects the gritty "reality" in order to narrate stories about a family of individuals who are struggling with questions of faith within a society that may not be entirely sympathetic. While some viewers find *Seventh Heaven* to be "unrealistic," it nevertheless attempts to narrate and reflect a particular ideological worldview, and the narrative and visual strategies help reinforce that worldview. Similarly, *Gilmore Girls* stems from a desire to reflect a small-town existence that is, generally, absent from mainstream primetime, to represent a relationship between a mother and daughter that is not often seen on television but that, nevertheless, is becoming more common in the "real world," and to represent a young woman who is sexually naïve and academically driven. Setting *Gilmore Girls* in the fictional Stars Hollow allows Sherman-Palladino to tell these stories, but, at the same time, the cost is that it removes the plotlines and characters from the larger historical and political context, and thereby undermines the possibility of engaging in any overt political commentary upon them. The stories, then, are about personal lives and choices, not about the "broader political and social" situations.

Another consequence of this strategy, then, is the lack of commentary upon racial inequalities within society. While Stars Hollow is quite small, and although it "exists" within a historically white section of Connecticut, within the cast of characters are found a number of racial and ethnic minorities, including Michel Gérard, Mrs. Kim, Lane Kim, Gypsy, and Caesar (the two recurrent characters without last names, according to the cast credits on the Internet Movie Database). These five characters constitute only a small portion of the cast, and they are all secondary characters. Furthermore, they all have service economy jobs. Realistically speaking, it is possible that, in that particular locale, people of color might well be consigned to service sector jobs, but this possibility is never overtly examined. In addition, the fact that these five individuals live within a predominantly white community might well have an impact upon their everyday lived experiences, but if it does, it is not reflected within the narrative world. Perhaps even more glaring are the omissions. For example, one of the most prominent of these secondary characters is Michel. From within the narrative framework, it appears that Michel is one of the only, if not the only, black man in Stars Hollow. And although race does not have to inform every action or conversation, Michel is far more concerned with diet, appearance, dancing and auctions than with the ways in which his Otherness might affect him in this small Connecticut town. As another example, Rory leaves Stars Hollow to attend Yale University and apparently neither meets nor befriends any students of color.

Amy Sherman-Palladino's television writing career is already long and distinguished. She began writing for *Roseanne* (1990–1994), *Love and Marriage* (1996), *Over the Top* (1997), and *Veronica's Closet* (1998–1999). But it was on the *Roseanne* show that Sherman-Palladino began to engage in social issues. The Conner family, living in a small town in Indiana, struggles, like so many did in that place and time, to support their three children. They also struggle with raising their children within the larger social context. One of the most acclaimed episodes, written by Sherman-Palladino (with Jennifer Heath), was "A Bitter Pill to Swallow," in which Becky asks her mother to take her to the pharmacy to get birth control pills. But even here, the emphasis is on the personal choice and upon the personal reactions and responses (e.g. Dan threatens to go kill her boyfriend) rather than upon the larger social factors—the availability of birth control, the legal consent to obtain the pills, the responsibility for birth control (hers and his), the relationship between the availability of contraception and teen pregnancy, and so on. From this, then, it seems that throughout her career, Sherman-Palladino has written from a postfeminist perspective.

The same ideological emphasis is evident in *Gilmore Girls* in many of the characters, but Rory and Paris illustrate it most clearly because they are, unlike Lorelai, outside the protective confines of Stars Hollow. Rory and Paris both work as editors of the newspaper of the elite prep school, Chilton. Later, both serve as editors at the *Yale Daily News*. And while both Rory and Paris face difficulties in balancing work and school, both strive to cover meaningful stories, and both work to be exemplary journalists, their difficulties stem largely from personal choices. Unlike the systemic marginalization and undervaluing of female executives in the newsroom on *The Mary Tyler Moore Show*, on *Gilmore Girls*, the focus is on the personal, not the political. After graduating from Yale, Paris is accepted by every graduate program — medical schools and law schools— to which she applies. Her success is a testament to her intelligence, skills, and work ethic, but her success is the result solely of her abilities, and the show does not acknowledge or dramatize any potential failings as a result of social structures or biases. In reality (both historically and currently), women struggle to achieve parity in graduate and professional schools, but here Paris overcomes all of that through personal determination and ability. On the other hand, prior to graduating from Yale, Rory applies for the Reston Fellowship at the *New York Times*, which she does not get. Instead of wondering who the other candidates might have been, who might have garnered the prestigious positions, whether or not she might have failed because of anything other than pure ability and merit, Rory assumes that the winners must have been better qualified and better suited. In part, Rory's response is in keeping with her personality, but it is also part of the larger ideological perspective of *Gilmore Girls*.

As a part of her personal development, Rory has three significant romantic relationships, and she learns something from each of them. Far more than the focus on Lorelai, I would argue, the show focuses on Rory's development. Whereas Amy Sherman-Palladino expressly sought to represent a sexually-naïve young woman, by the end of the series, Rory has developed into an experienced (without the negative connotations of that term) woman. And, while she was always intelligent and driven, she learns from experience where her interests and her self lie. Because of her sense of self, she is finally able to stand on her own and stand up to the wealthy, experienced, worldly Logan Huntzberger. Just as Mary Richards walks out on the marriage proposal from a doctor, Lorelai Leigh Gilmore walks out on the marriage proposal of an old-money entrepreneur. While Rory begins as a sexually and socially naïve young woman, she struggles (and errs) along the path to become a confident and independent woman.

In "Gilmore Girls Only" (7.17), Rory realizes that Logan has continued to behave in an immature manner, and when she goes to Mia's wedding (largely to escape Logan) and he follows her, she stands up to him for the first time. "Wow, I can't believe you're still doing this. This is so last year's Logan.... You think you can just fly anywhere I am and overwhelm me by just showing up and — I'm just not impressed anymore by your grand gestures." In the penultimate episode, "Unto the Breach" (7.21), Rory is alone in the apartment, spackling the walls, when she tries on the engagement ring. As she looks at it on her hand, she smiles, a move aimed at eliciting the expectation among viewers that she will accept. Instead, she tells him, that, although she loves him and the idea of being married to him, "there are just a lot of things right now in my life that are undecided. And that used to scare me, but now I — I kind of like the idea...." She concludes by telling him, "And if I married you, it just wouldn't be." Although she rejects Logan's offer, she knows that she, personally, has options and that her decision will be based on whatever works for her.

Despite the temptation to become (or the possibility of becoming) her grandmother, who skillfully and elegantly arranges D.A.R. meetings and socializes with bluebloods, Rory realizes that it is not the life she would choose for herself (6.05, "We've Got Magic to Do"). While she proves to be skillful and creative — indeed, she out-organizes and out-fundraises even Emily Gilmore — she eventually realizes it would not be a fulfilling life for her, that it would be a deviation from her personal plan. Despite the temptation to become her mother, who escapes the stifling atmosphere of Hartford, elite society, and her parents' household and remains in a sort of perpetual adolescent fantasy world wherein her material and emotional needs are met by others, Rory realizes that, as difficult as it will be, she must leave the comfort of Stars Hollow, close friends and townsfolk, and her mother's household and make her way into the world at large.

Despite its "shortcomings" in terms of so-called "realism," and despite its "failures" to fully engage social issues such as race, class, and sexuality, *Gilmore Girls* does follow in the footsteps of a number of its predecessors in their post-feminist arguments. The lyrics of the theme song, "Where You Lead" by Carole King and Louise Goffin, seem to be intended more ironically than literally. Lorelai Gilmore did not follow in her mother, Emily's, footsteps. In many ways, despite the original promise that Lorelai and Rory are mirror images of one another, the youngest Lorelai, Rory, does not follow her mother, either. While her grandmother pulls her in one direction, toward one particular set of values, her mother pulls her toward another set of values, which is often little more than a reaction to Emily's ideology. And while Rory wavers back and forth between them, torn between allegiances and her own life experiences, she manages, over the course of seven years, to find a pathway that suits her. That personal and ideological struggle for Rory can also be read as a metaphor for the series. As Rory struggles to negotiate a pathway for herself, as she seems to lose her way, the series seems to lose its way, as well. In the end, however, I would suggest that as Rory discovers an authentic self, finds a way out of the other-worldly utopia of Stars Hollow and out into the world — of politics, no less — she finds more independence than her mother was ever able to find at the Independence Inn. In Rory's return to her goals, *Gilmore Girls* returns to its goals, as well. In this return, *Gilmore Girls* remains faithful to its original post-feminist ideology, and Rory's decisions regarding school, relationships, and career are the result of personal choices, not institutional structures and practices. For Rory to find her self and her pathway, "the personal is political" means that she must examine her own personal choices, not the larger social structures around her.

The Essays

When I sent the call for papers out into cyberspace, I had very little idea of the kinds of responses I would get (if any, at all). And to be sure, I received a number of crank e-mails almost immediately, mostly to ridicule the very idea of this collection. My favorite among them was a response to a blogger who had posted the call for papers. The comment simply read, "wtf." My next concern was that I would simply get fan mail, or essays that simply and uncritically sang the series' praises. To my relief, that was not the case. Despite reservations about the collapse of the division between fan and critic, many of the writers herein identify themselves as fans of *Gilmore Girls*, but they are nevertheless willing and able to engage with the series through a critical lens (as are those fans of Joyce's *Ulysses* and Whedon's *Buffy*). But what surprised (and pleased) me the most about the entries received was the geographical variety, the mixture of female and male authors, the number of co-written essays, and the willingness and ability to engage with the series critically. All of these speak to the appeal (and hence effect) of the show; it confirms, in my mind, the richness and appeal of the text for critical analysis. As I mentioned above, however, the essays are not, despite some inevitable overlap, homogeneous, nor are they comprehensive. And while I have my own perspective and interpretation of the series, I have tried not to impose my own perspective upon the writers; it has been my intention to have different and differing perspectives represented.

Notes

1. According to Amy Sherman-Palladino, *Gilmore Girls* was initially slotted on Thursdays against *Friends*, which turned out to work to her advantage. "'Since we were against the monster show of all monster shows, [...] all we had to do was survive. All we had to do was basically get here on time, turn the cameras on, and have a cocktail afterwards. That's all we had to do. Because nobody expects us to take out *Friends*, for

god's sakes. And then when the critics— god love 'em, every one of 'em —chimed in and validated the studio and the network's feelings of being behind this, it just sort of grew. Then slowly but surely we built a tiny little audience that got bigger and then a little bigger'" (LaTempa). In the last several seasons, *Gilmore Girls* often aired in the same time slot as *American Idol*, an even bigger juggernaut.

2. I recall, however, sitting in an apartment in São Paulo, Brazil, watching *Gilmore Girls* on cable. I remember wondering, as the Portuguese subtitles flashed by, how a show that seemed so completely rooted in a U.S.-based ethos could translate into another language and culture.

3. Now that both *Gilmore Girls* and *The New Adventures of Old Christine* are gone from prime-times line-ups, that number is near zero. As of October 2007, the five networks air only one female-led sitcom, *Girlfriends*. *Christine* is scheduled to return as a mid-season replacement; a new sitcom entitled *Miss/Guided* is scheduled also to appear mid-season. The new Amy Sherman-Palladino series, *The Return of Jezebel James*, is also slated to appear mid-season. This shift takes place at approximately the same moment that Christopher Hitchens writes a piece in *Vanity Fair* in which he argues that "women aren't funny." This analysis, however, excludes made-for-cable shows such as *The Sarah Silverman Program*. The blog The Hathor Legacy notes that "Warner Bros president of production Jeff Robinov has made a new decree that 'We are no longer doing movies with women in the lead.'" Subsequent blog posts note that Warner Brothers has denied the statement and policy; nevertheless, many others have been wondering about the dearth of female-led vehicles.

4. A new series for the 2007-2008 season, *Women's Murder Club*, may fall into this category, as well.

5. Dow's suggestion is echoed by Amy Sherman-Palladino in regard to *Gilmore Girls*: "I really believe there's something for everybody in the show, [...] and I've structured it in my mind to that end. As lovely as it is that we have young girls watching the show, some of my favorite stuff is done with Emily and Richard (Lorelai's parents) and the generational stuff" (LaTempa).

6. This assertion is supported by the fact that, during seasons 4, 5, and 6, when Lorelai and Rory really were more involved with relationships, the popular appeal in the series and the characters waned.

7. In some ways, these same generational conflicts are mirrored within the Kim household.

Works Cited

Battis, Jes. *Blood Relations: Chosen Families in* Buffy the Vampire Slayer *and* Angel. Jefferson, NC: McFarland, 2005.

BetaCandy. "Remember When I Said They Teach You Not to Write Screenplays with Women as Leads?" The Hathor Legacy. 7 Oct. 2007. 13 Oct. 2007

Bird, Rick. "Get to Know 'Gilmore Girls.'" The Cincinnati Post. 4 May 2004 <http://www.cincypost.com/living/2000/girls100500.html>.

Bodroghkozy, Aniko. "Where Have You Gone Mary Richards?: Feminism's Rise and Fall in Primetime Television." Iris (Fall 2004): 12. 28 December 2006 <http://proquest.umi.com/pqdweb?did=791851621&sid=6&Fmt=3&clientld=48296&RQT=309&Vname=PQD>.

Dow, Bonnie. Prime-Time Feminism: Television, Media Culture, and the Women's Movement since 1970. Philadelphia: University of Pennsylvania Press, 1996.

Freeman, Michael. "'Gilmore Girl.'" Electronic Media 20.8 (2001): 16.

Hanisch, Carol. "The Personal Is Political." Feminist Revolution: An Abridged Edition with Additional Writings. Ed. Kathie Sarachild. New York: Random House, 1978.

Hitchens, Christopher. "Why Women Aren't Funny." Vanity Fair January 2007. 25 May 2007 < http://www.vanityfair.com/culture/features/2007/01/hitchens200701>.

LaTempa, Susan. "The Best of Friends." GilmoreGirls.org. 29 April 2002. 4 May 2004 <http://www.gilmoregirls.org/news/211.html>.

Macdonald, Myra. Representing Women: Myths of Femininity in the Popular Media. London: Edward Arnold, 1995.

McLoone, Tracy. "Single White Females." Pop Matters. 1999-2004. 4 May 2004 <http://www.popmatters.com/tv/reviews/g/Gilmore-girls.shtml>.

Pfefferman, Naomi. "Nice, Jewish Maidel: Amy Sherman-Palladino Turns Gilmore Girls into a Homage to the Catskills." The Jewish Journal of Los Angeles. 2004. 4 May 2004 <http://www,jewishjournal.com/home/print.php!id=10275>.

"A Bitter Pill to Swallow." By Amy Sherman-Palladino and Jennifer Heath. Roseanne. CBS. 17 September 1991.

Ward, L. Monique and Kristen Harrison. "The Impact of Media Use on Girls' Beliefs about Gender Roles, Their Bodies, and Sexual Relationships: A Research Synthesis." Featuring Females: Feminist Analyses of Media. Ed. Ellen Cole and Jessica Henderson Daniel. Washington, DC: American Psychological Association, 2005. 3-23.

"Would Life Be Better If We All Spoke Like Shakespeare?" Talk of the Nation. NPR.com. 26 April 2007. 11 May 2007 <http://www.npr.org/templates/story/story.php?story Id=9849018>.

Yaszek, Lisa. "I'll Be a Postfeminist in a Postpatriarchy, or, Can We Really Imagine Life after Feminism?" Electronic Book Review 29 Jan. 2005. 14 Oct. 2007 <http://www.electronicbookreview.com/thread/writingpostfeminism/(fem)sci-fi>.

Zoonen, Liesbet van. Feminist Media Studies. London: SAGE, 1994.

Z Staff. "Editorial: The Personal Is Political?!" Z Magazine July 1997. 29 March 2007 <http://zena. Secureforum.com/Znet/zmag/articles/julyeditorial97.html>.

Zuckerman, Diana and Nicole Dubowitz. "Clash of Cultures: Women and Girls on TV and in Real Life." Featuring Females: Feminist Analyses of Media. Ed. Ellen Cole and Jessica Henderson Daniel. Washington, DC: American Psychological Association, 2005. 59-69.

Welcome to Stars Hollow

Gilmore Girls, *Utopia, and the Hyperreal*

ERIN K. JOHNS AND KRISTIN L. SMITH

Beginning with the pilot episode, *Gilmore Girls* established itself as a dramedy that indulges in an idealized world, a fictional utopia known as Stars Hollow. The show, known for its excessive displays of both food and knowledge, is a witty juxtaposition of popular culture and high brow education. *Gilmore Girls* is unique in its blend of idyllic 1950s community and contemporary culture, which can be more explicitly explored through the lens of Richard Dyer's 1977 essay "Entertainment and Utopia." Looking at *Gilmore Girls* through Dyer's essay, we will show that the portrayal of Stars Hollow as utopia provides the backbone around which the show is built, both for the audience at home and for the characters within the show, reproduced as a doubling of simulation Jean Baudrillard would call the hyperreal.

In "Entertainment and Utopia," Dyer looks at the importance of utopia in musicals. Even though *Gilmore Girls* is not a musical, his perspectives on one-dimensionality, created through representational and nonrepresentational signs, function in a similar way in this particular television show, creating the utopia of Stars Hollow for the express purpose of providing entertainment. Dyer writes,

> Two of the taken-for-granted descriptions of entertainment, as "escape" and as "wish-fulfillment," point to its central thrust, namely, utopianism. Entertainment offers the image of "something better" to escape into, or something we want deeply that our day-to-day lives don't provide. Alternatives, hopes, wishes— these are the stuff of utopia, the sense that things could be better, that something other than what is can be imagined and maybe realized [273].

According to Dyer, the utopian ideals entertainment provides as a means of escape or wish-fulfillment point to specific inadequacies or tensions in society

23

created by capitalism. Thus, a utopia represents community, transparency in communication and relationships, and energy/intensity in addition to offering abundance as a solution to fragmentation, manipulation, dreariness, and poverty/scarcity (277–78). Overall, *Gilmore Girls* as a television show accomplishes all of the above aspects of utopia, manifest in Stars Hollow. It does so by combining both representational signs—pointing to the way the world is and drawing from the audience's concrete experiences—and nonrepresentational signs—pointing to how things could be better (Dyer 279)—to create not a literal model of a utopian world, but "what utopia would feel like rather than how it would be organized" (Dyer 273).

The representational signs of the utopian ideal of community are obvious in Stars Hollow, a small town where every character knows everyone in the community. Rumors spread quickly from person to person—particularly through the sex-on-the-mind Miss Patty and the nosy, gruff-voiced Babette. Whether good news or bad, the spreading of gossip shows the interconnectedness of the community. This is evident as early as the pilot episode, in which Rory tells Dean, who is looking for a job, to check with Miss Patty because "she just kind of knows everything that's going on in town" (1.01, "Pilot"). This sense of community is reinforced throughout the series, as every event becomes a community event, from the Town Hall meetings, to the reenactment of the "legendary Battle of Stars Hollow" (1.08, "Love and War and Snow"), to the Festival of Living Art (4.07, "The Festival of Living Art"), to finally the graduation party thrown for Rory as she completes Yale (7.21, "Unto the Breach").

Dyer's utopian ideal of transparency in communications and relationships is also present in Stars Hollow, predominantly in the characters of Lorelai and Rory, who have a somewhat abnormal mother-daughter relationship. This is also clear from the pilot episode. When Rory has second thoughts about entering the prestigious Chilton Preparatory School, Lorelai tells her, "We've always had a democracy in this house. We never did anything unless we both agreed." At the end of the episode, when Luke pleads with Rory to put down her coffee because she doesn't want to grow up to be like her mother, Rory replies, "Too late." The characters argue, struggle, and have downfalls, but generally these issues are swiftly reconciled. Considering the rapid pace of the show through dialogue, the short periods of time between the initial argument and reconciliation seem logical—emphasizing the "life in hyper-speed" theme of the show. The arguments between the characters tend to be surface level, which allows them to be resolved quickly and easily, and therefore viewers rarely receive sustained glimpses of the characters' internal struggle. Occasionally, conversations reflect basic conflicts for a character, but these are usually rapidly paced and short conversations that skim the surface of major psychological issues. It is this absence of internal conflict, both in the mother and daughter whose bond drives the show, and in the characters with whom they interact, that makes them transparent and one-dimensional. This transparency permits the witty banter that so heavily relies upon pop-culture and education. The one-dimensionality allows characters to pull in these references (often referred to as Gilmorisms), because there is no need to elaborate on conflicting communications or internal strife. In both the communications between Lorelai and Rory and between them and their respective best friends, Sookie and Lane, all there is to know is already out on the table. That's not to say that the characters aren't complex — Lorelai has commitment issues with men (Christopher, Max Medina, Jason "Digger" Stiles, Luke); likewise, Rory has her own relationship troubles (Dean, Tristin, Jess, Logan) — but none of these relationships matters without the primary mother-daughter relationship which, extraordinary as it is, exists only as a result of the utopia in which they live.

Throughout every relationship in the show, communication through fast-paced talking and quick quips becomes an essential element of the narrative structure. The energy and intensity that Dyer mentions is evident in the characters' rate of speech. In general, and especially for Lorelai and Rory, the characters' dialogue is produced as a rosy-cheeked and breathless tumbling out of words — quirky conversations engaged in with a rapidity that might rival a speed addict's, whether as the result of over-consumption of coffee or a natural inclination to lightning-fast thought processes. Not only is the dialogue energetic and intense, but it is full of obscure pop culture references, facts about authors, and rare, if not completely unheard of, inquiries about music — wordplay which has become the hallmark of recognition for *Gilmore Girls* and has earned the nickname of Gilmorisms. The centrality of relationships — whether mother/daughter, friend, family, or intimate — exposes a lack of boundaries through not only speech, but also continual contact between the characters.

Work and play become synonymous, disintegrating the boundary between leisure and the daily grind. Lorelai works with her best friend Sookie; Rory often appears at the inn to visit or help out; other family/friends/boyfriends occasionally appear at or call the inn to talk on company time; etc. In this utopia there is none of the routine drudgery or predictability of usual work life. It is this, in part, that provides the characters with endless energy, drama, and excitement, along with the intensity of what Dyer would call "affectivity for living" (278) that seems to be contagious in the Stars Hollow community. Town events, celebrations, and festivals — like the annual "Charity Picnic Basket Lunch Auction" (2.13, "A-Tisket, A-Tasket"), "Movie in the Square Night" (2.19, "Teach Me Tonight"), the annual "End of Summer Madness Festival" (3.01, "Those Lazy-Hazy-Crazy Days"), the "Stars Hollow Dance Marathon" (3.07, "They Shoot Gilmores, Don't They?"), etc. — take precedence over all else. These events become the topic of endless preparations, decorating, and chatter among townspeople, demonstrating Dyer's ideal of energy/intensity, and are strongly tied to the sense of community Stars Hollow provides. The characters' quick, witty banter, plentitude of obscure references, and constant contact leads into the last of Dyer's utopian ideals: abundance.

Not only do Lorelai's and Rory's puns and references demonstrate an abundance of education, whether in popular culture (as is often the case with Lorelai) or in academia (as is usual with Rory), but abundance in Stars Hollow is often portrayed as consumption. Dyer emphasizes a point made by Hans Magnus Enzensberger that consumption functions as spectacle. In a utopia, people will want for nothing; therefore, consumption must be displayed. In *Gilmore Girls*, consumption is primarily of food and coffee. The pilot episode opens with Lorelai walking into her favorite place to eat, Luke's diner. As soon as she enters, Lorelai grabs a large coffee mug and approaches Luke, begging for coffee. When Luke asks, "How many cups have you had this morning?" Lorelai lies and says, "None." Luke knows better, however, and when he presses her, she admits, "Five, but yours is better." When Luke chastises her and tells her, "You have a problem," Lorelai can only respond, "Yes, I do."

Lorelai receives her coffee — her sixth cup that morning — evidence of abundance and excessive consumption from the very beginning. As the show continues into later seasons, Lorelai and Rory's abnormally large consumption of coffee and food becomes a staple of their life and the show. They get coffee multiple times a day, order entire columns from the Chinese menu, and pizza exists as its own food group. In addition, their food consumption often corresponds with their own entertainment. Whenever they sit down to watch a movie or a television series, Lorelai and Rory first collect an assortment of sweets, frozen foods like tater tots, and pizza. Even at the inn where Lorelai works, elaborate spreads of food are always on display, courtesy of Lorelai's best friend and the inn's chef, Sookie. In this world, no one goes hungry.

Community, transparency, energy/intensity, and abundance, the utopian ideals Dyer asserts are the solutions to societal inadequacies created by capitalism, are all present in the community of Stars Hollow through the representational signs within the show, creating a utopia for the characters who live there and thus completing wish-fulfillment for the characters through a world that creates its own contemporary utopian solutions. Dyer suggests that the utopia is one-dimensional because those solutions "imply wants that capitalism itself promises to meet" (278); the ideals present in entertainment provide "alternatives *to* capitalism which will be provided *by* capitalism" (279). Yet this one-dimensionality is often fragmented and complicated by the nonrepresentational elements of entertainment, because for entertainment to be effective, "the utopian has to take off from the real experiences of the audience" (279).

The nonrepresentational elements of *Gilmore Girls* function to make the viewers a part of the utopia of Stars Hollow that already exists for the characters. For the most part, this is accomplished through visuals and music. Visually, the town is filled with small, historic-looking wooden houses that give the nostalgic impression of a 1950s community. This, perhaps, may have been the intention of the show's creators, who chose to use the set of a town originally constructed in the 1940s on the Warner Brothers' property (Thomas) and whose familiar building façades were used in classic shows such as *The Dukes of Hazzard* and *The Waltons* ("Trivia"). Big business is absent in the town, which consists mainly of shops and markets, and all major events occur in the town square. By choosing to stress this time period in the set, *Gilmore Girls* partially removes itself from time and space to a period that could be believed to be a more "free-and-easy stage in American development," as Dyer suggests is one technique of musicals in creating utopia. This removal is only partial, however, because the show simultaneously includes many elements of the present moment: technology such as cell phones, computers, the internet, and hybrid cars (Rory gets a Toyota Prius for graduation [3.22, "Those Are Strings, Pinocchio"]), as well as frequent references to current politics, other television shows, and music. It is this connection of the past and the present, offering the best of both, that help solidify the utopia, and Stars Hollow becomes for viewers a place of retreat or escape from everyday hustle and bustle — a place that offers, as Dyer says, "Alternatives, hopes, wishes" (273). The audience comes to feel like a part of the Stars Hollow community, a feeling reinforced by another non-representational element of the show: the music.

The show's theme song by Carole King, "Where You Lead," contributes to viewers' feelings of utopian community not only because it expresses the sentiments exhibited by the characters of Lorelai and Rory, but because it invites the viewers themselves to "follow" both the storyline of the show and the examples set forth by the characters. Stars Hollow becomes a place where the viewer wants to live and is filled with characters that the viewer would like to imitate. The show obviously tries to illicit this very response through the *Gilmore Girls* official website, linked to the network CW's homepage. One selection on the page offers viewers a chance to "Be your own Gilmore Girl with CW style!" (*Gilmore Girls* 2006). Clicking here takes viewers to a page where they can search apparel shown on the show by brand, character, episode, or product — offering them a chance to imitate the show, and thus a chance to become a part of the utopian Stars Hollow community. Further fan participation is encouraged on the official website with the recent additions of "Kirk's Town Tours" — videos viewable online, alongside a town map, narrated by Kirk and interspersed with episode clips, added weekly to ensure fans' return to the site — and the "Play Like a Girl" trivia quiz game with which fans can test how pop culture savvy they are by answering questions about the Gilmorisms featured in the video-question clips. The character music playlists found on the quiz page offer fans a further opportunity to imitate the show and its characters by downloading ringtones "the citizens of Stars Hollow [would] have on their cell phones" (*Gilmore Girls* 2007). Doubts regarding the demand for such information regarding characters' clothing brand names or favorite music and viewers' desires to participate in the Stars Hollow community can be put to rest by visiting the CW Lounge, a message board for *Gilmore Girls* fans also accessible through the official website, and browsing the usernames of those who have posted. Such names appear as "gilmoregirlxoxo," "iheartgg," "iwant2Bgilmore," etc., suggesting that the fans are, indeed, buying into the utopia that *Gilmore Girls* provides.

The music of *Gilmore Girls* not only invites viewers to feel a part of and participate in the utopia of Stars Hollow, but it also accompanies the characters' actions, almost giving the impression that the characters have soundtracks to their lives. For example, at the beginning of the pilot episode, when Lorelai goes to Luke's for her sixth cup of coffee, "There She Goes" by The La's plays in the background. Later in the episode, when Lorelai goes to Hartford to see her mother and father, Emily and Richard Gilmore, to ask them for financial help so Rory can attend Chilton, we hear the song by Sam Phillips "Where the Colors Don't Go." These songs are present for the audience only, but they seem to match the narrative so well that they almost seem one and the same, suggesting, as Dyer describes, that "utopia is implicit in the world of the narrative as well as in the world of the numbers" (281).

Another nonrepresentational aspect of the show that contributes to the notion of Stars Hollow as a utopia, which the townspeople don't seem to notice but which is obvious to viewers, is the color scheme. Stars Hollow is filled not only with quirky, colorful characters, but with vibrant colors and fabrics in the set and scenery, whether in the opening montage that depicts a bird's-eye view of the town, with its white steeple contrasted with the deep greens and reds of early autumn, or in the characters' living rooms, filled with bright and fluffy furniture, blankets, and knick-knacks. The Stars Hollow characters wear bright clothing, as well, which serve to make them seem friendly and approachable. Lorelai, as the only character to live both outside and in Stars Hollow, seems also to be the only character aware of this contrast with the color schemes in scenes that take place outside Stars Hollow — like the home of the elder Gilmores. When "Where the Colors Don't Go," plays, we see Lorelai standing in front of her parents' home, a large stone house that blends in with the scenery. The muted color scheme exists within the home, as well. Emily leads Lorelai into a living room decorated in ivory, complete with crystal chandeliers. Everything in the room is stiff and symmetrical (including Emily herself) and gives the impression of a formal parlor. The song plays in the background — "That's where the colors don't go/ That's where the colors don't show" — in keeping with Emily's visit to Stars Hollow several episodes later, when Lorelai tells her, "You will not come into my house and tell me I threw my life away. Look around, Mom. This is a life. It has a little color in it so it may look a little unfamiliar to you, but it's a life" (1.09, "Rory's Dance"). The music and the color scheme work together in leading viewers to experience the sense of dystopia that descends upon Lorelai and Rory when any of their relationships extend outside of the safe zone of the Stars Hollow utopia, for it is really only then that unhappiness and general discomfort settle in on that central relationship.

This sense of dystopia is further emphasized by the fact that Emily and Richard live merely a half hour away from Stars Hollow. Lorelai, who got pregnant at sixteen and ran away from home, has a rather adversarial relationship with her mother. In Hartford, a world so far away from Stars Hollow in perception but not distance, Emily and Richard are the epitome of New England wealth and decorum. In this world, Lorelai was forced to follow the rules of social etiquette and understand the role of duty as was passed along to her as the descendant of the Gilmore family which arrived on the Mayflower. Emily and Richard's house offers wealth and comfort, but not happiness. It is the strict rules and codes of behavior that make this world dystopian compared to the world of Stars Hollow. Lorelai finds her ideal life by leaving her home atmosphere and by entering into a community whose lack of parental rules creates a utopia by providing the personal freedom and individuality the utopian ideals represent. Instead of the adult world, which would have required Lorelai to marry Christopher and become a housewife similar to Emily, Lorelai escapes the Gilmore household and upper class society. When she moves to Stars Hollow, Lorelai escapes the possibility of marriage and the rules dictated by the wealthy society in which her parents live. Lorelai prolongs her adolescence, or perhaps more accurately, keeps her adolescence (considering that she is about seventeen). In moving to Stars Hollow, Lorelai takes on the adult responsibilities of motherhood without completely giving up the experiences she can gain through adolescence. Therefore, for Lorelai and the show in general, adolescence becomes a utopian construct — one of escape and comfort that represents a world free from adult rules. In essence, Lorelai grows up with Rory rather than inflicting the severe rules of her childhood on Rory. In this way, Lorelai create a safe space — the utopia of Stars Hollow.

In an era of reality television shows, *Gilmore Girls* strives to do more than just entertain. Anti-reality in that it portrays a vision of utopia, *Gilmore Girls* tries to show a utopian community that revolves around many of the current issues in the contemporary world — issues that are often left out of utopian visions. Dyer acknowledges the disadvantages of his discussion of utopia:

> The advantage of this analysis is that it does offer some explanation of why entertainment *works*. It is not just left-overs from history, it is not *just* what show business, or "they," force on the rest of us, it is not simply the expression of eternal needs — it responds to real needs *created by society*. The weakness of the analysis (And this holds true for Enzensberger too) is in the give-away absences from the left-hand column [the social inadequacies] — no mention of class, race or patriarchy. That is, while entertainment is responding to needs that are real, at the same time it is also defining and delimiting what constitutes the legitimate needs of people in this society.... Yet entertainment, by so orienting itself to them, effectively denies the legitimacy of other needs and inadequacies, and especially of class, patriarchal and sexual struggles [278].

Because *Gilmore Girls* does, in fact, focus on class and patriarchy, the analysis Dyer makes about utopia in musicals no longer applies. *Gilmore Girls* acknowledges the importance of these social structures and redefines them in order to establish the utopia of Stars Hollow.

One of the major propellants in the story around which *Gilmore Girls* centers is class. Lorelai, who felt trapped by the wealthy atmosphere in which she grew up, left her home with her infant at seventeen. She fled to Stars Hollow. Once there, she asked for a job at the Independence Inn as a maid. Wealth and money, which defines the upper classes, made her feel repressed and controlled. Lorelai left this privileged class and entered into the Stars Hollow community in the lowest class possible, because she had no money and no means of support. Despite this setback, Lorelai worked her way up the ladder at the Inn. In sixteen years time, Lorelai has become the successful manager of the Independence Inn. In this utopian world (as is the case in Voltaire's *Candide*), hard work is one of the requirements of the utopia. Money is not in abundance, but Lorelai is able to establish a middle-class life for herself. She rejects the class she was born into in favor of one that requires her to do something with herself, which is obviously an implication about class and its role in society. This is further emphasized when Rory moves from Stars Hollow High School to the prestigious Chilton Academy. At this new school, the offspring of the upperclass surround Rory. Although she eventually fits into this world, it is ultimately dystopian. She is often fighting with the strong-willed and highly self-motivated Paris Geller, which leads to her excommunication from the society of Chilton in many instances. When she enters the world of the upper class, Rory over-compensates through hard work and education. Conversely, it is not until Lorelai enters the working class that she exhibits the quality of hard-work. In their utopia, both Lorelai and Rory can use hard work to enter into and adapt to new surroundings. Also, Paris flushes out this equation — like Lorelai, she has a strained relationship with her parents. Although she is very much a part of the upper class, Paris still exhibits a hard working mentality — often to the point of over-achievement. By removing Rory from this atmosphere, Lorelai enables Rory to find a middle ground between the privileged upper class and the working class. For example, Paris feels that both her hard work and her family name should be enough for her to be accepted into Harvard. However, Paris's attitude and overachievement is the very reason that she is not accepted. Rory, who has the best of both worlds, is accepted into not only Harvard, but also Yale and Princeton.

Rory only deviates from this established norm of hard work and education when she encounters others in that upper class world at Yale — particularly Logan Huntzberger and the Life and Death Brigade. With this exposure, Rory has the opportunity to work for Logan's dad, Mitchum, a newspaper tycoon. While working for him, Rory begins to doubt her abilities as a journalist. This doubt eventually causes Rory to drop out of Yale for a while — living instead with her grandparents and becoming an active member of the Daughters of the American Revolution (D.A.R.). At first, this lifestyle seems perfect for Rory; she is free to be adrift in adolescent indecision. As she becomes more efficient at the D.A.R., Rory's life focuses on throwing fancy parties and playing the perfect hostess. Eventually, the lifestyle Rory was accustomed to (Lorelai's lifestyle) again confronts the strict parental rules of the Gilmore household. Rory eventually realizes that she is turning into Emily after a confrontation with her old Stars Hollow life through the figure of Jess. Although Rory has been interacting with people from Stars Hollow, like Lane, it is the opposition of her new life with her old life (through a dislike of Emily's rules and Jess) which prompts her to escape the upper-class dystopia of the Gilmore house for the utopian Stars Hollow. Like Lorelai, Rory leaves the controlling atmosphere implemented by both her grandmother and grandfather, which enforces a traditional class power structure also carries assumptions about male power.

The role of the patriarchy is also tied into the globe of Lorelai's parents—the world from which Lorelai escaped. In this world, Richard is a successful businessman. Emily is an active member of the D.A.R., arranges frivolous parties, and meddles in other people's business. Emily's place, though, is highly linked with her class. It is understood that this was what women of Emily's class should accomplish with their money. Her only job in life is to complement the success of her husband by using his money for her own interests and maintain her husband's and her social standing. Emily does not work, but because of her class, she is not even confined to the repression and depression of the 1950s housewife. She arranges menus for dinner, but never actually has to cook a meal. Emily is meticulous and manipulative, which leads her to dismiss many house maids.

This social order in which Emily was raised, and which she takes to be her natural privilege and of the highest good, is a product of the patriarchal ideology particular to her class. Her beliefs about the natural, hierarchal order of things are most vividly exemplified in her treatment of maids. To her, maids are expendable life forms, who must fulfill her every whim. In her rejection of a life of privilege to become a maid at an inn, Lorelai assumes the lowest class in her mother's eyes, as well; she assumes the position of the disposable maid, but this is further complicated by Emily's sense of duty and family. This emphasis on duty is what leads Emily to lend the money to Lorelai for Rory's schooling. Although Lorelai disposes of her upper-class standing and the duties of the Gilmore name, Rory remains as the link between Lorelai and Emily as well as the hope for the continuation of the Gilmore name as something to be honored and respected. By setting up the plot in this way, the patriarchal order still exists as a result of money and class. When they exit this world to go to Stars Hollow, Lorelai and Rory become two independent women, who have established themselves outside of these social structures, escaping the patriarchy of the upper class to a place where women's relationships can be primary. This leads to a series of questions. Why, if utopias are supposed to exist outside of the realm of these social structures, does *Gilmore Girls* explore these structures? Why include these dystopian notions in a utopian world?

To answer these questions, we must reach back to the original quote from Dyer included at the beginning of this essay. Dyer writes that the role of utopia is to be an escape and to obtain wish-fulfillment (273). In order to explore this, Dyer briefly explores the role of semiotic development and use of the sign and the signifier. In this, he includes both representational and nonrepresentational signs. So far, this essay has explored how both the representational and non-representational signs function within the show to create a utopia for both the characters and the audience at home. But Stars Hollow is more than just a utopia.

The most intentional sign used in the show is the representational use of language. The language makes *Gilmore Girls* memorable; therefore, it appears in the show in excess. But why are these Gilmorisms so significant? *Gilmore Girls'* use of language functions as more than simply a means of communication between characters and between television show and audience; it is an experiment in what Jean Baudrillard named the hyperreal. In cultural studies, television and film often function as examples that achieve hyperreal status, which is exactly what happens with the show *Gilmore Girls*. Baudrillard writes:

> It is no longer a question of imitation, nor of reduplication, nor even of parody.
> It is rather a question of substituting signs of the real for the real itself; that is, an
> operation to deter every real process by its operational double, a metastable, pro-
> grammatic, perfect descriptive machine which provides all the signs of the real and
> short-circuits all its vicissitudes [366].

Here, Baudrillard stresses that the system of signs is simply a comparison to or a rewriting of that which it is signifying. At some point, that which is real no longer exists. The only thing that exists is this sign that represents the real, which is the hyperreal. *Gilmore Girls* uses this chain of signification to its advantage by incorporating the hyperreal into the television show itself. In the end, the hyperreal functions on two levels: as hyperreal for the audience at home and hyperreal for the characters within the show, a hyperreal within a hyperreal.

In *Gilmore Girls*, there is an interfacing of reality with television. The show *Gilmore Girls* gives an example of what the world should be like, which is expressed through the use of utopia. By watching the show, the audience begins to believe that this is what reality should be like, which helps to create a hyper-real atmosphere within Stars Hollow. Then, within the show, the characters are often making popular culture references—comparing their lives (which are reality's hyperreal) to the hyperreal of the television, books, and movies that the characters watch. This is why so much focus is given to the use of Gilmorisms in the show, because they are the hyperreal within the hyperreal. Not only is the viewing audience given a world which becomes the hyperreal, the characters on the show must maintain their status *as viewers* within their own hyperreal.

In order to do this effectively, a display of all things popular as well as high brow must first be established for the viewers at home through the characters' constant affirmation of their status as consumers of and experts on popular culture. In the pilot episode alone, there are many examples. For instance, as she tries to find a solution to pay for Rory's education, Lorelai tells the secretary at Chilton, "It doesn't give me a lot of time to pull a bank job" (1.01, "Pilot"). In this case, Lorelai equates the solution to her current situation with the desperation of robbers for money as is portrayed through film. As she discusses this same issue with her best friend, Sookie, Lorelai says, "There are several chapters from a Stephen King novel that I'd reenact before I'd consider that option" (1.01, "Pilot"). Obviously, in Lorelai's world, her current issue, although real in the television show, is continually equated with the hyperreal, with that which she can substitute in for the real.

Rory accomplishes this same effect, as well, but she refers to the highly educated realm of the hyperreal. As she engages in a conversation with the new boy at school, Dean, Rory says, "I know it's kind-of cliché to pick *Moby Dick* as your first Melville" (1.01 "Pilot"). In this instance, Rory judges herself by what should be the first Melville to read, which results from the established hyperreal in education and academia. Although it works well with television, the hyperreal also exists within the realm of literature, which is exactly how Rory applied it in her life.

When they are together, mother and daughter pass the wordplay back and forth — often with the daughter in the realm of academia and the mother in the realm of popular culture. Towards the end of the episode, Rory and Lorelai are standing outside of the house of Emily and Richard. Rory asks her mother, "So do we go in? Or do we just stand here, reenacting 'The Little Match Girl'?" To which Lorelai responds, "I know you and me are having a thing here. But I need you to be civil — at least through dinner. And then, on the way home, you can pull a Menendez" (1.01, "Pilot").

Although they are having a small conflict, Lorelai and Rory still default to the realm of the hyperreal in order to make each of their points. Rory refers to the realm of the fairy tale with all of its moral implications, whereas Lorelai exploits the current news and the implication of violence to parents. In either case, their argument is one-dimensional or surface level. It exists to fuel the realm of the hyperreal and the world of witty banter.

The Gilmorisms throughout the show emphasize the hyperreal, which in the end also stresses the utopian aspect of the show. In essence, the hyperreal is itself an image of utopia. When they make obscure references in the show, Lorelai and Rory actually imitate the interaction between the audience member and the show. Like most television, movies, and advertisements, the community or people depicted on a show are an ideal representation of the everyday world. This representation itself does not quite qualify as the hyperreal, but when the audience member begins to view *Gilmore Girls* as a reality, the show reaches hyperreal status. When they begin to use Gilmorisms or mimic the fashion on the show, viewers imitate the show in the hopes of achieving the same utopian status and vision. When the image becomes the real, the hyperreal occurs, which in the case of *Gilmore Girls*, is an attempt at obtaining the utopian world of Stars Hollow. The use of Gilmorisms in the show is meant to display the hyperreal within the hyperreal or the representational utopia within a utopia. Like the audience, Lorelai and Rory continually compare their lives to that of media representations. The language that Lorelai and Rory use actually attempts to place them as ultimate viewers and consumers. By doing this, *Gilmore Girls* destabilizes Baudrillard's concept of the hyperreal by indulging in a representation within a representation, which creates the necessity for the witty banter and quick thinking language throughout the show — all of which are required in the *Gilmore Girls* utopia.

This excess of language and the hyperreal all function together to tie back to the original implications of Dyer's argument of abundance in utopia. Although Stars Hollow is the hyperreal for the viewing audience, the characters have their own hyperreal that mimics its structure in society. Despite this, Stars Hollow functions as a form of entertainment and utopia. It provides a place where viewers can escape reality, which is in essence, the goal of the hyperreal. In either case, as Yo La Tengo quietly sings in the background at the closing of the pilot episode, "So welcome to my little corner of the world" (1.01, "Pilot").

Works Cited

Baudrillard, Jean. "Simulacra and Simulations." *Literary Theory: An Anthology*. Ed. Julie Rivkin, Michael Ryan. 2nd ed. Malden, MA: Blackwell, 2004. 365–77.

Dyer, Richard. "Entertainment and Utopia." *The Cultural Studies Reader*. Ed. Simon During. New York: Routledge, 1993. 271–83.

Gilmore Girls. The CW Television Network. 2006. 28 Dec. 2006 <http://thewb.warner-bros.com/shows/gilmore-girls>.

Gilmore Girls. The CW Television Network. 2006. 21 Apr. 2007 <http://thewb.warner-bros.com/shows/gilmore-girls>.

Thomas, Rachel. "*Gilmore Girls* Review, Synopsis and General Information." About.com. 21 Nov. 2006 <http://tvdramas.about.com/od/gilmoregirls/p/ggirlsreviewpro.htm?terms= gilmore+girls>.

"Trivia for *Gilmore Girls*." *Internet Movie Database Inc.* 1990–2006. Amazon.com. 28 Dec. 2006 <http://www.imdb.com/title/tt0238784/trivia>.

Rory Gilmore and Faux Feminism

An Ivy League Education and Intellectual Banter Does Not a Feminist Make

MOLLY MCCAFFREY

When the television show *Gilmore Girls* premiered in 2000, the audience was introduced to Lorelai Gilmore (Lauren Graham), a sexy and irreverent single mother who had raised her daughter by working as a hotel maid despite the wealth of her parents. Viewers soon found out that rather than give her daughter her father's name, this gutsy protagonist had simply named her after herself — Lorelai Gilmore, called Rory for short — a choice Rory (Alexis Bledel) describes as feminist in the first episode. Though Rory's father was willing to marry Lorelai and her parents were willing to let her reside at home during her pregnancy, Lorelai refused both offers of support, believing it was more important to raise Rory on her own than it was to compromise her integrity by living with parents who did not respect her or marrying a man she did not love.

In these ways, Lorelai seems to perfectly embody the values of a third-wave feminist as outlined in Jennifer Baumgardner and Amy Richards' *Manifesta: Young Women, Feminism, and the Future.* That is, she insists on both her independence and respect while also reveling in her femininity (Baumgardner and Richards 134–35). According to Baumgardner and Richards, women born after the 1960s grew up in an era of female empowerment thanks to the accomplishments of second-wave feminists. As they explain, "We have inherited strategies to fight sexual harassment, domestic abuse, the wage gap, and the pink-collar ghetto of low-wage women's work" (21). Baumgardner and Richards argue that for the current generation, feminism is like fluoride: "We scarcely notice that we have it — it's simply in the water" (17). Though this third wave of feminism builds on ideas inherited from the second wave, third wavers also tend to be more open about their sexuality than their predecessors. Like Lorelai, they do not necessarily shun make-up, skirts, or high heels but rather feel they can embrace their femininity without sacrificing their feminist ideals (136).

Because Lorelai fits this definition of third-wave feminism, it has been rather surprising to watch her daughter, Rory, make choices that not only do *not* fulfill her mother's feminist legacy but also contrast markedly with the values of her mother. What's most unsettling is that on the surface Rory appears to be a feminist: she's educated, articulate, career-oriented, and progressive. She also routinely makes comments that belie feminist leanings. But her behavior tells us otherwise. Throughout most of the show's seven-year run, Rory's romantic relationships are marked by dysfunction and inequity, her life decisions are often shaped by patriarchal influences, and her lifestyle becomes more and more dependant on money and privilege. In this way, Rory represents the many women today who claim to be feminist but actually exhibit qualities that are in opposition to feminist ideals, making one wonder if, as feminist scholar Toril Moi asserts, feminism today really is "languishing" (1735), a fear echoed by Baumgardner and Richards who worry that third wavers lack the political fight of second wavers and, thus, cause inequalities to continue (18).

Rory's faux feminism is most evident in her romantic relationships. From the very beginning, Rory is drawn to young men who, on the surface especially, appear to be "bad boys." Early in the show's history, that role is filled by Dean, Rory's first boyfriend, a new transplant to Stars Hallow who, in the show's first season, is depicted as an outsider. With his long hair, white t-shirt, blue jeans, and leather jacket and his tendency to pick fights with Rory's other suitors, he is clearly a contemporary reinterpretation of the original bad boy — James Dean in *Rebel without a Cause*. It becomes obvious not long after Dean has been introduced that he and Rory have little in common. The young Rory, a straight-A student, carries a book with her wherever she goes and keeps her dresser drawers filled with various literary classics rather than cluttering them with trendy clothes, but Dean does not like to read or watch classic movies, is not a good student, and has no plans for college. Rory's attraction to him seems to be based more on his mysteriousness and good looks than on anything concrete. As Lorelai points out to Rory's father, Christopher, in season one, "She has a Dean" (1.15, "Christopher Returns"), implying that it is not Dean as a person Rory is attracted to as much as the idea of a rebellious loner.

At the same time, Rory exhibits behavior that pays lip service to feminist ideals. In the beginning, Rory is more likely to stand up for herself than she does throughout most of the rest of the series. For instance, when her egomaniacal classmate Tristin tells her in season one that "The guy's supposed to buy the tickets" after he finds her waiting in line alone to purchase for tickets to a dance, she responds by asking, "Does Susan Faludi know about this?" (1.09, "Rory's Dance") and then goes on to say that she likes cheap guys, a clever way of saying that she is comfortable resisting gender roles. But later that same night, she is not bothered when Dean gets into a scuffle with Tristin and warns him to never come near her again, textbook machismo behavior. Though Rory points out that "having my boyfriend defend my honor. It's weird," she also admits to feeling good when she and Dean decide shortly thereafter that they are boyfriend and girlfriend (1.09, "Rory's Dance"). In contrast, when Christopher and Luke fight over Lorelai in season seven, neither one of them tell her about the incident because as Christopher says, "Well it's not something I'm exactly proud of. I mean this is what it's come to—I'm fighting the guy in the street" (7.14, "Farewell, My Pet"), thus demonstrating that even *he* knows that his actions are juvenile and off-putting and that any progressive person would see them that way. Unlike both of her parents, Rory actively participates in a relationship with Dean, a person who is unaware of this distinction, a person whom she barely knows, much less respects, behavior that reveals a deep lack of self-awareness on Rory's part.

Rory's behavior within her relationship with Dean is also categorized by girlishness. When Rory finally works up the nerve to tell Dean she's interested in him, she runs away after she's said it, much like a ten-year-old schoolgirl with a crush. What is more troubling is that, during season seven, we still witness Rory engaging in this type of immature behavior. When she develops an attraction for the teaching assistant who has taken over her grandfather's economics course at Yale, she communicates this interest by giggling nervously and stumbling over her words. This is the same character who can play verbal volleyball with her mother at one hundred miles per hour. Yet, when faced with an appealing member of the opposite sex, her intellect abandons her and is replaced in a split second by childish coquettishness.

Before her relationship with Dean has ended, Rory meets Jess, another good-looking "bad boy." Jess is an improvement over Dean because he and Rory share a love of books and culture and, thus, have a real, intellectual connection. But even with Jess, Rory finds herself, once more, without words. In one particular scene, Lorelai and Luke watch in disbelief as Rory and Jess mumble one-word grunts at each other in a rather pathetic attempt at communication. More important, though, is Rory's inability to stand up to Jess. One night in particular, Rory waits hours for Jess to pick her up, and when he finally arrives, her anger dissolves almost as soon as he smiles at her. On another occasion, she has difficulty telling him that she doesn't want to fool around at a party and is ultimately rescued by Dean. Rory's relationship with Jess comes to an abrupt end when he leaves Stars Hollow to be with his father in California, and it is notable that it isn't until after he is gone that Rory is able to communicate her true feelings to him.

Though Rory never lives alone during the show's seven-year run, she is single during her freshman year in college, a fact that she bemoans throughout season four while she is surrounded by other student couples, and it is this loneliness that drives her back into the arms of Dean. Despite the fact that he is by then married, Rory sleeps with him and, in the process, loses her virginity to a man who is largely unavailable to her. When Lorelai criticizes this choice, Rory defends her behavior by arguing that he is "my Dean" (4.22, "Raincoats and Recipes"), implying that her claim to him is greater than that of his wife. At the same time, Jess reappears in her life, showing up unannounced in her college dorm. Though Jess is single and wants her to go away with him for the summer, Rory opts to stay with the still-married Dean, a choice she makes presumably because there is less emotional risk involved.

The next year, Rory has a platonic relationship with another student at Yale; during the show's seven seasons, Marty is the only young man with whom she has a healthy, equitable relationship, the only one with whom she is able to truly be herself, and the only one who is not a stereotypical "bad boy." Marty and Rory binge on food and films in a way that seems eerily reminiscent of Lorelai and Rory's movie marathons. In this way, they seem to share real intimacy. Nevertheless, when it becomes apparent that Marty has romantic feelings for her, she dismisses him as only a friend. As she explains, "Marty's just a friend. Which is another great thing about college. You learn to have guy friends" (5.10, "But Not as Cute as Pushkin"). Rory's unwillingness to see Marty as more than a "pal" betrays her inability to understand that healthy, functional relationships are grounded in friendship. Soon, Marty, like Jess, is driven away by Rory's fickleness, revealing her desire not to be with a man who treats her as an equal and with respect.

Though Marty does not remain an active presence in Rory's life — only reappearing in season seven as the boyfriend of classmate Lucy — wealthy Logan Huntzberger is left in his absence. Marty knows Logan because he has catered parties where Logan has been a guest, and Rory's first view of Logan is a comical one; she and middle-class Marty both see Yalies like Logan — who travel in limos and participate in over-the-top stunts with The Life and Death Brigade — as immature, decadent, and materialistic. Though she is initially put off by Logan's irresponsible antics, Rory eventually becomes a willing participant in them as well as a reluctant member of his romantic harem. Logan is a womanizer, initially content to date Rory at the same time as other women. Though he ultimately decides that he wants to be in a monogamous relationship with her, the viewer is left to wonder why she would find someone like him appealing. This is especially the case when, during a short break-up, Logan sleeps with most of his sister's bridesmaids.

Ultimately, it becomes obvious that Rory is drawn to Logan precisely because he — like Dean and Jess before him — is a bad boy; he drinks to excess, spends money carelessly, travels to exotic locales, participates in dangerous stunts, and blows off his responsibilities at the *Yale Daily News*, where she first encounters him. In fact, it is his bravado at the school newspaper that initially catches Rory's interest. She — a meek, young journalist struggling for recognition — is awed by Logan's casual yet confident approach to his own articles and is no doubt impressed when she finds out that he is the son of one of the biggest publishing magnates in the country. Though Rory does not consciously admit that his family's business is part of her attraction to Logan, on some level, it must make him more appealing to her. Also, Logan is wealthy and well connected, and even though Rory and Marty have ridiculed him for this, her obsession with The Life and Death Brigade — and subsequent exposé about the group — belies a curiosity about status and privilege that is a running theme throughout the series. It is as if she wants to experience for herself the moneyed lifestyle that her grandparents epitomize and her mother has both rejected for herself and kept from her. The fact that Logan is the first romantic interest of hers of whom Emily and Richard approve is further evidence of Rory's desire to participate in their affluence.

Despite their less-than-traditional beginnings, in other ways Rory and Logan's relationship is rather old-fashioned. He surprises her with unexpected visits and buys her exotic gifts — the luxurious Berkin bag that her grandmother covets being the most obvious example — though she rarely returns the favor. Their relationship is also characterized by inequality, Logan most often holding the reins between them. For example, though Rory wants to visit Logan in London at the beginning of season seven, she puts off her own wishes when he announces he has bought her a plane ticket to visit months later during the Christmas holidays. In another revealing scene, Rory expresses a need to change out of her stuffy Daughters of the American Revolution clothes, and Logan stops her, claiming she has the "hot librarian thing going on" (6.04, "Always a Godmother"), effectively reducing her to a physical trophy. These are the ways in which Logan controls their interaction. There are hints of Rory's willingness to relinquish control to her romantic partner earlier in the show's history — most notably when she waits hours for Jess to pick her up — but with Logan, she has become the epitome of the woman in waiting — most often waiting for him to find time to fit her into his busy schedule. This is never truer than in the first half of season seven when Rory lives in Logan's apartment while he is in London running part of his father's publishing empire. Having recently graduated, Logan pays the rent while Rory finishes her senior year at Yale. She is not unlike a kept mistress, literally waiting for him to come home from London and have sex with her. When he does — on rare occasions — visit, it is notable that he has little time to spend alone with her outside of their lovemaking and even drags her along to spend time with his new colleagues. Latina feminist Ana Castillo asserts that machismo is "a defensive response to the racist and classist hierarchy under which most of modern civilization lives" (66). When Logan feels displaced and manipulated by his father, he uses Rory as a way to build himself up. Rory, pushed to the brink of frustration, finally stands up for herself, becoming most angry with him when he fails to mention that one of the coworkers, Bobbi, with whom he has been spending a good deal of time, is a woman. But even before the scene has ended, Rory is backpedaling, apologizing for her outburst. "Great," she says, "so now I'm not just an idiot, I'm an anti-feminist idiot, an anti-feminist who's standing here in the street arguing about things I don't really want to be arguing about" (7.05, "The Great Stink"). By calling herself an "anti-feminist idiot," Rory is revealing that on a conscious level, she thinks of herself as a feminist or, at the very least, that she should be a feminist and that not doing so is "idiotic." It is also notable that this is only the *second* time the word "feminist" has been explicitly used in the show's entire history, the pilot episode being the first. Her behavior is also telling because once again, Rory finds herself without the words to communicate her unhappiness about the newly feminized Bobbi and the lack of quality time she is getting with Logan in a healthy way. She is so flustered that one almost expects her to stomp her feet like an unhappy child unable to make her desires known. Though Rory is not able to adequately express her feelings in the moment, they come out to some degree in a passive aggressive fashion when, soon after this incident, she writes a scathing review of a launch party for one of Logan's business ventures.

It is important to recognize that Rory does finally stand up to Logan's attempts to control her. After she recognizes the vulnerable position she's put herself in by living in Logan's apartment, she comes to the wise conclusion that she must move out. It is unfortunate that Rory, who is bankrolled by her wealthy father at this point, passes up the opportunity to live on her own, instead choosing to live with Paris and Doyle, but it is still a step in the right direction — that is, a step towards independence. Nevertheless, it is soon revealed that despite her attempt to have a home separate from Logan, she has simultaneously become, as Mitchum describes, part of Logan's "team" (7.15, "I'm a Kayak"). Like her grandmother, she has become, in a sense, the woman behind the man. This is just another example of how, thus far, Rory fails to fulfill her mother's legacy and falls back on more traditional, heteronormative modes of behavior. As Emily notes in season seven, Lorelai is like a "kayak," rowing both sides of her boat independent of any man, while Emily is in a canoe with Richard, forced to rely on him in order to keep the boat from spinning out of control. As Emily explains, "I always thought I'd be someone's wife" (7.15, "I'm a Kayak"). In *Borderlands/La Frontera*, Gloria Anzaldúa points out that males make the rules while women reinforce them, thus "keeping women in rigidly defined roles" (17), and Emily is the perfect example of a woman who reinforces the rules of the patriarchy while also being oppressed by those same rules. Though Rory has demonstrated some assertiveness by vacating Logan's apartment, Mitchum's comment demonstrates that she is still suffering under this same system of oppression; she is, in fact, still much closer to her grandparents' canoe model than she is to the kayak personified by her mother.

It is also important to note the ways in which Logan, in typical patriarchal fashion, attempts to isolate Rory from her peers, a tendency that Castillo discusses in *Massacre of the Dreamers* (71). To her credit, Rory has never been the kind of person who feels the need to surround herself with a superficial posse of girlfriends. But when she does finally form a small social circle with Lucy and Olivia during her senior year at Yale, Logan sabotages those relationships by abruptly outing Rory's past with Marty, Lucy's current boyfriend. The end result is that Rory loses these new friends—at least in the short run—and is forced to rely on Logan for companionship more than ever.

There is evidence of similar behavior in previous plotlines. When Logan and Rory first meet, it is through Marty. Though Logan and Marty have been friendly in the past, as soon as Logan decides he is interested in Rory, he does his best to push Marty out of the picture by inviting the two of them to activities in which cash-strapped Marty cannot possibly afford to participate and generally competing with Marty for Rory's attention. Soon, Marty gives up—on both his romantic pursuit of Rory and their friendship—leaving her, once again, to rely on Logan and his crew for social interaction.

Logan's friends also mirror his inability to have equitable relationships with women. Though, for the most part, his friends do not engage in actual relationships with women, there is one notable exception: After a decadent summer in Europe, Colin returns with a Dutch milkmaid named Katrinka in tow. He claims to be in love with her, initially fawning over her beauty and iconicism. But when the novelty wears off, he ignores her until she ultimately gets the message that he's no longer interested, illustrating the fact that in Logan's world, women are seen as disposable. Rory's response to the situation is worth noting. Initially, she jokes with the boys about Katrinka, revealing that her need to fit in with them is stronger than her desire to stand up for her fellow woman; but later, she shares a moment with Katrinka, acting somewhat sympathetically towards the abandoned girl, thus creating a comparison of the two women — who both play second-string to their boyfriend's friends— in the viewer's mind.

Ultimately, what is possibly most troubling about Rory's love life is that — until the surprising series' conclusion — she never initiates or ends relationships and has no real sense of agency. Though we witness her mother proposing to Luke and best friend Lane pursuing first David and then future husband Zack, Rory has only been involved with men who have pursued her: Dean, Jess, and Logan. She even kisses long-time pursuer Tristin during season one despite the fact that she repeatedly expresses disdain for him. In this way, she is the epitome of a woman who is the object of the male gaze.

Similarly, Rory never breaks up with anyone—again, until the show's penultimate episode. While Lorelai repeatedly ends relationships with men who don't completely fulfill her—most obviously Max, Jason, and Christopher but also Luke, whom she leaves when he is unwilling to commit to a wedding date—Rory stays in relationships that don't satisfy her with Dean, Marty, and — for most of her junior and senior year of college — Logan until another, better alternative comes along. Similarly, she remains emotionally involved with Jess even after he has physically left her behind. It is notable that the only time Rory does take initiative in her romantic relationships is with Jess; when he moves back to New York, she very uncharacteristically skips school to visit him there. Then later, in season six, she travels to Philadelphia to see Jess on a whim. Though he has sent her an invitation to an open house at his publishing company, it is still a rare moment of assertiveness on Rory's part, the implication being that Jess inspires something in her that forces her to act.

Though Logan, like Christopher, appears to be the best "catch" on the surface — he's handsome, educated, charming, and wealthy — he does not offer Rory the type of equitable partnership that exists between the series' other couples: Paris and Doyle, Lane and Zack, or Sookie and Jackson. Even oddballs Kirk and Babette have more rewarding relationships with their significant others than Rory does with Logan. Though we never see Mrs. Kim's husband, no one could argue that she is not a strong woman, and his absence indicates that she is not overly dependent on him. Obviously, Richard and Emily clearly fit the model of the male-dominated, patriarchal family — he being the breadwinner and she being the domestic diva — but Emily makes it clear when she leaves Richard that even though he is the head of the household, she is not without a voice.

It is, in fact, one of the show's great ironies that, amidst a sea of functional couples, the superficially perfect Rory is unable to have a healthy, rewarding relationship and is often left feeling lonely and unfulfilled. Admittedly, we see a change in Logan in the second half of season seven when he is at her side during her grandfather's illness, but throughout the rest of their relationship, Rory plays second fiddle to Logan's other interests: first Colin, Finn, and The Life and Death Brigade and later Bobbi and his other colleagues in London. Perhaps it is impossible for Rory and Logan to have an equitable relationship given the fact that his money will always put them, to some degree, on an uneven playing field, but it is almost impossible to imagine that strong-willed characters like Emily, Sookie, Mrs. Kim, or even Gypsy would allow such an obstacle to get in the way of their quest for happiness. Like Lorelai, these women are not afraid to stand up to the men in their lives. Sookie resists Jackson's desire to have more children, albeit unsuccessfully, and Emily leaves Richard when he makes a business decision that she sees as unethical. No, these women would no more put up with Logan's self-absorbed behavior than Luke would tolerate cell phones in the diner, forcing one to ask whether or not Rory is meant to represent the problematic third-wave feminists who are ill-equipped to fight inequality (Baumgardner and Richards 18).

While Rory allows the men in her life to dictate the tenor of their relationships, Lorelai stands up to the men in hers. As already mentioned, Lorelai has a long history of both initiating and ending romantic relationships. When

Luke asks her to put off their nuptials, she agrees only so long as it is good for her mental health. Though it is of less importance, she also holds her ground when Luke wants her to sell her house and move to a bigger one in town. Similarly, she resists Christopher's attempts to get her to relocate in season seven. And though both Max and Christopher attempt to rush her into marriage, she removes herself from those situations when she sees they cannot possibly work. Of equal importance is the fact that she refuses to have a baby with Christopher before she is certain she is ready. Also, it is noteworthy that she — like her best friend Sookie — does not take Christopher's name after they marry despite the fact that he calls her "Mrs. Hayden" (7.07, "French Twist") upon their return from Paris. Lorelai's ability to hold her ground in her relationships is in stark contrast to her daughter who has so little self-determination that she goes to bed with a married man. Ultimately, Rory gives up far too much of herself to satisfy the needs of the controlling men in her life.

Interestingly, Lorelai's assertiveness is often misread as craziness from Rory's point of view. When she says to Rory that she has a crazy idea, Rory responds by saying, "Those are never comforting words coming from you" (1.13, "Concert Interruptus"). In contrast, on the few occasions when Rory is assertive in her relationships, it is covert. She tells no one about her spur-of-the-moment trips to see Jess in New York and Philadelphia. It is also revealing that, during season three, Rory suggests that she and Lorelai devil-egg Jess' car, arguing that "it's active. It's aggressive. It's destructive, but not too destructive" (3.6) even though it is, in truth, a passive way of dealing with both her and her mother's emotions.

Not only is Rory's behavior shaped by the men with whom she is in relationships, it is also affected by other outside influences, most of which are patriarchal in nature. Her grandparents are the most notable example of this. From the very first episode, the viewer watches as Rory gives up parts of herself to please Richard and Emily Gilmore. This begins with the Friday night dinners, a ritual to which Lorelai agrees in exchange for Rory's tuition at Chilton. Though Rory is initially unaware of this trade, it will forever color her interaction with her maternal grandparents as they will always have the upper hand. In that sense, Emily and Richard have a relationship with Rory that is similar to that of Logan; their money gives them power. Much to Lorelai's surprise, it isn't long after Rory meets her grandparents that she agrees to play golf with Richard, an activity in which she has no interest outside of her desire to get to know him. Throughout the next six seasons, Rory routinely goes along with the requests Richard and Emily make of her amidst Lorelai's mostly ignored protestations; she participates in an old-fashioned debutante ball, she spends a summer with her grandmother in Europe, she allows Emily to throw lavish parties for both her 16th and 21st birthdays, she takes a job at the Daughters of the American Revolution at her grandmother's suggestion, and, most importantly, she agrees to apply to Yale, Richard and Emily's alma mater. Even though she has made this concession, it is still shocking when Rory agrees to attend Yale, simultaneously allowing her choice of college to be patriarchally determined and giving up her lifelong dream of attending rival Harvard. It is this moment when the viewer realizes that Rory is no longer her own person. Even Lorelai goes along with this abrupt change of plans, telling her parents, "I know we've had our differences over where Rory should go to school, but that's behind us now. She's going to Yale, and, that's good" (3.18, "Happy Birthday, Baby"). Interestingly, the pressure that the senior Gilmores exert on Rory is most often related to her grandfather's desire for her to go to Yale even though both Emily and Richard went to school there.

If Rory's grandparents are a benevolent example of patriarchal control, Mitchum Huntzberger, malicious and manipulative both, is the malevolent other half of this male-centric equation. The first time the viewer witnesses this is when Mitchum, a publishing mogul, convinces a devastated Rory to take an internship with one of his newspapers the day after his family has insulted her by saying that she's not good enough for Logan. Though this opportunity might have been read as a peace offering at the time, later it becomes clear that Mitchum had nothing so generous in mind. When her internship is finished, he tells Rory that she is not cut out for journalism. She is affected so deeply that she drops out of school, effectively giving up her dream of becoming the next Christiane Amanpour. Granted, Mitchum's goal is to intimidate Rory, but the viewer cannot help but wonder why Rory allows him to do so. Her own mother points out that Mitchum is not to be trusted and that his is only one opinion, but rather than listen to reason, Rory lets Mitchum's criticism break her spirit. As a result, it is the patriarch of Logan's family who determines Rory's self-worth, demonstrating how malleable and weak she really is. What is equally telling is that when she recovers from this setback and encounters Mitchum again, she does not tell him how out of line he was. Instead, she is short but cordial, giving him the respect she must assume he deserves as Logan's father. Mitchum's cruel and dismissive assessment of her future and the Huntzberger family's rejection of Rory echoes feminist critic Astrid Henry's assertion that major systems of oppression — "whether based on race, sex, class, or sexuality — are interlocking" (1718). Rory allows herself to be deflated by Mitchum, the epitome of patriarchal control, while the Huntzbergers as a family deem Rory unworthy of Logan because of their prejudices pertaining to class. In this way, sex and class work in tandem to oppress Rory in the exact way that Henry describes in her essay, "Feminist Deaths and Feminism Today." When Mitchum attempts to manipulate her again by asserting the importance of Logan's move to London, she proves once more that she can be bent to his will by ultimately agreeing to help convince Logan to go. This pliant behavior continues even after Rory moves out of Logan's apartment. When Mitchum invites the two of them out for Logan's twenty-fifth birthday, he thanks Rory for convincing Logan to give London a try and tells her that "You're part of the team" (7.15,

"I'm a Kayak"), thus reinforcing the notion that, like her grandmother, she is putting the needs of her male partner ahead of her own while simultaneously revealing his own gendered ideas about the role of women.

In contrast, when patriarchal influences attempt to exert pressure on Lorelai, she consistently resists, allowing herself to make decisions, instead, in her own best interest. This is seen repeatedly throughout the series in Lorelai's interaction with her parents. On almost a daily basis, Lorelai questions their suggestions and refuses to take their advice. As a result, the hilarious and often gut-wrenching banter between Lorelai and Emily becomes one of the show's signatures. In a similar fashion, Lorelai, unlike her daughter, does not give any credence to Mitchum's caustic words about Rory's future in journalism.

But it is the premise of *Gilmore Girls* that most clearly demonstrates Lorelai's unwillingness to give into patriarchal pressures or shoehorn her life into heteronormative models. At the outset of the show, Lorelai is introduced as a woman who refused to marry her child's father, despite the objections of her parents and the tempting fact that Christopher's family had enough money to support them both. Subsequently, she also rejects her own parents' money and support when they were unwilling to respect her decision to raise a child on her own. Instead of living under the security of one of their luxurious roofs, she chose to live independently of them, both financially and emotionally. In fact, she demonstrated that she would rather work as a maid than be constantly subjected to either her parents' or Christopher's parents' negative assessment of her choices.

This is not the only time Lorelai maintains her independence in order to stay true to herself. When she needs money to finish building the inn that she and Sookie plan to open, it is also notable that she does not ask her wealthy parents for assistance, preferring instead to go to Luke, whom she sees as a person willing to give her a loan without strings attached. In fact, the only time she asks her parents for help is when she needs money for Rory's education.

Not only does Rory fail to inherit her mother's independence and confidence, she also fails to adopt her mother's attitudes about money and privilege, a fact already alluded to in the discussion of her relationship with Logan. As Henry asserts, contemporary gender issues must be considered "in tandem with other factors of identity, power, and privilege" (1719). Though Lorelai refuses her parents' money and support, her daughter is more prone to embrace the wealth and status her mother has rejected. This is never more obvious than in season six when Rory whines, "But I'm a Gilmore," after Logan's even more affluent parents' dismiss her as unsuitable for their only son (5.21, "Blame Booze and Melville"), demonstrating her willingness to use her status and position when it suits her.

But evidence of Rory's tendency towards materialism can be seen throughout the series' seven-year history. From the very first episode, Rory longs to go to Harvard and is willing to attend snotty Chilton, leaving her best friend,

Lane, behind to get there. When Lorelai and Rory's home is attacked by termites, Rory does not hesitate to go to Emily for financial support despite her mother's clear desire for financial independence. Without considering the consequences of her actions, she allows her grandparents to pay for her tuition at both Chilton and Yale, buy her a new car for her high school graduation, and decorate her freshman dorm room like a luxury hotel. After she finally begins her Ivy League education — again, on her grandparents' dime — she engages in the very lifestyle that she and Lorelai — and later Marty — once criticized.

The first change the viewer witnesses is Rory's wardrobe. Though her prudish school uniform was replaced by similarly unassuming sweaters and pants during her freshman year at Yale, her sophomore year heralds an era of fashionable tops, sexy skirts, and knee-high boots, signaling the metaphorical death of the young high school student who once filled the drawers of her dresser with books. Her attitude towards other material pursuits changes that year as well. Though at first she is wary of Logan and The Life and Death Brigade, eventually she joins their ranks. Her lifestyle changes even more drastically when she begins to date Logan, and before long, she is eating in expensive restaurants and riding in stretch limos on a regular basis. Her mother is as disgusted by this behavior as she was during season one when Rory agreed to golf with Richard at the country club but says nothing since she fears losing her daughter's confidence.

Later, like a stereotypical rich girl, Rory drops out of college and moves into her grandparents' pool house, which they promptly spend tens of thousands of dollars to redecorate, effectively spoiling their granddaughter in a fashion to which her mother would have never agreed. When Jess reappears in season six, he questions her new lifestyle: "I know you better than anyone! This isn't you," he says. "Living at your grandparents' place ... No Yale ... You going out with this jerk with the Porsche! We made fun of guys like this!" (6.08, "Let Me Hear Your Balalaikas"). In response, Rory can only offer a confused "I don't know" to his objections (6.08), signaling to the viewer that she no longer knows who she is and is willing to allow herself to be defined by both her grandparents and her boyfriend. Though Rory moves out of Richard and Emily's house and returns to Yale after this conversation, she stays in a relationship with Logan, indicating that only some of Jess's message has sunk in. In fact, by the beginning of her senior year, Rory is living in Logan's lavish New Haven apartment, where state-of-the-art appliances meet stylish décor. It is obvious that material possessions become a priority for Rory during her time at Yale, and it is fascinating to note that as Rory's sense of self shrinks, her wardrobe grows.

At the same time that Rory is becoming more accustomed to a life of luxury, her classmate Paris is shown adapting quite well to her new identity as a struggling college student after her parents' fortune is abruptly lost. Paris no longer has servants to fall back on or parents to call for emergency funds, but she soldiers on, almost stronger as a result of her financial hardships. In many ways, she appears to be carrying the feminist flag that Rory so casually drops.

It is also worth noting that Rory never lives alone. She moves from the security of her mother's house to a dorm room — and then pool house — decorated by her grandparents and from there to Logan's upscale apartment. Whenever she finds herself faced with the possibility of striking out on her own, she runs to a sympathetic party like Paris or her grandparents. In sharp contrast, Lorelai was on her own at the age of sixteen, unwilling to live with her parents or Christopher if it meant compromising any aspect of her identity.

Perhaps what is most disturbing about the character of Rory Gilmore is that when her mother — the most important person in her life, the person to whom she is the closest — tries to talk to her honestly about her choices, Rory refuses to participate in an open line of communication. The first time this happens is during season one when Rory begins to date Dean, and Lorelai is, in her own words, merely "okay-ish" with her daughter's new boyfriend (1.07, "Kiss and Tell"), who later accuses her of hating him. Lorelai is desperate not to repeat the same mistakes her mother did with her, and she expresses this desire to Luke when she says, "I have to make her understand that I'm okay with the guy thing. 'Cause not talking about guys and our personal lives. That's me and my mom. That is *not* me and Rory" (1.07). Later in the same season, Lorelai and Rory have another disagreement and Rory runs to her grandparent's house, a pattern that will become both more common and more disturbing as the series goes on. When Rory begins dating Jess, the pattern repeats itself with Lorelai worrying that Jess is a bad influence and Rory being unwilling to listen to her mother's concerns. Still, mother and daughter remain close despite Lorelai's attempts to redirect her daughter away from the bad boys to whom she is repeatedly drawn. But when Rory sleeps with a married Dean, Lorelai makes it absolutely clear that she does not approve, much to her daughter's disappointment, and Rory responds by shutting Lorelai out and running away with her grandmother to Europe. Upon her return, they make up, but Lorelai seems more reluctant to be honest with her daughter, and when, later, Rory gets drunk over Logan, she questions her daughter's desire to be with someone who causes her engage in such destructive behavior but is notably less insistent than she has been in the past, gently probing Rory rather than instructing her. At first, Lorelai is also tentative when Rory tells her, at the end of season five, that she is dropping out of Yale. But ultimately, Lorelai's strong will wins out, and she tries to tell Rory that she cannot drop out of school. Rory is so put off by her mother's unwillingness to see things from her point of view that she goes running, again, to her grandparents. Rather than consider if her mother's words have any value, she cries in her grandfather's arms, essentially begging him for a way out of her problems. The message is that she will run when Lorelai pushes her. Thus, Rory seems incapable of real self-awareness. She appears to have no desire to think critically about her choices. In contrast,

Lorelai is so hyper-analytical of the meaning behind her own actions that, during season seven, she even begins to question if all of her life choices have been affected by a desire to follow a path separate from the one her parents want her to take. At times like these, the difference between mother and daughter is palpable.

But Rory is never without promise. In fact, what makes Rory's bad decisions throughout the show's narrative arc so tragic is that she does possess the intellect, the upbringing, and the education to be a strong, independent woman. And, suddenly, at the end of season seven, the viewer sees evidence of this when we are treated to behavior that causes one to hope that she will get back on her original Susan Faludi-quoting path; Rory moves out of Logan's apartment, balks at Mitchum's promise of a position with one of his papers, interviews for jobs that might keep her away from Logan, and stands up to him when he blows off his responsibilities to party in Vegas. Still, none of these admirable choices make it any less surprising when Rory ultimately declines Logan's proposal of marriage in the series' penultimate episode. It is, in truth, this moment that most clearly defines Rory's character; she has the choice to marry Logan and move to the other side of the country — away from her mother and her friends, away from any of the jobs for which she has interviewed — or to stand on her own two feet, single and, for the time being, unemployed. If she agrees to marry him, she will likely never have to worry about money again. Logan's lucrative salary and sure-to-be-reinstated trust fund will allow her to live a life of relative ease. If she does not marry him, she will be on her own — a state we know she fears and avoids — without a job or an income. Nearly everything in Rory's past has led the viewer to believe that she wants Logan to take care of her, to make these big life decisions for her, and that she is incapable of choosing uncertainty over a clearly laid-out plan. But something shifts in Rory at that moment — most likely because of Logan's insistence that they either marry or part ways — and she turns him down, uncharacteristically opting for the unknown. At that moment, she finally becomes her mother's daughter, a woman who will not give up her independence to a man she just isn't sure about no matter how big his bank account. It is notable that moments before Rory informs Logan of her decision, she is shown smiling and laughing as she walks arm-in-arm with her girlfriends — Paris, Lucy, and Olivia — to their graduation ceremony; for the first time in the show's history, she is depicted as a young woman with a group of female peers she can both enjoy and rely on. The scene is obviously emblematic, representing the conclusion of Rory's education, both literally and metaphorically.

This wonderful but sudden shift in Rory raises the question, why was she depicted as weak and easily manipulated throughout so much of the show's history? If Lorelai — in her "Juicy" sweatpants (4.06, "An Affair to Remember") and body-skimming outfits — is a fictional embodiment of third-wave feminists who aren't ashamed to show off their figures while simultaneously demanding equality and respect, then one can't help but wonder what Rory is supposed to represent. Is it possible that, throughout most of the series, she is emblematic of the women of her generation? As Moi points out, young women today "no longer make feminism their central political and personal project" (1735). Rory Gilmore spends most of the show's seven years only superficially fulfilling her mother Lorelai's legacy of feminism, her strength during that time about as deep as her fashion-forward wardrobe. Throughout most of high school and college, she is the epitome of a weak, dependent woman who, unlike her mother, is controlled by the various men in her life. But before the final curtain comes down, Rory overcomes her insecurities as well as patriarchal influences in order to reject the watered-down feminism that is so prevalent in our society in favor of a much stronger model. A model that features independence, risk, and the road less traveled. In this way, the show uses the character of Rory to demonstrate the behavior mothers like Lorelai hope to see their daughters embrace. She not only talks a good feminist game, she also lives it, finally filling Lorelai's awfully big shoes with the courage they deserve.

Gilmore Girls, therefore, makes the argument that feminism is more than an Ivy League education and witty repartée. In reality, feminists are not always who we think they are, and they come in all different types of packages. They are not just urban women with trendy clothes and sparkling resumes; they are also the Lorelais, Sookies, and Mrs. Kims of the world, the small town and suburban women who have successful careers and healthy relationships while quietly making statements about what it means to be a strong woman. I know women like this. We all do—whether we realize it or not. And the show's creator, Amy Sherman-Palladino, understands how important it is to shine a light on both these overlooked heroes and the potential of their still malleable daughters.

Works Cited

Anzaldúa, Gloria. *Borderlands/La Frontera: The New Mestiza*. San Francisco: Spinters/ Aunt Lute, 1987.

Baumgardner, Jennifer and Amy Richards. *Manifesta: Young Women, Feminism, and the Future*. New York: Farrar, Straus and Giroux, 2000.

Castillo, Ana. *Massacre of the Dreamers: Essays on Xicanisma*. New York: Plume, 1995.

Henry, Astrid. "Feminist Deaths and Feminism Today." *PMLA* 121.5 (Oct. 2006): 1717–21.

Moi, Toril. "I Am Not a Feminist, But ...": How Feminism Became the F-Word." *PMLA* 121.5 (Oct. 2006): 1735–41.

Reinventing the Bitch

The Dynamicism of Paris Geller

ANGELA RIDINGER-DOTTERMAN

When E. M. Forster coined the terms "round" and "flat" to distinguish between dynamic and static characters,[1] he surely had not envisioned *Gilmore Girls'* Paris Geller. For to call Paris round or imply that there is any roundedness to her personality would be to commit the sort of imprecise use of diction for which the young despot would surely excoriate us. Indeed, though her character marks one of the most interesting experiments in dimensionality in the history of television, Paris's character is decidedly angular, defined by her sharp edges. Paris is just as apt to deliver a scathing diatribe on Forster's fiction as she is to fashion a shiv from a page of *Howard's End* and hold a foe at bay.

The character of Paris Geller marks an innovation in the ways in which American popular culture, and television in particular, have presented the archetype of the bitch, or more particularly, the ways in which female power and aggression have been portrayed and politicized in American popular culture. The following discussion situates *Gilmore Girls'* caustic character in the long history of representing "mean girls" in popular culture, and examines the ways in which Paris both follows and departs from the existing models of representation.

Before we begin examining historical treatment of the "bitch" archetype in American popular culture, it is perhaps useful to clarify exactly what we mean by "bitch," for it is an overused (and abused) phrase. Most of us with even a hazy recollection of the Clinton White House remember the awkward moment when Newt Gingrich's mother, Kathleen, confided to Connie Chung in a hushed whisper amplified on prime time television that the Speaker of the House thought Hillary Clinton was "a bitch." Gingrich's estimation of the then–First Lady is an example of the common overuse of the term. Because most of our culture casually applies the moniker to any woman asserting power or representing a threat, most of us have become comfortable making the

50

commonplace defense that if a man were to act like (insert bitch's name here), he would be called powerful, a good businessman, etc. To be clear, this isn't what I mean here when I say bitch. By those loose standards, even the doe-eyed Rory could on occasion qualify as a bitch. A real bitch isn't to be confused with a strong woman or even a woman exhibiting a moment of impoliteness. Paris Geller isn't simply a strong woman, nor is she a woman whose impoliteness is contained in moments. The nature of her character is that she is almost frequently unpleasant, undemocratic, and unkind. Whether there is excess in her behavior isn't up for debate. Paris is a bitch through and through.

Now, certainly we've seen plenty of bitches before, and without question popular culture will continue to reproduce these women; they make for good entertainment. However, generally bitches seem to undergo one of two fates in their representations. The bitch either retains her edge and exists as the woman we "love to hate," or she enters a process of education, rehabilitation, and transformation into a "nice girl." Both modes of representation are at their basis psychologically satisfying. The woman "we love to hate" is merely another configuration of the villain. The psychological satisfaction of the villain is universal. We need only think of most fairy tales (real and Disney-ized) to see that at the heart of each is a villain: the wicked stepmother, the big bad wolf, the sea witch, the evil king. Villains are psychologically satisfying for both simple and complex reasons.

On one hand, as embodiment of "bad" attributes and deeds, the villain in all his/her "badness" highlights the goodness and moral desirability of the hero/heroine figure. Though in real life seeing people as all good or all bad is an indicator of Borderline personality disorder, in fiction the simplicity of this viewpoint is highly functional. The audience of a work of fiction can witness a struggle between good and evil in understandable, safe terms. In real life, evil often triumphs over good. We like fiction; indeed, we like villains, because we know we are safe from them. The rules of storytelling dictate that they won't win. We can watch (or read) with smug satisfaction as they are punished, and in the process, our sense of right and wrong is reinforced.

However, this explanation for why villains satisfy us does little to explain why we find ourselves more delighted by *Othello*'s Iago than the morally good Othello, Desdemona, or Cassio, or why we inwardly cheer when *Mean Girls'* Regina George deflates the junior varsity jock by telling him to go shave his back (for which he calls her, not coincidentally, a bitch). The impulse is the same one that prompts us as children to want to be the robber instead of the cop. There is something viscerally savory about imagining acting outside the rules. In real life, we are healthily bound by consideration for others and anticipation of repercussions. Most of us want to be liked most of the time by most people. In other words, our psychological need for inclusion and approval outweighs our desire to behave in ways that violate our social code. Villains, at least the compelling ones, act in ways that we find satisfying in part simply because their ability to defy social convention allows them more power and levity of behavior than we enjoy in real life. This is not to say that we sympathize with villains, at least not in the same way that we sympathize with heroes and heroines. We don't really want to bring harm to people. We do, however, harbor dark "what ifs" that villains act out for us.

As villains, bitches psychologically satisfy us in both of these ways. Everyone is the victim of someone else's cruelty in some measure, and by the time we have transitioned out of elementary school, at least some of this cruelty has come at the hands of a female. When we see bitches pitted against a protagonist with whom we identify, and witness the bitch's comeuppance, we feel that in some way we have taken a little of our dignity back. As a child, I drew great satisfaction from watching reruns of *Little House on the Prairie* where young Laura triumphs over Nellie Olson. Watching Laura run fresh-faced and vindicated down the dirt road of Walnut Grove while Nellie's red face seethed behind her window pane made it a little easier to endure the real life bullies of second grade.

I'm not sure that bitches satisfy the dramatization of the dark "what ifs" for men in the same way that they do for women, but for most women, or at least most whom I can imagine reading this article, bitches satisfy a longing in us to occasionally breach the (dare I venture?) unequally narrow boundaries of acceptable female behavior. Without negating my distinction between a bitch and a powerful woman or impolite woman, it is nonetheless a fact of life that demonstrations of female power that threaten the male establishment or impoliteness of any sort are the domain of the bitch. As such, a bitch represents an albeit extreme manifestation of the power that women find themselves at a lack to express without incurring social sanction. Beyond this, however, the bitch provides access to desires for power and, somewhat paradoxically, inclusion that most of us are unable to realize in real life. To better explain, we might return to the example of the popular film *Mean Girls*. In writing *Mean Girls*, Tina Fey used as her basis the psychological study *Queen Bees and Wannabees*, an examination of the precarious lives of adolescent girls. As embodiment of the Queen Bee, Regina George secures her power within the community of the high school through overt and covert acts of social terror. Yet, like any formidable villain, Regina's consolidation of power is contingent upon her possessing qualities that others find desirable (otherwise she could be dismissed from the high school zeitgeist altogether). Even while engaged in trying to disarm Regina of her wiles, including her "man-candy" Aaron and her "army of skanks," Cady finds herself desiring Regina's approval and friendship. This is an important component of the bitch who survives in fiction. She must be compelling to us in some way; we must admire her even as we dislike her. In part, we revile her; in part, we want to emulate her. We carry with us a faint hope that she might like us. This is the origin of the psychological pleasure the bitch provides for us.

Of course, because the bitch figure represents a threat to social harmony, and to the social harmony of men in particular, we should not be surprised that rather than functioning as the person we love to hate, the bitch has more often served in fiction as a project of moral and social reform. Usually at the hands of a man, the bitch finds herself chastised, chastened, repentant, and reformed. Sure, she might still be a little sassy (insert patronizing wink here), but she knows who's boss. The figure of the reformed bitch dates back at least as far as Shakespeare. Most popularly, the spirited Kate the Cursed (*The Taming of the Shrew*) is subdued by Petruchio, her bitchiness replaced by an uneasy obedience. In American popular culture, the reformed bitch figure began appearing as early as the late eighteenth century. This figure emerged in many of the novels espousing moral value and guidance, and written for young female consumers (perhaps to deter any would-be bitches). In Susanna Rowson's *Charlotte: A Tale of Truth* (1791), Mademoiselle La Rue cruelly lures the hapless semi-heroine Charlotte from the safety of her family and friends in England to a life of infamy in America, topping her act off with turning a pregnant Charlotte out onto the street in the dead of winter. It's no mistake that Rowson's novel ends with Charlotte's parents and daughter finding Mademoiselle La Rue homeless on the street, much as Charlotte years before, and sorry for her long life of sin. The reformed bitch makes lower-stakes appearances in fiction throughout the nineteenth century in the best-selling novels written for female consumers. Susan Warner's *The Wide, Wide World* (1850) is primarily a novel dedicated to the moral maturation of the already angelic Ellen Montgomery. However, a minor character in this novel is Nancy, the granddaughter of old Mrs. Vawse. Throughout the early portions of the novel, we see how our poor Ellen endures Nancy's torments—the taunting, the tickling—persisting in setting the good Christian example of somber self-sacrifice promised on her mother's deathbed. Not surprisingly, Ellen's goodness prevails, and Nancy is inspired to amend her bad ways. Similarly, Little Eva in Harriet Beecher Stowe's *Uncle Tom's Cabin* (1852) reforms the lawless Topsy through Christian love.

The pressure to suppress ire on the basis that it signals an un–Christian and unfeminine emotion also appeared in relation to female characters who fell short of being bitches, but were simply unconventional. In the beloved *Little Women* (1868), Jo March—perhaps the most likeable saccharine character of the century—is urged by her mother to forgive her younger sister Amy for burning her manuscripts. When Amy, still out of Jo's good graces, falls through the ice and nearly drowns, Jo comes to Marmee to "'fess." "It's my dreadful temper! I try to cure it; I think I have, and then it breaks out worse than ever.... It seems as if I could do anything when I'm in a passion; I get so savage, I could hurt anyone and enjoy it. I'm afraid I shall do something dreadful and some day, and spoil my life, and make everybody hate me" (79–80). It is interesting to note that the impulse to forgive and reform is put on Jo, the least feminine and conventional of the March sisters. Marmee confides to Jo that she too once had a bad temper, but was "cured" by Mr. March. "He helped and comforted me, and showed me that I must try to practise [sic] all the virtues I would have my little girls possess, for I was their example" (81). The suggestion seems to be that to arrive at a happy womanhood (marriage and motherhood), Jo must subvert her assertion of her will and sense of the value of her writing (for this is what puts Jo "in a passion" to begin with). Indeed, when Jo does meet her husband-to-be Mr. Bhaer, she foregoes her own identity as an author and begins to assess her values through his "mental or moral spectacles," concluding that the stories she writes are "trash," and that by writing them she has hurt her herself "and other people, for the sake of money" (344). The tale ends with Jo terminating her career as a sensationalist author and accepting a proposal for marriage from Mr. Bhaer.

Looking at these historical representations of the bitch (or in the last case, the potential bitch) illuminates some of the important social encoding that underlies the diachronic treatment of this stereotype. Dating from the Early Modern Period in England, women's legal status as *femmes couvertes* was justified on, among other things, the basis that public expression rendered a woman unchaste. To publish — or to speak publicly — was to be a woman of infamy. Even as the laws of coverture receded, the viewpoint that a woman's mode of verbal expression indicated the quality of her moral character — indeed, her sexual purity — was retained.[2] In the 1650s and the 1850s, and indeed even in the 1950s, women were taught to believe that said that femininity was attached to self-negation and silence. It is a short leap, then, to understand that the bitch as villain is a product of a long historical progression of men's fear of women's expressive power, and that the stereotype encompasses more than just "mean" behavior. The bitch isn't a desirable sexual mate. Consider even contemporary representations of bitches. More often than not, they are girls or women who are either promiscuous or mannishly asexual. "Mean girls" aren't "nice girls." Indeed, this representation is in keeping with the etymology of the word. The *Oxford English Dictionary* notes the term "bitch" was "applied opprobriously to a woman" to signal "strictly, a lewd or sensual woman." This use of the phrase is first noted in literature in the anonymously authored Chester Plays, as early as 1400, and continued to appear commonly in literature throughout the nineteenth century. While the modern use of the word is simply "a malicious or treacherous woman," representations of the bitch figure suggest that the word retains its original baggage.

Consider some of the bitches who appeared in major motion pictures at roughly the same time that *Gilmore Girls* hit the air. In the awesomely bad cheerleading flick *Bring It On* (2000), representations of the promiscuous bitch figure abound, clad in spankies and toting pompoms.

Within the film, the sprightly and earnest Torrance Shipman finds herself pitted against the world of competitive cheerleading, an unwitting squad captain trying to restore credibility to her team after learning the previous captain has stolen their past championship-winning routines from an inner-city high school. In attempting to lead her jejune minions to an earned national title, Torrance faces opposition from a bitch duo, Darcy and Courtney, who typify the bitch-as-whore archetype. Through Torrance's good example, Darcy and Courtney see the light, acquiesce, and reform to become team players. Thus, the film simultaneously reinforces the patterns of representing the bitch as hypersexual and the bitch as a project for reform.

In MTV Films' brilliant revisitation of high school politics, *Election* (1999), the perky but ruthless Tracy Flick controls the petty power at Carver High School. Without any apparent display of conscience, she brings about the social destruction of not one but two of her male teachers. At the heart of the teachers' undoing is an affair between Tracy and her teacher, Mr. Novotny. The liaison discovered, Mr. Novotny is fired, while Tracy remains unscathed and stands poised to win the student council presidency. When confronted by Jim McAllister about the affair, she gives this hoary reply, leaving the teacher wide-eyed and wordless:

> I don't know what you're referring to, but maybe if certain older, wiser people hadn't acted like such little babies and gotten so mushy, then everything would be okay, ... and I think certain older people ... shouldn't be leching after their students ... and they certainly shouldn't be making slanderous accusations, especially when certain young naïve people's mothers are paralegal secretaries at the city's biggest law firm.

The representation of Tracy in *Election* is interesting, as she is on the one hand depicted as the teen nymph who has seduced the dimwitted Mr. Novotny and made familiar overtures to Mr. McAllister, and on the other asexualized, an ineligible mate for her male peers. Tracy dresses like a member of the PTA, and draws little attention from the boys of Carver High beyond insults. Nonetheless, while the film creatively dabbles in subverting both the bitch-as-slut and bitch-as-man stereotypes, it fails to resist either one.

Returning our attention to Paris Geller, it is my contention that Paris's development from girlhood to womanhood and the acquisition of a sexual identity marks one of the more interesting evolutions of her character, one that both reinforces and departs from traditional representations of the bitch. When we meet Paris in the first season of the television series, one of the things that stands out about her character is that she is without the lacquered façade of her female peers. Where the Lorelais, played by Lauren Graham (mother) and Alexis Bledel (daughter) are, through a combination of nature and (we can presume) cosmetics, physically attractive and soft in appearance, Liza Weil's Paris is comparatively broad-faced and plain, an effect which is also partly achieved through the use (or lack) of cosmetics. Her sturdiness contrasts with Rory's bookish daintiness. The difference in physical appearance is surely no mistake. I'm not suggesting that Paris is presented without insecurities in season one. In fact,

her insecurities create the opportunity for the founding of her quasi-friend-
ship with Rory. I simply wish to point out that the character of Paris is consciously constructed on several levels to appear as something other than a sweet,
fresh-faced girl of sixteen.

The development of Paris's character in the first season begins by following a fairly predictable pattern. When Rory enters Chilton as "the new girl,"
she transgresses on Paris's territory. While Paris isn't a "Queen Bee" in the typical sense of the word, she is not without her own sort of status. Paris sees herself as the "smart person" at Chilton, an impressive distinction at the Ivy League
mill. Studious Rory, with her shared goal of making it to the hallowed halls of
Harvard, represents a threat. Paris is also not without her cronies. Madeline
and Louise reinforce Paris's tyranny, isolating Rory from the social life at Chilton
on her command. Madeline's and Louise's devotion to Paris is one of the great
mysteries of *Gilmore Girls;* the reason for their allegiance to her (or Paris's allegiance to them, for that matter) is never made clear. Played as overindulged
and underengaged heirs to Connecticut's social aristocracy, they seem to have
nothing in common with her. Nonetheless, they appear for the first three seasons as Paris's sister harpies. What is fully clear is that Paris "runs" Chilton; in
a school constructed to usher the students in to the top tier, Paris gets her hands
on all the hot "commodities" that pad college applications: the student council, the school newspaper, etc. Paris achieves this consolidation of Chilton's
opportunities primarily through her acerbic speech. For all her insecurities,
Paris pulls no punches when exploiting her peers' foibles. For example, target-
ing Rory's naïve likeability, Paris snaps, "Maybe someday I'll stumble into a
Disney movie and suddenly be transported into your body, and after living
there a while, I'll finally find the beauty within myself" (2.07, "Like Mother,
Like Daughter"). Who can forget her torture of Broadway Brad before the
Chilton speech competition (3.16, "The Big One")? Or several years later, Paris's
potshot at a fellow speed-dater's brave attempt at small-talk? When Paris tells
him her name, and Jack asks if her parents traveled a lot, she retorts, "No. Did
your parents change flat tires a lot? ... Or plug the phone into the wall a lot?"
(5.10, "But Not as Cute as Pushkin").

Perhaps most deliciously vicious of all is her reply to the dippy co-ed who
asks a visibly drenched Paris if it's raining outside. "No, it's national baptism
day! Have your tubes tied, you moron!" (4.17, "Girls in Bikinis, Boys Doin' the
Twist"). As entertainment value, Paris's verbal down-dressings of her hapless
victims are priceless. In the world of the television series, her insults collude
with her plain face to make her an unattractive mate for her male peers.

In the episode "Rory's Dance" (1.09), we begin to see the ways in which
Paris is socially isolated even as she seems to have it all. Selling the tickets to
the Chilton dance, Paris sells two to the Chilton hottie, Tristin. We watch as
Tristin inconsiderately flirts with Paris, even as he plans to ask Rory to the
dance. The night of the dance, Paris's date hits on Rory, and when Rory rebuffs

him, we learn that Paris's escort for the evening is her cousin. Sure that Rory will use the information to expose her vulnerability to the rest of the school, Paris loudly confronts her rival.

> Now you can just go all over the school and just tell everyone that Paris Geller couldn't get a date to the dance.... [S]he had to get her mother to ask her cousin Jacob to take her, and ... give him gas money just to make him do it.

Paris's admission here is an indication that her sharp tongue is partly used to conceal an insecure, hurting psyche. We are tempted to think that she will enter the path of rehabilitation; her façade penetrated, Paris will become a nice girl.

In one of the first signs that Rory and Paris can exist as something other than archenemies, Rory helps Paris dress for a Rory-arranged date with Tristin (1.18, "The Third Lorelai"). Paris's relative insecurity about the date stands in contrast to her abrasive projection of superiority, and as viewers, we can't help but hope that Paris will find love (or whatever it is that people find when they are sixteen). Paris's social awkwardness creates for viewers the opportunity to feel empathy. Up to this point in the season, we have rightly regarded her only as a foe. We don't go so far as to like her, at least in the way that we like Rory, but we invest in her fate with a wish other than seeing her downfall. The next morning in the school room, we can't help blush for Paris when we learn she has called Tristin five times to tell him she had a good time, or sting with her when he tells her they should go out again "as friends." That we hurt for Paris signals that she has become something other than our stock bitch figure. We are not glad that she has been rebuffed, and are not happy that Tristin really desires our heroine Rory.

The sequence leading up to Tristin's rejection of Paris seems to reveal that the writers of the television series were working within, and ultimately against, the preexisting narratives of the bitch figure. When Paris places her awkward self in Rory's capable hands to prepare for the date, we wonder whether she is, in fact, on the road to rehabilitation. We believe, at least for part of an episode, that Paris is on the verge of a transformation. Will the ugly (or, more accurately, awkward) duckling become a swan? Will the "mean" girl reform and receive the alpha male as her reward? Tristin's rejection of Paris ends this possibility. The moment of vulnerability gone, Paris rearms and resumes her torment of Rory, breaking her assault only for occasional self-serving entreaties for Rory's assistance (for instance, as a student council running mate). However, Paris doesn't then evolve into the bitch we love to hate. Instead, though the dimensions of Paris's character continue to bump up against the preexisting narratives of female sexuality and aggression, the character manages to become something other than what has come before her. She is a whole new kind of bitch.

The volatility of Rory's relationship with Paris defines the three Chilton years of the series, culminating in yet another interesting milestone in Paris's sexual development. Throughout the eighteenth and nineteenth century, most popular fiction strayed little from the reiteration of the sex = death formula; the act of premarital sex so ruined the prospects for a woman's life that the only way to handle her was to kill her off, usually slowly and with a great deal of pathetic sentiment. Even to the end of the twentieth century, the pattern survived in horror films, the promiscuous teen slaughtered, the virgin surviving, a trope so recognizable it was parodied in the 1997 hit *Scream*.[3] Of course, by the end of the twentieth century, other models for female teen sex had also emerged. We gritted our teeth through another "very special *Blossom*" as Six and Blossom agonized whether to do "it" or not, and sat on the edge of our seats as *Beverly Hills 90210*'s Brenda Walsh did and regretted it. Buffy (*Buffy the Vampire Slayer*) even enjoyed sex, though the act seemed to summon the wrath of hell. The *American Pie* girls gave it up on prom night in trysts ranging from awkward to comically bawdy, all surviving to appear in the first sequel. However, variations aside, none of these amorous moments approached Paris's "first time."

In the episode "The Big One" (3.16), Paris and Rory find themselves ordered to collaborate on a speech to be given at the Chilton Bicentennial, televised on C-SPAN. As they reluctantly meet to plan their speech, Paris confides to Rory that she and her boyfriend, Jamie, had sex. She characterizes the moment in this way. She says that she'd gone to his house and they just "did it." Paris was "surprised" by the moment because she "wasn't wearing anything particularly alluring" and because they had been "discussing modern day Marxism in America, which is not what I would have deemed a come-and-get-it sort of conversation, but nevertheless, he came and got it, and I have to figure out what that means to me on a psychological level."

We learn in this moment (along with Lorelai, eavesdropping in the hallway) that Rory hasn't had sex, even though the first three seasons have in part been devoted to her emerging sexual identity. We also learn that Paris enjoyed sex, and that the act, though spontaneous, wasn't a moment of recklessness. "It was a regular After School Special." The next day, however, Paris arrives late to the Chilton bicentennial, with a crazed look in her eye and her rejection letter from Harvard clutched in her fist. Though sex doesn't equal death for Paris, she does claim that doing the deed keeps her out of Harvard.

On one hand, we can smartly argue that Paris not getting into Harvard has nothing to do with her having sex, but more to do with the creative direction of the television series. By the end of season three, Paris had become such a compelling character that the show would have suffered from her absence. Rory changes her lifelong dream of attending Harvard to attending Yale, and Paris has to follow her to Yale, so that everyone can stay within proximity to Hartford and Stars Hollow, and the crux of the narrative — Rory's relationship with Lorelai — can remain intact. On the other hand, coming as it does on the heels of her "first time," we can see the writers of the series framing Paris's sexual foray in terms of the traditional representation of premarital coitus, the sex equals physical death formula. Lorelai's whisper to herself after hearing in the hallway of Paris's deflowering, "I've got the good kid," suggests a traditional attitude about sexual purity, and makes us wonder if, perhaps, Paris is being punished (just as, ironically, Lorelai was sixteen years earlier), as does Paris's confession to Rory after the Chilton bicentennial disaster that she fears she has become part of the stereotypical teen sex narrative. "I can't believe I slept with Jamie.... What if he doesn't love me anymore? What if he doesn't think I'm special anymore" (3.16, "The Big One").

Ultimately, however, *Gilmore Girls* resists punishing Paris for sex. Yes, she doesn't get to go to Harvard, but she does get to go to Yale. Jamie doesn't lose respect for Paris and never speak to her again. In fact, it is Paris who lets go of Jamie a year later, in what again is a relationship that plays along with and resists a common narrative of female sexual experience. When Richard introduces Paris and Rory to his friend Professor Asher Fleming, we hardly imagine that Paris's interest in him will amount to more than a prospective letter of recommendation. Surprised we are when, with Rory, we see Paris and Asher lip-locked after the Harvard-Yale game. The relationship between the sixty-year-old professor and the frosh Paris begins with Paris's complete absorption in the relationship. Staying out late, dangerously close to neglecting her studies, Paris displays the tell-tale signs of infatuation. In the episode "A Family Matter" (4.12), Jamie comes from Princeton to visit Paris, only to be ignored and then coldly dumped. Paris's dismissal of Jamie effectively foregrounds her utter lack of loyalty to him and emphasizes her bitchiness. Reflecting on Rory's accusation that she has been unfair to Jamie, Paris concedes, "I've been pretty mean." She eases her conscience by picking up the phone, dialing Jamie, and gently breaking the news to him. "Hey, it's me. We've gotta end this— now. There's just no reason to prolong it. Sorry you came all the way down here." Rory sums up the moment well, commenting that Paris used "all the tact of a Nazi Storm Trooper."

As the relationship between Paris and Asher develops during the season, we begin to suspect that Paris will fall victim to Asher's usury, the naïve young girl seduced and forgotten by the older, more experienced man. Indeed, the show drops several hints of this, like Paris's wistful remarks on spring break in Florida that she thought Asher might have invited her to the academic conference he is speaking at in Denver (4.17, "Girls in Bikinis, Boys Doin' the Twist"). We find ourselves waiting for Paris to get her comeuppance for her lack of judgment and her cruelty to Jamie. The play on our expectations, our subconscious allegiance to a preexisting narrative, culminates in the episode "Luke Can See Her Face" (4.20).

In the immediately preceding episode, Paris and Rory attend Professor Fleming's bookstore reading of his newest novel, where they find themselves in the company of a number of young women clamoring for the attention of the "academic dreamboat." We learn through the editor of the *Yale Daily News*, Doyle (the next Mr. Geller), that Professor Fleming has a "new girl" every year, and deduce that Paris is just one in a long pattern of delicious young things consumed by the good professor with an appetite for youth (4.19, "Afterboom"). However, in "Luke Can See Her Face" (4.20), after Paris resolves to break up with Asher, concluding that he is losing interest, we are surprised to discover that Paris is the exception in Professor Fleming's long chain of young conquests. Asher's apparent coolness—his hints that she shouldn't join him in England for the summer — stem from his own insecurities about Paris's affections, not from a lack of genuine interest in Paris. Thus, though we have expected Paris to finally be the one to be dumped, she's not. Asher and Paris take flight to Oxford at the end of season four, leaving viewers behind to marvel at Paris's surprising maturity and Asher's respect for her.

All good things must come to an end, however, and at the beginning of season five, we learn that Asher has died of a heart attack while at Oxford. Left mouths-a-gaping by Paris's assurance to Rory that Asher does not die during sex — "No, Rory. This great man was not brought down by my vagina" (5.03, "Written in the Stars") — we watch as Paris begins to search for a new relationship. We are a little surprised, but in that "we should have known" way, when Paris and Doyle discover a match in each other at speed dating (5.10, "But Not as Cute as Pushkin"). After over a year of working together at the *Yale Daily News*, Paris and Doyle begin a relationship that is defined by its strangeness, its sensuousness, and its occasional volatility. In other words, though viewers have by now learned not to expect the expected from Paris's love relationships, the partnership between Paris and Doyle is, oddly, what we might expect. The dynamic of the relationship between Paris and Doyle is not one of equality; Paris "wears the pants," and Doyle is happily "emasculated." This is visually emphasized for us the evening Paris kicks Doyle out of their apartment, when he winds up pouring his heart out at the bar to Rory and heads back to Paris's apartment looking rather like an awkward pimp, clothed in Rory's very girly coat (6.16, "Bridesmaid Revisited"). However, their relationship resists being more than whip-and-mule. While the power is not shared equally, there is elasticity in their exchange. Consider Paris and Doyle's study of Krav Maga. The two spar together, an exchange that suggests both equality and playfulness (6.16, "Bridesmaid Revisited"). Doyle and Paris are also sensual; Rory's unwitting walkings-in-on are common. In the episode "Knit, People, Knit!" (7.09), we even see Paris and Doyle "scorching the floorboards" at a party, Paris clearly feeling free to express her femininity and her sensuality in public. In this relationship, Paris has come a long way from the teary-eyed Chilton overachiever wondering if she was a slut, or the college frosh sneaking around with Professor Fleming. Paris has achieved a security in her sexuality, and she has done this with Doyle.

The final resolution of their relationship — insofar as we are forced to accept that one exists by the series ending—is that Doyle comes to love Paris fully, without any expectation for her reform. In the episode 7.19, "It's Just Like Riding a Bike," Paris breaks up with Doyle so that she can decide which graduate school to attend without attaching her decision to concern for a man. It's a move that is cold and heartless—thoroughly bitchy—but also refreshingly true to Paris's goals. As she explains to Rory, "This decision is the culmination of everything I've ever worked for, everything. I should choose a school based on its merits, not based on its proximity to some guy." Though Paris is resigned to live with her self-inflicted heart-break, Doyle is not. Returning to her apartment to find that Doyle has refused to move out, Paris reminds him "We're broken up." Doyle refuses to accept her decision, proclaiming "I love you, Paris Geller. You are the ... most exciting woman I have ever met in my entire life, and there is no way I'm gonna let you go." When Paris tells him he doesn't "have a choice," Doyle sticks to his position. "Sure, I do" he says. "Just because you don't want to base your decision on me doesn't mean I can't base my decision on you." When Paris pretests that they are too young, Doyle counters, "Maybe you are, but I'm older and a heck of a lot more mature."

Perhaps inspired by his years with Paris, Doyle finds his spine. However, Doyle's bravery (for it is only a brave man who can love Paris) comes in the form of his decision to follow Paris. Paris demonstrates a new kind of bravery in this moment, too. Characteristically suspicious and distrusting of everyone, certain in her conviction that she has to look out for herself, Paris lets Doyle follow her. She exhibits the confidence that she's worth following.

More importantly, Paris has not been tamed. She remains as sharp-edged as ever, her laser tongue knowing no mercy, even for a friend. How apt are her words to Rory in the first episode of season seven. Deriding Rory for her friendliness to a SAT tutee, Paris scolds, "Today's work was shoddy, at best. Between the overt coddling and the inappropriate flirting, I feel like I'm running a bordello." She tells Rory that none of her students fall in love with her because "you don't fall in love with people that make you want to crap your pants" (7.01, "The Long Morrow"). But Doyle has fallen in love with Paris, as did Asher and Jamie before him. In this mystery lies one of the greatest achievements of the character of Paris Geller, for while *Gilmore Girls* has successfully avoided succumbing to pat, anticipated narratives about female sexuality, and the bitch in particular, the series has managed to do something even more amazing. In allowing Paris to remain a bitch (and how!), while simultaneously casting the affections of interesting, smart, worthwhile men upon her, the series has succeeded in reinventing the bitch archetype. The bitch, represented by Paris, can retain her edge, and while we can't deny her caustic behavior, we can love her both because of and in spite of it. Paris's bitchiness—her intolerance for any inadequacy around her—stems from her own high standards and personal accomplishments. She tolerates nothing less than excellence in others because she tolerates nothing less than excellence in herself. Without ignoring the excess of her perfectionism, and certainly without failing to acknowledge her bitchiness, we begin to see Paris as more than just a villain and embrace her as a strong, albeit imperfect, woman. In the sexual maturation of Paris, we see her evolve from the insecure Chiltonian to a sensuous woman, her sexuality represented not as a fault to judge or an agent for her reproof, but as one expression of a multidimensional, formidable character.

Notes

1. Forster's discussion of round and flat characters appears in *Aspects of the Novel*, Harcourt, 1927.

2. For a more extensive discussion of the *femmes couvertes* in Early Modern England, see Margaret W. Ferguson's "Renaissance Concepts of the 'Woman Writer,'" *Women and Literature in Britain*, 1500–1700, ed. Helen Wilcox, Cambridge: Cambridge UP, 1996. For illustration of the concepts transformation and transplantation in 19th century American, see Joyce W. Warren, "The Gender of American Individualism: Fanny Fern, the Novel, and the American Dream," *Politics, Gender and the Art: Women, the Arts, and Society*, ed. Dotterer and Bowers, Seligsgrove, PA: Susquehanna UP, 1992.

3. This is voiced by the character Randy (Jamie Kennedy) when he explains "the rules" for surviving a horror film.

Works Cited

Alcott, Louisa May. *Little Women*. 1868. Introduction Susan Cheever. New York: Modern Library, 2000.

Bring It On. Dir. Peyton Reed. Perf. Kirsten Dunst, Eliza Dushku, Jesse Bradford. Universal Studios, 2000.

Election. Dir. Alexander Payne. Perf. Matthew Broderick and Reese Witherspoon. MTV Films, 1999.

Gingrich, Kathleen. Interview. *Eye to Eye with Connie Chung*. CBS. 5 Jan. 1995.

Mean Girls. Dir. Mark Waters. Perf. Lindsay Lohan, Tina Fey, and Rachel McAdams. Paramount Pictures, 2004.

"Bitch." *Oxford English Dictionary*. OED Online. 3 Jan. 2007

Rowson, Susanna. *Charlotte Temple*. 1791. Introduction Cathy N. Davidson. New York: Oxford UP, 1986.

Scream. Dir. Wes Craven. Perf. David Arquette, Neve Campbell, and Courtney Cox. Dimension Films, 1996.

Stowe, Harriet Beecher. *Uncle Tom's Cabin*. 1852. Introduction Elizabeth Ammons. New York: W. W. Norton and Company, 1994.

Warner, Susan. *The Wide, Wide World*. 1850. Afterword Jane Tompkins. New York: The Feminist Press at CUNY, 1987.

Drats! Foiled Again

A Contrast in Definitions

ANNE K. BURKE ERICKSON

Gilmore Girls is a pleasant, upbeat series that relates the story of Lorelai Gilmore (Lauren Graham), a single mother who left an affluent home as a teen to independently raise her daughter, Rory (Alexis Bledel), in the rustic, idyllic, small New England town. When Rory's academic success leads to the path that Lorelai herself rejected — specifically private school, although other trappings are not far behind, Lorelai returns to her parents — Richard and Emily — to seek assistance. The still-grieving-the-separation parents agree, on the condition that Lorelai and Rory become actively involved. Due to this situation, many of the myths of this show are offered in contrast to their realities, revealing the oft-insisted on roles of the script are actually false, but tacit acceptance and verbal insistence, prevents this illusion from being deconstructed on the show. Close examination, however, reveals cracks in the ideal Mother image, the self-made woman image, the "good" daughter image, and what is or isn't effective communication.

If one were to watch the entire series of *Gilmore Girls*, one might notice how often Lorelai describes Rory as a "good girl," but, over time, it becomes clear that this simple description is overly simplified. In the course of the series, "good" Rory accomplishes much that is good, and much that is problematic — morally and legally. Rory manages to stay out all night after a high school dance, sleep with a married man, break up his marriage, miss her mother's college graduation because she skipped school to visit someone in New York City, become estranged several times from her mother, quit college, and commit grand larceny. Through a series of foils, we are presented with other young adults who are comparatively worse, distracting the viewer from questioning this frequent assertion that Rory is, in fact, a good girl. As a result, the casual viewer may miss the greater implications of morality, maturity, and parenthood implicit in this series.

Continually, Rory is represented as good or perfect. Her being sweet, kind, and good means she won't say no to Emily regarding golfing with Richard, nor to Luke regarding tutoring his wayward nephew Jess. Generally, Lorelai is proffering these claims, and they frequently belie the current situation. "That's not Rory.... Rory doesn't throw fits" (1.04, "Deer Hunter"). "Rory is never late, almost annoyingly on time." She even tells Rory who she is: "You don't lose it in class; that's not part of the Rory personality description." In the big blowout with Emily after Rory stays out all night the night of the Chilton dance, Lorelai says Rory is "smart and careful, and I trust her and she's going to be fine" (1.09, "Rory's Dance"), although staying out all night is neither smart nor careful, and the episode does shake Lorelai's faith, providing yet another conflict between claims and behaviors. For the most part, however, Rory's sweetness and kindness makes her vulnerable, and in need of protection. She falls victim to the Huntzbergers whose privilege allows them to pronounce her unworthy to marry into their family or to pursue a career in journalism. Her timidity and desire to go along with the flow consistently gets her into trouble, while making her a likeable character. Whether it is being entangled in Marty's hiding their previous friendship, or navigating the Paris-as-editor-in-chief storyline, Rory is kind, sympathetic, and appealing.

No matter how "totally low maintenance, like a Honda" (1.02, "The Lorelais' First Day") Lorelai defines Rory (as to Headmaster Charleston), episode after episode proves otherwise. Rory struggles academically her first year, accidentally trashes Paris' very elaborate project, is caught breaking into the Headmaster's office, and has a meltdown during a test. She misses her mother's college graduation because she skips school to visit Jess in New York (and then grounds herself). While these can be justified — transferring late, a stuck locker, and trying to "join in" as demanded by the administration — the plotlines belie these claims, enabling the show to have tension-filled plotlines and sufficient drama to attract the huge following *Gilmore Girls* has. These plotlines become increasingly mature as Rory's character also does, including Rory's first sexual encounter being with a married man and her "no-strings" relationship with Logan. As a result, over the span, there seems to be a disconnect between the *Gilmore Girls'* being a well-advertised Family Friendly Programming Forum's Script Development,[1] with the requirement to have a "responsible resolution of issues" and a show that parents and kids can watch together. As one of the FFPF's most successful investments, it is still highly promoted by the FFPF, despite Rory's degrading moral character. This conflict — between the idea of a perfect fictional character who is good and sweet, and the need for a driving plot line — produces interesting challenges throughout. Because half of the appeal of the show is a desire to identify with the Gilmore Girls, these characters must navigate interesting plotlines while maintaining their appeal. In fact, the proposed plotline to rescue the show from its slump and possible non-renewal was the season ender in which Rory loses her virginity to the already-married Dean — a plotline Amy Sherman-Palladino pitched (Shaw). This high-lights the conflict between family-friendly plotlines and viewer shares.

A tandem assertion is that the mother and daughter do not fight, which is also negated as often as it is expressed. Rory and Lorelai argue over whether she will attend Chilton when Rory has cold feet and is attracted to Dean, a new boy in town. Sookie explains to Lorelai that mothers and daughters do fight, but Lorelai asserts, "we don't fight" (1.01, "Pilot"). Thus, right from the very beginning, the reader is provided with a fictional history of this family dynamic which makes a small spat seem noteworthy. The disagreements and subsequent periods of not communicating with each other will grow more serious as the seasons pass, partly so the characters can express how "unusual" this fighting is, and partly so the storylines can escalate to avoid repeating the same old conflict. The situation of the fights' growing more severe just so they can claim this is not something they do adds a layer of irony.

Season one involves the squabble over Dean, and season two brings dis-agreements about Jess and how Rory treats Dean. Season three brings a fight between them during a dinner party. By season four, Rory is in college and by the end, Lorelai catches her sleeping with the married Dean, leading to a long silence that carries into season five, which climaxes with Rory's stealing a boat and quitting Yale, and another long silence between the two. At this point, Lane says to Rory, "You two? It will blow over....You and your mom will talk again. You and Lorelai have gone too many years without fighting" (6.04, "Always a Godmother"). The clash between Lane's statement and the reality of their rela-tionship is not observed or admitted. All parties ignore the elephant in the room and pretend that Lorelai and Rory have perfect and consistent communication between them, when their battles provide the bulk of plot tension in the show. Based on the elevating conflicts between mother and daughter, it is hard to imagine that this statement could go unchallenged, but it is only because the relationship Rory has had with her mother is much more open than the rela-tionship that Rory's best friend Lane has with her mother that it does not sound like a bold-faced lie and can be accepted as some version of truth.

Yet, Rory does also have an appeal. Richard, who had no time for his own daughter, takes her to the club and finds, in discussions with members regard-ing their granddaughters, that Rory is, in fact, a "good girl," who shares the gossip from the ladies' steam room and in whom he can take pride. Even Rachel says, "That is one really not annoying kid. I might consider doing the whole Mom thing if I could be guaranteed that I could get one just like her" (1.19, "Emily in Wonderland"). Having all these characters constantly praise Rory enables the show to whitewash over any plot events that contradict, because surely these folks can't all be wrong — instead the event must be an anomaly. Coupled with the idea that Rory is prone to being the victim and if she does commit an offense, then she must have a good excuse or reason, Rory's appeal can continue.

Rory's real appeal, however, is that she seems "good" in contrast with the other characters.[2] In contrast with the Chilton/Yale set, Rory is the proverbial Middle Ground between the socially inept, scholarly overachievers like Paris and the giddy and overly social chums like Madeline and Louise. Rory is able to score a handsome boyfriend, even inspiring a dramatic testosterone clash as Tristin and Dean spark rivalry at the various functions, showing she has the appeal to get a guy who is not her cousin, and keep him. As Logan later puts it, Rory is girlfriend material. All of these various male suitors and female companions, who are either too loose or too abrasive, indicate that Rory is the best possible option, for all her faults and strengths, but only by comparison.

Rory is also "good" in comparison to Lane, which is a tricky feat, since Lane herself is a conflict in morality. She has created a whole secret life, which is lived in closets and loose floorboards. She began this life at age six or seven, when Mrs. Kim told her the Cookie Monster was one of the Seven Deadly Sins—gluttony. Since then, she has hidden her fanaticism for rock music, danced, worn makeup, and eaten contraband foods. In contrast, Rory shares much of her life with her mom, and, although they have frequent and long communication breakdowns, there are truths between them, and little white-washing. Rarely does Rory actually lie, and the one time she does, it is so that she and Lane can double-date, at Lane's request to be set up with Troy. Rory doesn't want to put Lorelai in the awkward spot of lying to Mrs. Kim, so, as Lorelai puts it, "bits of information were left out of the mom packets" (1.12, "Double-Date").[3] Lorelai is adamant that Rory does not lie to her and suggests Mrs. Kim's over-controlling parenting might produce negative effects. Lane's need for deception and rebellion is so ingrained that she hides the Korean boyfriend she meets at a Chilton party from her mother and creates such elaborate schemes that eventually he opts out of the relationship.

Offering a sharper contrast for Rory, and proving that opposites attract, Jess joins the cast. When Luke agrees to take on the troubled nephew, he's pleased that Jess is attracted to Rory and hopes she can help to influence him. Jess is depicted as "bad" as Rory as "good." While Rory is the Ice Queen of Stars Hollow, Jess is the devil incarnate, staging faked crime scenes, to gain attention and flirt with Rory. He also goes further, stealing balls and gnomes and destroying snowmen. Rory find this all amusing and appealing, becoming seduced by the playful aspect of his mischief and its undermining of sleepy town charm. Town Meetings are held to discuss his negative effect on the town, and Lorelai has to defend both Danes men. While Rory is a perpetual part of Stars Hollow, Jess is transient, leaving to pursue his father, and running off to New York. When they have their car accident that totals the car Dean made for Rory and breaks Rory's wrist, the whole town blames him, although having him drive and taking the detour were her decisions. The fact that the whole town, without knowing the facts, presumes that Jess led Rory astray and endangered her is very telling. The base myth—that Rory is good—and the initial impression Jess leaves with the town — that he is evil incarnate — determine how all their actions will be interpreted and further information is not needed. Of course, Rory is incapable of correcting the misconception people hold, and then feels trapped and uncomfortable.

Jess has intellect on par with Rory, but scholastically he fails. Later, when he writes his book, he redeems his failure, which challenges Rory to overcome her failure and get back to Yale. Again, contrast is very purposeful. Jess, now professional and responsible, criticizes the unhealthy and irresponsible behavior of boyfriend Logan. When they were dating, Jess was irresponsible and Rory spent her nights waiting for him to call, but he can also criticize Logan for heading to South America for a Life and Death Brigade stunt. Even though Luke hoped Rory would be good for Jess, eventually Jess helps Rory to redefine her life's purpose and get her back on track. Of course, because he is the Black Sheep, his important contributions to reforming Rory go unacknowledged. The parallels between Jess and Logan are thus established, as Logan's pomposity and Rory's acceptance, because she loves him, run counter to the way Rory accepted Jess' taking her for granted. Jess' great failure was that he was unwilling to follow the beaten path; although he was smart, he did not attend classes and complete the work he saw as trivial and pointless. Pursuing this other path, he is now a partner in an avant-garde publishing community, being part of the "in" group which flaunts the establishment just enough, and is also aware of where the line lies. Logan constantly lures the underclass into his world, shares generously, but then reminds others that they don't match up. In a way, both are very aware of societal constructs and flaunt them on occasion, although Jess does so primarily when he feels they are stupid. Although this is also elitist, it is an elitism that is available to any person — built on self-education and personal drive, not entitlement.

A frequent theme is that of knowing someone, especially within the Emily-Lorelai-Rory trio. Emily frequently challenges Lorelai to let Rory try things connected to the affluent life that Lorelai left behind. Due to Emily's challenges, Rory experiences the country club, a debutante ball, etc. Emily posits that Lorelai is afraid that Rory will have a good time, and Lorelai encourages Rory to live (much like Auntie Mame[4]) and try it, and discovers that Rory does enjoy it. This makes Lorelai aware that she and Rory are not the same, and that maybe all her alleged familiarity with Rory was only due to her limitations on Rory, coincidental, shared beliefs. Each challenge is an assault on the claim that Lorelai knows Rory. Lorelai does consistently point out how little Emily knows them, but she does not fault herself for her own misinterpretation of Rory. Ironically, she can waive her blame because she encouraged Rory to try it, although Rory's initial position was often based on an assumption that Lorelai would not approve, based on Lorelai's complaints about her childhood and people of privilege. It is ironic that Lorelai contributes to the inhibitions, alleviates the inhibitions, and eventually Rory pursues things to become a person separate from Lorelai and her expectations.

The main charge leveled against Emily is she never knew Lorelai or tried to "get her." One of the most emotional scenes is when Emily goes to Stars Hollow for Rory's birthday and discovers she doesn't know Lorelai, as she experiences for the first time the "family" and "home" which Lorelai created for herself. The events reveal to Emily that Lorelai was right and this awareness has the potential to allow her to redefine her role. Later, when she decorates a room for Rory, she will take some time to get to know her and consider her interests, although she will still miss the mark, by putting up 'N Sync posters. A runner-up for emotion is the scene where she finally meets Mia, the owner of the Independence Inn who acted as surrogate mother to Lorelai in Stars Hollow. Mia completely understands Emily's need to meet her and promises to deliver scads of photos of the girls. Mia seems to "get Emily" although Emily is horrified and ashamed of the entire events surrounding Lorelai's departure. The problem is Emily's lack of knowledge coupled with her meddling. A person can't advise what's best for another without knowing that person, so Emily's objectives misfire — such as her insisting the two teens marry in the first place, her provoking Christopher to lure Lorelai from Luke, and her breaking the plan to get Rory back to Yale by letting her stay in the pool-house. In all of these situations, Emily misses the objective and proves she is clueless.

Ultimately, Rory is the one who knows best — at least she knows Lorelai, and she speaks her mind. She is the one who realizes Max is good for Lorelai, even while Lorelai develops cold feet. She warns Chris to back off, and let Lorelai's and Luke's relationship have a chance. Although Emily does catch Rory off guard, Rory manages to keep a fairly even pace with her, through honest discussions and quiet acceptance. Rory's keen understanding of Lorelai is really an essential part of their success and their failings. She is also often the conduit for peacemaking. Her discussions with Richard help to reconcile his estrangement with Emily. Even in Rome with Emily, Rory manages to maintain the peace and keep Emily happy. Whenever Rory errs, she yells at herself and can predict Lorelai's concerns. The long silences between them are most often imposed by Rory, who needs to wait to be able to confront Lorelai's real reaction until she's processed her imagined reaction. This is understandable, however, since Lorelai herself is not sure what her reaction should be, given that she's torn between being a friend and a mom. Even when Rory does approach Lorelai, the latter sends mixed messages as she struggles to define her role as mother. There are even times when news indirectly reaches Lorelai so she can have her initial reaction and then develop a planned response. In this manner, their communication failures ironically contribute to improved communication.

Not coincidentally, there's a lot of overlap between Lorelai and Rory, and this leads to their ability to understand each other. Lorelai's problem in fully understanding Rory is that she and Rory are also different. Throughout the show, Lorelai compares the two and discusses their similarities. The pilot episode ends with Luke serving coffee to Lorelai and Rory, but then he begs Rory to put it down. "You do not want to grow up to be like your mom." "Too late," Rory retorts and both ladies giggle into the fade out. Critic Joy Press describes it as: "the two have a symbiotic, almost creepily close relationship." Once Lorelai learns of Dean, she overreacts, concluding, "after all, you're me, ... someone willing to throw important life experiences out the window to be with a guy" (1.02, "The Lorelais' First"). Lorelai repeatedly compares the two, using the Freudian slip, substitutions, and drawing connections. While Rory also draws these parallels, she often does so in reference to her genetic inheritances. The pairing of the two of them is the centerpiece to the story, the attractive the mother and daughter who are also sisterly, as the mother's growth was stilted and she is still just a "girl" in many aspects, almost waiting for her daughter to grow up until she continues her life. Although she has taken on the financial responsibility, emotionally Lorelai is stunted and unable to establish a solid relationship with a man. While Rory is definitely "girlfriend material," Lorelai is not, continually initiating and ending relationships. Rory's return to Dean is more like her mother's relationships than either realizes or admits. In Rory's case, she is young but still criticized by Lorelai. When Lorelai got back together with Christopher, at least until he found out his wife was expecting, Rory was cautiously supportive.

The best expression of this overlap is when Lorelai has an outburst at Chilton because Rory was not allowed to take the Shakespeare test. "We have studied.... My God, we're just one person" (1.10, "Forgiveness and Stuff"). This slip indicates an inability on Lorelai's part to separate herself from her daughter, and to see they have different objectives. Although Lorelai did study with Rory, Rory's trip, late arrival, and inability to take the exam all occur without Lorelai. This is echoed when, upon discovering at Thanksgiving dinner at Richard and Emily's, in front of other guests, that Rory has applied to schools in addition to Harvard, "We've applied to other schools?" (3.09, "A Deep-Fried"). Just as Lane lives vicariously through Rory, so too does Lorelai, to the point where she is blind to certain possibilities, and blurs the line between them. An example is the dream for Harvard, as Lorelai cannot remember where it began: "Was it my dream that you went to Harvard, because I never got to do the big, fancy college thing, and maybe all this time I am thinking it's all for Rory, when really it wasn't?" (1.10, "Forgiveness and Stuff"). This indicates a growing awareness that she was possibly guiding Rory into a life as predetermined as any Emily had had for herself, only the means by which it was achieved were far more subtle. In many ways Lorelai's coercion seems more like Althusser's Ideological State Apparatuses than the Repressive State that Emily represents.

Lorelai also says, "I left that life, you know, the club, my parents. I left it as soon as I could. It just never occurred to me that she [Rory] might want it. It occurred to my mother though" (1.03, "Kill Me Now"), and here we see the import. Because Lorelai sees herself in Rory, she cannot see those aspects of Rory that differ. The series traces constant challenges to Lorelai's perceptions as she comes to discover where the line is between herself and Rory. It also signals a central conflict, since their dream is for Rory to gain the educational opportunities that Lorelai missed, but not necessarily the social trappings of the upper class. Thus, as Rory approaches graduation and becomes more involved with Logan, Lorelai fears losing Rory to that life.

When Rory and Dean fall asleep at Miss Patty's studio after the dance, Emily exclaims that Rory is going to get pregnant and do the same thing Lorelai did. Lorelai rejects this, stating Rory is "a good kid, Mom. She's not me." This conversation immediately shifts focus as Emily asks, what kind of mother are you to let this happen? Lorelai pounds the parallel: "Uh, I don't know, Mom. What kind of mother were you?" (1.09, "Rory's Dance"). Of course, Lorelai can say this because she sees the two as so very different. Rory is "smart and careful," and Lorelai says she trusts her. Lorelai calls herself a "horrible, uncontrollable child" and claims that Emily would have lost her with or without the pregnancy, because Emily suffocated her. As Emily becomes more a part of their lives, Lorelai develops an awareness and resentment, realizing that Rory is not her carbon copy, and, even more frightening, that Lorelai might share aspects of parenting with Emily. Lorelai then becomes more fully aware of herself, despite criticizing Emily for not knowing her.

When Lorelai thinks about dating Max, she explains that Rory is her "pal" (1.05, "Cinnamon's Wake"). Even Dean acknowledged the intense friendship: "Rory has her own mind, but you're her best friend. If you don't like me, Rory won't" (1.07, "Kiss and Tell"). And the girls from Chilton find the bond between Lorelai and Rory fascinating — both the closeness and friendliness. They note that Lorelai is cool and more like a big sister. These bonds attract attention and their affection seems to be what sets their relationship apart, but it is clear that there are communication struggles, especially regarding boys and sexuality.

Rory wants to talk to Lorelai about important issues, but develops an inability to do so. Due to Lorelai's outburst when Dean causes Rory to reconsider going to Chilton, Rory doesn't share details about the budding romance, including their first kiss. Rory runs to Lane's and blurts out the details. She's excited and says that she wants to go tell Lorelai, only she's also nervous, and ultimately does not. Instead, Lorelai finds out from Mrs. Kim, who overheard it all. By finding out indirectly, Lorelai can adjust and digest. Rory does not learn that Lorelai stalked Dean and talked with Luke (who told her she could not kill the bag boy) and she says that this failure in communication is typical of the Lorelai-Emily conversations, but she had thought her relationship with Rory was different, and they could "tell each other everything" (1.07, "Kiss and Tell"). She then realizes she will need to react differently than Emily would have, and calm down. Lorelai, therefore, seems to react well in front of Rory, but the whole episode makes her aware that there is a gap between herself and

Rory and that she and Emily have more in common than she would like to admit.

Ultimately, Lorelai is not a best friend, but a mother. She has to use the "Mom card" periodically to override what is otherwise a democracy. Rory's Chilton buddies learn this when they skip out during the Bangles concert to party. Lorelai keeps knocking on doors until she recovers the girls. She reads them the riot act, saying it's insane to take off and drink strange drinks, and if they do anything like this again, it won't be around her kid! Even Rory understands Lorelai's need to be the un-cool Mom, and in Paris' eyes, the act elevates Lorelai's status. She has, along with Madeline and Louise, appreciated Lorelai's coolness, but she appreciates Lorelai's motherly commitment and effort, expressing that she's not sure her own mother would look for her, although she might send someone.

Given Rory's apparent maturity and close bonds with Mom, it is hard to rationalize her contradictions—the best friend who won't speak for months on end, the "good" girl who is an Other Woman and Home-Wrecker. Lorelai often suggests one possible cause: that it all boils down to dating and guys. In the lengthy conversation between Lorelai and Mrs. Kim after the girls are caught lying and double-dating, Lorelai claims that Lane respects Mrs. Kim. Mrs. Kim says lying is not respectful, and Lorelai excuses her: "she's sixteen. She had a crush on a boy.... Teenagers sometimes slip up." (1.12, "Double Date"). Lorelai isn't just urging Mrs. Kim to be tolerant. She uses various excuses herself to explain away any of Rory's transgressions. She rationalizes the rifts between herself and Rory as being the result of Rory's relationship with boys, and while some of them are (Dean vs. Chilton, Jess, sleeping with Dean), there are many others (choosing Yale, leaving Yale), which result from Rory's own decisions or the Gilmore's influence.

One source of Rory's breaking away from Lorelai is the Friday night dinners which bring Rory into the debutante life that Lorelai rejected. The exposure to wealth and a new lifestyle via the Gilmores brings new facets to Rory's character and drives a wedge between Lorelai and Rory. Perhaps the earliest signs of this involve jealousy over Richard—a recurrent aspect of season one. After golfing, Richard calls Rory to chat about shared interests in rare texts. Lorelai is jealous and picks a fight with Rory over a sweater. When Richard's angina strikes during a Gilmore Christmas party, to which Lorelai had been uninvited, she realizes that Richard worked and she escaped—there were no moments over which they might nostalgically romanticize while he's in the hospital. Rory's developing bonds with Richard cause Lorelai pain because, despite her claims that she and Rory are the same, the fact is, Lorelai was a disappointment to them and Rory is all that they had hoped for in their daughter. The tension between Emily and Lorelai tends to be over who gets possession of Rory. It is ironic that Lorelai's "better" mode of parenting produces the type of "success" in life that Lorelai herself rejected.

Lorelai addresses this irony when she confesses to Sookie: "You know, little white gloves and coming-out balls.... I just never thought I raised that kind of kid" (1.03, "Kill Me Now"). Lorelai is an interesting conflict in motives and goals, because she was consciously raising the kind of kid who would live in that world, attending schools like Chilton and Harvard. She also jokingly addresses the conflicts that are bound to arise, when she shares the news with Sookie that Rory has been accepted to Chilton: "This is it. She can finally go to Harvard like she's always wanted and get the education I never got and get to do all the things that I never got to do, and I can resent her for it and we can finally have a normal mother-daughter relationship" (1.02, "The Lorelais' First"). Although Lorelai usually discusses the trappings of that life — the balls, gowns, rules, and social expectations— with denigration and mocking scorn, here she implies that Rory's ability to experience what Lorelai *could not*, rather than *chose not to*, indicates that Lorelai's rejection of that life is not so simple, and the competition between Rory and Lorelai for that world, particularly for affection from the grandparents, will differentiate the two and cause conflict. Further, as Rory grows closer to her grandparents and finds acceptance and appeal in the trappings, Lorelai does develop resentment because Rory has the type of relationship with Emily and Richard that Lorelai did not. Lorelai does not seem to realize the irony that their relationship with Rory is better, in part, because of what Lorelai has taught them.

In addition to a relationship with Richard and Emily that confounds Lorelai and in addition to Rory's emergence in the world of balls, Rory is also beginning to find her own independent ideas and perceptions. One of the earliest indicators of this burgeoning independence is the Donna Reed episode which Lorelai and Rory mock in front of Dean, clearly indicating a Lorelai-brand of feminism and the family tradition of Reed-bashing. Challenged by Dean, Rory opts to research Reed's accomplishments and offers her own tribute — paying homage to Donna Reed while she is cat-sitting. Rory shifts from denouncing the male constructs and servile women to discover that Reed was an uncredited writer/producer on her show and a pioneer in media. With this information, she grows and develops her own opinion about Donna Reed, one that is independent of Lorelai's, and considerate of Dean's opinions. In this episode, risking Lorelai's mocking, Rory begins to individualize, to develop opinions for herself and to break free from ingrained training. While sometimes Lorelai, egged on by Emily and sometimes by Paris, does encourage Rory to try new things (attending balls, opening doors to college parties, etc.). Rory doesn't really ever try to explain her pursuit so Lorelai is somewhat unaware of the influences.

In the critical analysis, Donna Reed takes on greater dimensions. As Cara Wall points out, Lorelai appeals to a viewership of married mothers, who envy Lorelai's youth, physical fitness, camaraderie with her daughter, ability to date and be free from marital constraints, and ability to parent and be free from co-parenting constraints or compromises. Wall calls her "the anti–Donna Reed — not the mother who's perfect in the way others want her to be, but the mother living the life all mothers secretly want to lead." If Lorelai is the anti–Donna Reed, then Rory's embracing of Reed is a blow to Lorelai and the generation of successful professional women who waited to have children after education and careers. Then again, as Lorelai tells Mrs. Kim, she does not want Rory to grow up to be like herself, so once again Lorelai's goals for Rory contradict values Lorelai holds.

Running away to avoid facing reality becomes a habit for the youngest Gilmore. After she and Dean split on their anniversary, she can't handle that all Stars Hollow assumes "good" Rory was wronged, so she escapes to the Gilmores,' where Emily is tickled over her status elevation.[5] In this circumstance, the Gilmores offer refuge. Also, when Rory becomes the Other Woman, she opts to go to Europe with Emily, who, in a parallel story, has recently discovered that Richard has been lunching with Pendleton Lott all these years. As both discover flaws in their lives, they escape, and escaping from Lorelai is definitely part of Rory's agenda. Rory can't even really talk to Lorelai until she has processed her own guilt and decided to write to Dean. As Rory grows and faces greater challenges, she turns away from Lorelai, rather than to her, which indicates a lack of communication, and she also shows an inability to face the grown-up consequences that are linked to her poor choices and failings. Lorelai, on the other hand, was willing to take on the challenges and face the consequences, running away to face them by herself. While both young women ran when confronted with challenges, Lorelai ran to responsibility whereas Rory ran away, suffering only from having to re-enact *A Room with a View* with Emily. In fall, returning to the *Yale Daily News*, Rory also realizes she neglected responsibilities to her professional development, as she has fallen behind and is struggling to think of relevant story lines while others have been published in the *New York Times* and interned.

Even later, when Mitchum Huntzberger shakes her faith and aspirations, the despondent Rory retreats to the grandparents to take time off from school and her objectives— which have been so central in defining who she was. Her love for school and pursuit of life's goals have been the driving force behind the broad plot lines, and yet the words of Mitchum deflate her hopes and dreams and cause her to question her own abilities and skills in a way that utterly shuts her down and causes her to flee from reality to the Gilmore pool-house.

Rory's relationship with class is ambiguous, as well. Raised with limited resources, she finds their first home, the old potting shed at the Independence Inn, to be pretty with a view of the pond, despite its lack of walls around the bathtub. She mocks the rich with Jess and eventually becomes the rich she mocked, defending the boorish Logan for behaving abysmally and offensively, implying that Jess is uneducated, poorly read, and inadequate. Later with Logan she mocks the rich at one of his gatherings, and he points out that she's living in his place, paid for by Mitchum Huntzberger, and attending college which her dad is funding through his inheritance (because Christopher never did achieve success on his own). When Rory makes her court appearance for stealing the boat, she cops a plea to criminal mischief, third degree. The judge, criticizing rich privileged children treating the world as their playground, gives her a sentence much harsher than the cozy deal previously agreed to. Rory is in a constant battle between the two worlds—the world she actually inhabits and the world from which she came. Even the internship experience which goes astray indicates her on/off relationship with access and privilege. She is offered the coveted internship because the Huntzbergers were awful at dinner, saying she was not worthy to marry Logan. She tries to turn him down, but he points out that any door opened is worth thinking about, even if unearned. Then he offers a critique that causes her to question her whole career goal and leave school. Finally, an article quotes him as mentoring Rory, which enabled her to become editor at the *Yale Daily News*. Rory rides this rollercoaster with indignation and ultimately finds herself of neither the middle class nor the affluent class.

Lorelai is similarly divided, claiming that Stars Hollow is enough for her, although she's entertaining job offers with international duties. Rory leads Lorelai into having long-term relationships and she also precedes her into coming to some acceptance with privilege associated with money and status. Rory's progression challenges Lorelai to do the same. Lorelai breaks engagements, falls into bed with old flames, and sabotages most of her relationships. When she demands that Luke instantly decide to marry her or not, and he hesitates, she runs straight to Christopher, eventually marrying the now fabulously wealthy father of her child, after his conspicuous consumption in paying a Paris restaurant to re-open and feed them in the middle of the night. Lorelai has been wondering if her rejection of wealth was a rejection of all things Emily, and becoming the anti–Emily, but not really becoming Lorelai, and this is part of the unresolved issue as to who Lorelai Gilmore really is.

The notion that Lorelai is somehow not fully formed or formed with flaws is one challenge to the oft-repeated myth that Lorelai is independent, but only the most recent incarnation. This meta-myth goes unquestioned. Lorelai says to her mother, "I had to figure out how to live. I found a good job.... I worked my way up. I run the place now. I built a life of my own with no help from anyone" (1.01, "Pilot"). Her mother does not question this assertion, but reminds her she could be in a much better place if she had accepted help, saying she was "always too proud to accept anything from anyone"(1.01, "Pilot"). In fact, Emily provided excellent training, good schooling, among other things, and Emily's constant critique of service personnel would have been very instructive. Lorelai's ability to placate and please guests comes from years of dealing with Emily choosing to act in diametrical opposition to Emily. When Lorelai interacts with the Inn's guests, she is catering to Emily and her ilk. Whereas Emily has ex-employees filing law suits, Lorelai's compete to give her better gifts. Christopher thinks that she is Wonder Woman, complete with lasso and boots. This self-made premise is repeated often, going unchallenged, and yet this whole concept is false.

When Lorelai came to the Independence Inn, she had no service skills at all. Mia took her in and gave her a job. Although there are no flashbacks to this time, we do know Lorelai worked hard and stood out in comparison to the other maids. (Also not mentioned is how the infant Rory was supervised during this time.) While Lorelai's eventual management of the Independence Inn is very profitable for Mia, it is not sufficient for Lorelai to pay for Chilton. While Rory has "earned" admission, the point is clear — money grants access and Lorelai wants Rory to have that access, and the same advantages Lorelai had taken for granted in her own childhood. Ultimately, we see Lorelai borrow money for the Dragonfly Inn (from Luke), and for termite treatment (from a bank with Emily's help). She is inept with home repairs and cooking, so those around her are constantly called to provide help. Given that, it is no coincidence her two closest pals are cooks. Luke is constantly repairing her house, and Lorelai uses the annual Basket fundraiser to recruit home repair help. When insurance issues arise, Lorelai turns to Richard. Even when planning to open the Dragonfly, Lorelai tells Mia she will need her help, and we actually see Luke coaching Lorelai through business plans. Lorelai is willing to accept Richard's investment payoff and while independence is laudable, Lorelai is clearly dependent financially and skirts between the behaviors, objectives, and access of the Haves and the Have-Nots. Amy Benfer, reviewing the representation of the single mother on Salon.com in November of 2000, asks, "How does one assert one's independence as a parent when one is, in some ways, still in need of financial and emotional parenting oneself, in a culture that sees teenage mothers as nothing short of monstrous?" It is a hypocrisy, clearly, but one which is never noted in the *Gilmore Girls*.

Lorelai has not been alone in parenting Rory; the whole town of Stars Hollow has pitched in. Lorelai tells Dean that Rory is much beloved, clearly signaling that the town had much to do with raising her. Also, when Christopher arrives (the first time), the very daring Miss Patty flirts, "You know, Christopher, we're all like Rory's parents around here, and I'm one of her mothers, and since you're her father, well ... that would make us a couple.... Come back and see me" (1.15, "Christopher Returns"). Indeed Rory's upbringing seems to have been a testament to the Hillary Clinton child-rearing model, but this jars against the oft-repeated insistence that she did it all alone, as Chris says in the same episode, "God knows she doesn't need anyone besides you, but if you give me a chance." The myth that Lorelai has done it all alone is so often repeated that it goes unchallenged, and when acknowledged the contradiction is not even noticed. For example, when Dean wants to date Rory, Lorelai explains this small town he's moved to: "The whole town is watching you.... She's not going on your motorcycle" (1.07, "Kiss and Tell"). Dean has already been interrogated by Babette, so he has had a taste of this and understands.

Motherhood is a central theme in this series. Lorelai's model is clearly held up as the best option. Lane comments that the Rory-Lorelai bond is so strong, they must go through periods of non-communication to even out the cosmos. As has already been described, Lorelai's parenting is first and foremost being a best pal, and only pulling the "Mom card" when needed. Emotionally stunted, she finds Rory outgrowing her, but she still serves as the primary motherhood model for the show. The reason for this is the series of Anderson-esque Grotesques presented to the viewer. Paris' mother serves as a fine example. The one time she makes an appearance is at the Chilton's Parents' Day, and although Paris begs her to come to her literature class, Mrs. Geller is preoccupied with her divorce and comments publicly on Paris' acne. "I bet I'm looking pretty good to you right now," quips Lorelai to Rory, making a joke of a central truth (1.11, "Paris Is Burning"). Later plot developments reveal Lorelai and teacher Max Medina kissing in his classroom, which sets the school atwitter with gossip and proves that comparisons are relative.

Mrs. Kim and Emily represent all that is oppressive and overbearing. Control is exerted over diet, religion, and behaviors, and the result is rebellious children who make drunken phone calls, asserting independence. Their children eventually break free and tentative, newly adopted roles must be forged that respect the child's independence. This is however, a constant struggle or negotiation. When Mrs. Kim's mother comes for Lane's wedding, it is clear that Mrs. Kim had been raised repressively and she also rebelled.

On the other end of the spectrum, Luke's sister was an awful mother to Jess—who became too wild for her to handle, but Liz's character reveals an honest, affectionate, albeit detached model. With her new husband T. J. and with age, parenting the second time around will be different, as is indicated by the second delivery at home with a midwife. Liz and Sookie serve as the modern examples who seem to take the right approach and balance involvement with natural approaches. Yet, we rarely see them actually parenting, and the balance of Sookie's work and parenting is rarely addressed, except for her bedrest and "maternity leaves."

The final Mom model is even more modern—a female version of Richard—as Sherry is so work-obsessed that she can't pause to deliver, and eventually she runs away to Paris, abandoning the young Gigi to Christopher's care (and the nanny's). Although her repentance offers some redemption, it seems more like a plot contrivance to remove the toddler from Lorelai's and Christopher's life. Sherry does serve as a feminist message of warning that certain parenting models don't fit either gender.

It's difficult to discuss motherhood without discussing fatherhood, and yet until Luke's new-found daughter April's appearance, fathers are discussed more often in the abstract or negation. Like Richard, Christopher is absent, but not because he's working. When he does appear, he's sporting a false success and greets Lorelai and Rory in public, by asking Lorelai to remove her shirt. He says he wants to be a father to Rory, offering to be another pal. Lorelai keeps reminding him that he is the dad, and that can involve more than being a pal, and that Rory could use both.

Lorelai's rejection of suitors to serve as fathers is both a sign and symptom of her relationship failures. Lorelai's rules of dating prohibit date-child interfacing and because she rarely dates for long, so there are few questions as to the role of the new beau with Rory. Max finally raises the issue, as they near their wedding date, and Lorelai tells him that Rory is all raised and doesn't need him to be a dad. Her central inadequacy in relationships is a result of her inability to share her life. She uses Rory as an excuse to distance herself from potential suitors and to avoid realizing her "inability to commit." The few men she rotates in her relationships have previous relations with Rory although it only works because these men accept the myth that Lorelai has done it alone and the men defer to her decisions.

Meanwhile, Lorelai's relationship with Luke makes his paternal tendencies more evident even while Christopher is seeking to redefine his roles with Rory and Lorelai. Luke has been providing nutrition to Rory and serving as her primary male role model even previous to his dating Lorelai. The culminating scene is at Richard and Emily's vow renewal, when both Dad figures happen upon the amorous Rory and Logan. Luke points out that Chris missed Rory's chicken pox, high school graduation, college dorm moves, etc. Through his actions, Luke has been filling these obligations. Luke does this all while respecting Lorelai's greater claims. With the exception of a rather snippy double-date, Luke lets Lorelai call the shots and dictate their take on the situation.

The situation shifts with the revelation about April Nardini. Unlike Christopher, who chose to leave, Luke never knew about his daughter because Anna didn't tell him. She explains they are fine and don't need him (financially or otherwise). Slowly, Luke asserts his rights, first to see her, and then to seek custody (when Anna needs to relocate to Arizona). She bursts out that the move is none of his business and that he has no right to make any promises to her daughter (7.09, "Knit People"). He replies, "She's not just your daughter; she's my daughter, too.... I can never get back her childhood, but she's *our* kid, not just yours.... Why do I even have to say that? You can't just decide things.... I will fight you if I have to. I am her father, and I have rights." Finally, Luke grows a backbone, although he previously accepted Anna's dictate to keep Lorelai out of April's life, which drove a wedge between the couple. Emily, who is coming to accept the engagement, makes an attempt to know April and criticizes Lorelai, who awkwardly defends the plan. In this instance, Anna's imposition of a ban on Lorelai creates a schism between the engaged couple which only grows more painful. Luke, however, allows the dictatorial mother to determine the rules, until she threatens to take April away and deny his rights.

The question of Luke's commitment becomes central to the love triangle among Luke, Christopher, and Lorelai. When Richard is hospitalized, Luke is there to do subservient chores for Emily and to support the Gilmores. Meanwhile, jealous husband Christopher won't even take Lorelai's calls, because he is hurt about her letter in support of Luke's custody of April. The letter asserts how Luke has been supportively "there for" the Gilmore Girls, a fact which must smack the irresponsible Christopher's sensibilities.

Christopher and Lorelai are together such a short time that negotiating the parenting of young Gigi was never determined. Christopher's relationship with Gigi is definitely different in this second go at parenting, similar to Liz's experiences. This time, he is there for the birth, and he is the one who sticks around. He has to become the Super Dad, when he and Gigi are abandoned. He has not, however, learned to be the supportive husband, instead, always feeling insecure and inadequate.

It is interesting that those statements which are the most often repeated in this series seem to fail when compared to the actual events of the scripts. Even after six years, Rory's status as a "good" girl is only jokingly challenged (like when Lane implies that she is a slut — again, by contrast with virginal Lane whose mother is "stuck in her head" — or when Rory quips she killed a man to her roadside cleanup crew compatriot). Despite huge conflicts with these overarching claims, their fiction is supported because the scripts are full of grotesque characters, so bizarre and intense that anything, by comparison, seems normal. Indeed, it would be hard to be a slut in Miss Patty's town, after she shamelessly flirts with Richard, Dean, and Chris. Compared with Druella, the vile harpist, even Michel, the Dragonfly's acerbic manager, seems pleasant. Allison Weiner notes that Stars Hollow presents a conservative utopia — idyllic festivals and family values— and then flips this image as the group celebrates a wedding shower at a transvestite club or a funeral for a cat. This shows the same conflict between presentations that makes the show complex and nuanced, especially if one is attentive to the seeming contradictions.

These quirky characters help to shape a fantasy-land that is attractive due to its character and idyllic peace. There Lorelai is able to raise Rory and work on raising herself, as well. These characters provide a sense that Lorelai herself is within the bounds of "normal" as even sensible characters dash through town with trash bags of marijuana, looking for safe disposal sites, or as reverends approve the breaking of the incessant church bells. Lorelai proclaims to her mother: "You will not come into my house and tell me I threw my life away.... This is a life. It has a little color in it, so it may look unfamiliar to you, but it's a life, and if I hadn't gotten pregnant, I wouldn't have Rory" (1.09, "Rory's Dance"). If these characters and plot lines differed, and if Rory had not been so "bad," and Rory and Lorelai had not been torn apart, this series would not have lasted nor attracted the following it had.

Notes

1. Andrea Alstrup organized the Family Friendly Programming Forum in 1999 to bring advertisers together to offer financial incentives for networks to develop programming suitable for multiple generations without shocks. WB was the only initial broadcaster, as many had unfounded concerns over the editorial control. Amy Sherman-Palladino, the creator of *Gilmore Girls*, herself was surprised to find a show based on an unwed teen mom was chosen, but felt it reflected new ideas about family (Frutkin). In its second season, at least, *Gilmore Girls* hit the mark, as it was the most watched show in its time slot by women 12–34 years old (Weiner).

2. Ironically, she can also be used to compare to herself! "She was so sweet when she was little," Taylor says, after Rory seizes the blue and pink ribbons that signify whose side (Lorelai or Luke) of the breakup any given townsperson took (5.14, "Say Something"). Rory has returned home to nurture her mother and seizes Taylor's ribbon supply, demanding he stop meddling and dragging the town into her mother's life. Rory here has matured and is standing up to the insensitive Taylor, protecting her mother.

3. It is noteworthy, however, that information does not need to be included in the daughter packets, because Lorelai does not share that she is dating Max or Digger, or that she is engaged to Luke and married to Christopher until well after the fact. Although she encourages Rory to come and talk with her before things happen, the events of her own life reveal she can't control it or share with Rory. And yet, when Emily and Richard are temporarily separated, Lorelai provokes her until she will share. There is a constant call to share more information, but no one responds.

4. Mame's advice to all is that: "Life is a banquet and most poor suckers are starving to death!" Coincidentally, this is the advice she offers to Gooch, when she inadvertently sends her out on the evening from which she would eventually return pregnant and alone.

5. Ironically, this directly contradicts what she said to Mia. When Mia explains how Lorelai arrived at the Inn, she did what she hoped someone would do for her daughter-take her in and help her. Emily says she would have sent the child home. In this instance, she shows that she is a hypocrite, although she does call Lorelai to let her know where Rory is.

Works Cited

Benfer, Amy. "Knocked Up Like Me: What's Cooler Than Being a Middle-Class Teenage Mother? Having a TV Show All about You." Salon.com. 2 Nov. 2000 <http://archive.salon.com/mwt/feature/2000/11/02/gilmore_girls/index.html>.

Frutkin, Alan James. "Family Affair." *Media Week* 18 Mar. 2002. 20+.

Press, Joy. "The Gilmore Girls." *The Village Voice* 27 Oct.–2 Nov. 2004: 113.

Shaw, Jessica. "Mother of Reinvention." *Entertainment Weekly* 11 Feb. 2005: 32.

Wall, Cara. "The Dark Secret of Stars Hollow." Salon.com. 27 Sep. 2005. <http://dir.salon.com/story/ent/tv/feature/2005/09/27/gilmore_porn/index1.html?pn=1>.

Weiner, Allison Hope. "Golden Girls: How the WB Hit *Gilmore Girls* Became the Surprisingly Racy Standard for Family-Friendly Entertainment." *Entertainment Weekly* 22 Mar. 2002. 66+.

Good Girls, Bad Girls, and Motorcycles

Negotiating Feminism

Alicia Skipper

There is a Henry Wadsworth Longfellow[1] poem that I remember distinctly from my childhood; at least I remember the first stanza, as it was the one I heard most frequently:

> There was a little girl
> Who had a little curl
> Right in the middle of her forehead
> And when she was good
> She was very, very good
> But when she was bad
> She was horrid.

Undoubtedly, the reason that this stands out in my memory is that my mother would recite this stanza whenever she felt that I was not being a "good girl." This, coupled along with her other favorite adage, "pretty is as pretty does," was a sure indication that I was doing something below her standards, although I don't remember doing anything that could truly be classified as "horrid." Of course, most children are told at some point to "be good." However, often for females, being good is associated with pleasing others, being pretty, and fulfilling societal expectations in regards to gender roles. For most women the notion of being "good" begins at an early age and continues throughout their adult lives. As a result, "good girls" often become "good mothers," thus, further perpetuating the stereotype. One of the most common characteristics of being good is putting the needs of others before the needs of one's self, and this notion of self-sacrifice plays heavily into societal expectations of motherhood.

Feminists have sought to revamp the expectations and the roles of women in society since Betty Friedan's groundbreaking *The Feminine Mystique*.[2] Yet, feminists have had to struggle with the media and in recent years the media and cultural backlash has become even more pronounced. Since we are a culture based very much on television and other forms of digital media, television characters become ideal ways to perpetuate the stereotype of what it means to be "good." As a result, images of women that pervade the media and our lives reflect these same ideologies that have been inculcated in us since childhood.

Two such images that immediately come to my mind are *Leave It to Beaver*'s[3] June Cleaver from the 50s, who maintained an immaculate house wearing high heels and pearls, always ready with a smile for Wally, Ward, and of course, the Beaver and Donna Stone from *The Donna Reed Show*,[4] who maintained her family in much the same way. Then who could forget Carol Brady,[5] of the 70s, mom and step-mom to the Brady children, aided of course by Alice, who decidedly did most of the work around the Brady household? For many scholars Lucille Ball, of the *I Love Lucy* show, stands out as the quintessential 50s wife, yet in spite of Lucy's deference to the roles assigned to her by the patriarchy she lashes out in what scholars such as Patricia Mellencamp have classified as an act of feminism:

> Held to the conventional domesticity of the situation comedy Lucy Ricardo was barely in control, constantly attempting to escape domesticity — her "situation," her job in the home — always trying to get into show business by getting into Ricky's "act," narratively fouling up, but brilliantly and comically performing in it. Lucy endured marriage and housewifery by transforming them into vaudeville; costumed performances and rehearsals that made staying home frustrating yet tolerable [48].

Lucy's unrest is emblematic of the frustrations of many women with limited options. And while there are other issues regarding the depictions of the relationship of Lucy and Ricky,[6] the show stands as a testament to the limited options of women of the 1950s. In response to the depictions of women using humor Mellencamp notes: "Given the repressive conditions of the 1950s humor might have been women's weapon and tactic for survival, ensuring sanity, the triumph of the ego, and pleasure; after all, Gracie and Lucy were narcissistic, rebellious, refusing to be hurt" (55). Therefore, for women of the 50s, sitcoms became a means of coping with a world that they were ill equipped to change. Yet, the changing face of society calls for a change in the depictions of families and women on television.

According to the 2004 National Center for Health Statistics, 35.7 percent of all the women who gave birth in the United States that year were classified as unwed mothers. When one speaks of unwed mothers it is important to clarify that this distinction is given to women who have not ever been married to the fathers of their children, unlike single mothers who are divorced and are raising children without a live-in spouse or women who have been widowed.

Somehow, having been married at some point provides some level of legitimacy in a society in which women are still expected to marry. However, when one thinks of representations of motherhood on television there are few single mothers and even fewer representations of unwed mothers, even though they are clearly present in the population. Jane Juffer[7] discusses the power of television and the necessity of creating more such characters:

> TV has the potential to make what's going on at home seem weird and different to everyday and "normal." This is another reason it's important to have more single moms on television — it lessens the stigma, the sense of otherness that can come from being a child of a single parent if you live in an area when nuclear families are still the norm [65].

Of course, it is likely that television executives balk at the risk of encouraging the destruction of "family values," in spite of any accuracy that such depictions may, in fact, represent.

Instead, when one thinks of motherhood on television, it is common to think of the iconic mothers that I discussed earlier, mothers who established sickeningly impossible standards of beauty, housewifery, and cheerfulness. I can think of fewer depictions of single moms on television like the feisty Ann Romano, from *One Day at a Time*, who constantly struggled with the bills while managing the problems of two teenage daughters. Then there was Alice from the television show of the same name; she worked hard as a waitress while raising her son. And although both shows were comedies, these images often centered on the hardships they endured, which were more realistic than vacuuming in heels and pearls. Serafina Bathrick comments upon the role of situation comedy in relation to cultural understanding: "Situation comedy situates us more than any other television genre, it provides us, as viewers whose everyday experiences may be shaped by TV's presence and programming, with a powerful model for private life in the age of broadcast culture" (155). Yet, it is impossible to note that these women are not thriving or prospering without a man. These shows could even be seen as warnings for women who might be caught up in the second-wave feminist furor of the 1970s; if you don't stay married, this could happen to you, as well. Yet, despite the changing face of the American family, television shows typically reflect the traditional American family with a mother and father. That leaves the question: why are there so few examples of unwed mothers on television?

One can only assume that this is because this idea defies "family values," the emphasis of many politicians and right wing Christians who make up a large number of the American viewing audience. The most famous television show depicting an unwed mother to date is undoubtedly *Murphy Brown,* and that fame was largely due to comments made by Dan Quayle in 1992 as he used the character Murphy Brown's decision to have a child without a spouse as an example of the decline in "family values" in America. This reference in his speech was inflated in the media and detracted from Quayle's real point, which was more problematic than his indictment of a television character as Bonnie Dow explains: "Quayle's claims in his speech that poverty is traceable to a lack of moral fiber, that single, poor women are inadequate mothers, that, poor mothering is responsible for inner-city problems, and that marriage will save the inner city from decline are the most interesting and disturbing claims to the Commonwealth club" (154). The fixation on the Murphy Brown aspect of Quayle's speech and the furor surrounding it is a testament to the power of television in American culture and its perceived reflections of everyday life.

Undeniably, there are many negative stereotypes associated with unwed mothers, particularly unwed teens. While unwed pregnancy is common, it is problematic in regards with addressing the issue without seemingly glamorizing or advocating the problem. Yet, for the past six seasons there has been one television show that has challenged these stereotypes and others regarding the roles of women and in the process has created a strong feminist character in Lorelai Gilmore. That show is *Gilmore Girls*, which answers Lisa Johnson's call for a need of more diversified depictions of feminism on television: "Portraying women as either domesticated victims of male patriarchy or angry man-hating feminists doesn't permit the nuances of real women's lives to continue to come into clear view, just as assumptions that single women who long to be married must be 'unfeminist' obscures a more complete picture of contemporary women's psyches" (141). This essay will focus upon the character Lorelai (Lauren Graham) and her daughter Rory (Alexis Bledel) in the first season of the show and the ways in which Lorelai represents feminism and challenges prevailing hegemony regarding unwed mothers, the notion of the good girl and bad girl, and traditional gender roles.

While there have been many feminist figures represented on television throughout recent decades, it is significant, particularly considering the current conservative political and social climate, whenever a character is specifically labeled as a feminist or claims for herself the identity of feminist. While the decade of the 70s ushered in what has been termed as the second wave of the women's movement in America, the decades since have experienced a large degree of feminist backlash, thus prompting many women, even with those with feminist ideals and living feminist lifestyles, to preface any discussion of their political or social ideologies with the phrase, "I am not a feminist, but...." Many feminists are torn between the affect that this reluctance to openly embrace feminism is having on the movement. Long-time feminist activist and Congresswoman Eleanor Holmes Norton feels that the implications of denying feminism are not having an adverse affect on the movement at larger:

> The difference between our generation and our daughters' generation is less important than it may seem, because the daughters grew up in a world where feminist aspirations were accepted as the way the world operate. That some women have not embraced what we call feminism or do not use the feminist label had no effect on the pace of feminist change [147].

Norton excuses the attitudes of many feminists as the result of a lack of aware-ness or need to fight for rights being denied them. She makes the distinctions between the types of feminists noting that women of her generation were cat-alytic feminists, while women of recent generations are functional feminists. While Norton does not elaborate on her distinctions, it is easy to ascertain that her generation was the "catalyst" responsible for the change. Yet, I am not cer-tain that "functional feminist" accurately describes the situations of those denouncing feminism or feminists who deny the label. Women living today who enjoy the rights gained by earlier feminists while renouncing feminism are more accurately, and perhaps more harshly, "complacent feminists," and com-placency is dangerous in regards to social change. Yet, some women may be so adjusted to the new social order that offers more equality than past generations that the complacency, while problematic, may be justifiable. As Norton notes, "Even traditional families act on a revised view of who a woman is. The aver-age American may not call herself a feminist, yet the substance of feminist rev-olution is a potent guide to the way she lives her life" (148). As discussed previously, the perception of feminist as bad is largely due to the political cli-mate and the depictions of feminism in the press. In this second Bush era of ultra conservatism and "family values," the word feminist, like the word lib-eral, is much maligned in the media. As a result, many women are often reluc-tant to proclaim themselves as feminists even as they espouse or emulate feminist ideologies in their own lives. Therefore, it becomes important in terms of progressing feminism and in subverting the hegemony regarding feminism as "bad" if feminist characters on television are shown in a positive light, par-ticularly if those characters are active in naming themselves as feminists. Nonetheless, shows like *Ally McBeal* and *Roseanne* were heralded as presenting strong lead female characters that defied cultural norms. More recently CBS's *Judging Amy* offered a strong feminist protagonist, and ABCs *Commander in Chief* offered a groundbreaking presentation of a female president, which indi-cates that there is a feminist audience present, even if in some areas it is on the decline. Frankie Gamber discusses this decline of feminist presence in the media: "There may be a smattering of strong feminist presences in mainstream popular culture—*Gilmore Girls*, the national V-Day campaign around *The Vagina Monologues*, even Oprah—but our choices seem far less vibrant than they used to be" (46). While, one cannot deny a feminist presence on televi-sion, it is important to demand such a presence and even celebrate the femi-nist roles that are presented, such as *Gilmore Girls*' Lorelai Gilmore.

Lorelai Gilmore's feminism is made apparent to viewers from the begin-ning of the series. Lorelai has named her daughter after herself, though this becomes shortened to Rory. In the pilot episode Rory explains to her future boyfriend, Dean, upon their first meeting that she and her mother have the same name. Of Lorelai, Rory says, "She was lying in the hospital thinking about how men name boys after themselves all the time. She says her feminism just sort of took over." Rory does attempt to diminish the acknowledgement of feminism noting that "Personally, I think a lot of Demerol went into that decision" (1.01, "Pilot"). This quasi-disclaimer may have been a conscious decision on the part of the WB, the network that aired *Gilmore Girls*, which undoubtedly has viewers that may be less inclined to embrace feminism, yet there is no disguising the fact that Lorelai's actions are blatantly feminist. Based upon the previous discussion of feminism and feminist backlash, the use of the word feminism in direct association with Lorelai firmly entrenches her as a feminist in the minds of the viewers. This is significant as it is the first episode of the series, the one traditionally responsible for introducing the characters and providing some insight into their personalities and lives. Therefore, naming plays a double function in this episode; Lorelai is named as a feminist and Rory bears the name of her mother. The act of naming Rory for herself is significant in that Lorelai refuses to relinquish her own identity, in the form of a name, or her daughter's identity to the expectations of the patriarchy. Lorelai not only assumes the traditionally patriarchal act of naming her daughter for herself in the manner in which male sons have traditionally been named for their fathers, she also gives her daughter her surname of Gilmore instead of following the traditional practice of giving her daughter the father's surname of Hayden. Historically, taking on the name of the father provided legitimacy for the child; children lacking a father's name on their birth certificates often had their birth certificates labeled with the words "illegitimate." While viewers can be fairly certain that Christopher Hayden's name does appear on the birth certificate, one cannot deny the fact that Rory stands to represent the family name of her mother Gilmore, hence the naming of the show, *Gilmore Girls.* This act of naming is also accentuated by the appearance of the show's title. "Gilmore" appears in capital letters while "girl" appears in lowercase. Typically both words in the titles would be capitalized, but Gilmore stands out to viewers as the primary focus.

Aside from merely challenging basic ideals of language and tradition, the naming of Rory Gilmore challenges perceptions of ownership. Women and children typically take the name of the father as signifying a sense of belonging to then man for the purposes of protection and various legalities. Ultimately, this act signified ownership and for many feminists the assertion that being forced to renounce one's maiden name was tantamount to a loss of identity, thus prompting the practice of women retaining their maiden names upon marriage. Hyphenating the two names, the married and the maiden, becomes another solution commonly practiced by many feminists as it acknowledges both the male and the female identity of the union. It is a response to the naming dilemma, which allows children to take the name of both parents, although more commonly the children still retain the father's name. This is not to say that one cannot be a feminist and take on the spousal name; it is to highlight the fact that women have a choice in naming themselves which was not available prior to the second-wave feminist movement. This discussion is merely intended to highlight the naming debate and accent the relationship between naming and belonging and naming and identity. This issue of the need for mothers to be identified with their children is so compelling that often women choose to retain their married names in divorce settlements so that they will continue to share the same last name as their children. Yet, Lorelai chooses the name of Gilmore as she is intent upon retaining her own identity and proclaiming her independence. As a result, she distances herself from the life that her parents and Christopher would impose upon her, a life of marriage to Christopher, a marriage in which the name Hayden would undoubtedly be expected to supplant Gilmore. Lorelai chooses to completely reject the expectations of the patriarchy and proclaim her daughter as an extension of herself, and in keeping with the patriarchal notions of ownership, as belonging to her. Oddly enough, despite the rarity of the situation, it is never discussed in much detail on the show. Christopher even seems to be quite accepting of Rory's Gilmore status. In "That Damn Donna Reed" (1.14), he appears unexpectedly in Stars Hollow and, when questioned about his sudden appearance, he explains that he was on his way to visit his parents in Connecticut and thought that he would stop by to see "the Gilmore Girls."

Perhaps Christopher's lack of concern in regards to his offspring bearing his name is due to his lack of participation in other areas of his daughter's life. Although it is made clear to the viewer that Lorelai rejects Christopher's offer of marriage as well as her own parents involvement in their lives (1.01, "Pilot"),[8] Lorelai does not seem to deny Christopher access to Rory. She allows him to stay in their home when he arrives announced for a visit (1.14, "That Damn Donna Reed") and when Lorelai is confronted by a former high school acquaintance (1.06, "Rory's Birthday Parties")[9] she acknowledges that Christopher calls once a week, although viewers may even doubt this level of Christopher's involvement since Lorelai seems unaware of Christopher's recent business success until it is announced by her parents during one evening at dinner. Nonetheless, the willingness on Lorelai's behalf is apparent.

Another indication in regard to Christopher's level of involvement is Christopher's delayed bodily entrance into the series. He does not physically appear until episode 1.14, while most of the recurring characters were introduced in the pilot or, at least, within the first three episodes. Christopher's entrance highlights Lorelai's single status as well as her independence in regards to raising Rory. Her self-sufficiency and success at caring for them both reflects the feminist principles that men are not necessary to ensure survival and security. It also functions to identify a common problem in society, that of the absentee father. At the risk of essentializing women, the sheer essence of biology more often than not makes them the primary care givers. Luce Irigaray discusses this reality in *The Sex Which Is Not One*: "of course, children are conceived by women and men together, but conceived only. The work of gestating, giving birth, breastfeeding and mothering is up to women" (76). Yet, for Lorelai her role of mothering also includes procuring the financial means to be able to support herself and her daughter. It is doubtful that life would really be better for Lorelai had she married Christopher (despite what her mother believes). Many women, both married and single must balance the issue of work and home. Margaret J. Heide discusses the conditions of women in an analysis of society in relation to the television show *thirtysomething*. She says of the expectations placed upon women:

> They are encouraged to work at the same time it is assumed that they will still be the primary caregivers for home and family; defining oneself outside of one's own relationship to a man is cheerfully advocated while at the same time women are made to feel less than whole without a man or child. Thus, despite the gains women are still trying to conform to earlier culturally defined scripts about appropriate female behaviors and roles while they assume new roles and behaviors [36].

Clearly the male/female social role is varied, and for females a bit more complicated, as they are expected to perform more of the duties in regards to both manual labor around the home, but more specifically in preserving the home. This difference can be examined in the differences between the lives of Christopher and Lorelai. While both Lorelai and Christopher were sixteen at Rory's birth, there is a significant difference in the manner in which the two have approached their lives. Lorelai has a stable job, a home, a support system in the community, and a strong sense of responsibility when it comes to providing for herself and her daughter. In contrast, Christopher is free to pursue his own life and goals with little changing in regards to his planned path. Unlike Lorelai, pregnancy did not cause him to forego college, travel, and the pursuit of his own career goals. Christopher's freedom is exemplified in his sudden arrival via motorcycle (1.14, "That Damn Donna Reed").

The motorcycle is an important image in the first season of the *Gilmore Girls* and is emblematic of the dichotomy between the good girl/bad girl struggle. Of course, the motorcycle is symbolic of the freedom of the open road and Christopher's lack of responsibility. It is also a reminder of the allure of the "bad boy." And who is attracted to bad boys? Good girls. One need only recall Marlon Brando's iconic performance in *The Wild One*[10] to immediately associate the images of leather jackets with an erotic vision of danger. Yet, Lorelai herself longs for that same excitement as she immediately exhibits a more than cursory knowledge of the motorcycle as it roars into town. When Rory asks if the motorcycle is a Harley, Lorelai responds: "That is a 2,000 Indian, 80 HP, 5 speed, close ration transmission, and I want to get one." This knowledge reaffirms Lorelai's tenuous existence between the good girl/bad girl classifications. How does she know so much about motorcycles and is this knowledge one stereotypically expect from a female?

It is also the vision of Christopher that causes viewers to reflect on Lorelai's initial reaction in the pilot episode to the prospect that Rory wanted to avoid transferring to a different school upon meeting Dean. Lorelai is doubly horrified by the humiliation she had to endure in order procure the money necessary to secure a spot at Chilton and most of all, that Rory might be willing to throw her dreams of Harvard away for a boy. In the middle of the argument Lorelai demands: "Does he have a motorcycle? Because if you're going to throw your life away, he'd better have a motorcycle!" (1.01, "Pilot"). The motorcycle imagery also appears again when Lorelai has her conversation with Dean regarding the rules for dating Rory. One of the rules is, "She's not going on your motorcycle" (1.07, "Kiss and Tell"). When Dean protests that he doesn't even have a motorcycle, Lorelai repeats herself again. For Lorelai the motorcycle is representative of sex and danger. Therefore, when Lorelai says, "she will not get on your motorcycle," she is warning against any sexual interactions and denouncing the possibility of Rory repeating her own mistake resulting in teen pregnancy. This becomes even more apparent when Rory and Lorelai stand in the front yard watching Christopher leave at the end of his visit. When discussing her feelings for Christopher she responds wistfully explaining, "He's my Dean." This identification of Dean as Christopher has Freudian implications in that Rory would be looking for someone to mirror her father. In one episode, Lorelai notes to Luke that Dean looks like Christopher, which causes her concern. Instead of viewing Rory's attraction to Dean as a way to fulfill her needs regarding her father, Luke instead attributes Rory's attraction to Dean as a reflection of Lorelai, noting that since they are so much alike it makes sense that they would have similar tastes in men, possibly, as Lorelai fears, with the same end result.

The appearance of Christopher, as well as the specter of Christopher that looms over preceding episodes in references to Lorelai's pregnancy and the accusations of her parents, makes it apparent that Lorelai's rejection of Christopher is not based upon lack of love and desire for him. It is purely based upon preservation of her own future as well as both Rory and Christopher's futures. With an insight that exceeds the maturity of her sixteen years, Lorelai recognizes the dangers of an imposed marriage; therefore, in a feminist fashion, she chooses to strike out on her own instead of conforming to the societal (i.e., patriarchal expectations) that she and Christopher marry. As a result, she runs away with Rory. Lorelai's opposition to marriage is the main focus of season one, and one of the ways in which she clearly defies patriarchal expectations and the stereotype that all women are just dying to get married. While being pregnant in one's teens is certainly not the norm, more women are prolonging marriage until later in their lives: "This attitude towards marriage is commonplace among the third-wave generation. Journalists and sociologists are sitting up and taking notice of the growing number of women staying single longer, and the abundance of never married women and their stereotype shattering lives" (Johnson 146). Like the women Lisa Johnson discusses, Lorelai would fall into the Generation X range and despite the fact that she was pregnant had other ideas and clear choices for the future. Lorelai's parents are clearly still angry about her decision and berate her for it during the first of the Friday night dinners (1.01, "Pilot"). In their eyes, Lorelai's life would have been better and she would have been able to maintain her upper class status because their parents would have been able to help them. But Lorelai is unapologetic for any of her choices, and in true "bad girl" fashion, she defies her parents once again.

During a time when time when society has changed to the extent that many people are choosing to have children out of wedlock, more specifically in the case of Lorelai, unwed motherhood need not be a situation that naturally results in poverty. Although it may be statistically unlikely that most unwed mothers will be as successful as Lorelai at this stage in her life, and thus a possible cause for criticism of the show, viewers understand that Lorelai did have her financial struggles. She supported Rory and herself by working as a maid at the inn in which she is now executive manager and the two lived in a one-room potting shed on the property with bathroom conditions that were addressed during tenement reform in New York City in 1899.[11] Despite these conditions both Rory and Lorelai remember those years in a positive manner, and it is important to remember that Lorelai rejected wealth and chose this life. This is another way in which she defies the norms in a society obsessed with conspicuous consumption and the motivation of wealth; this is clearly represented in the show through the actions of ostentatious displays of wealth by Lorelai's parents, Richard and Emily Gilmore. Emily's viewing of the potting shed (1.19, "Emily in Wonderland") prompts one of her most emotional arguments with Lorelai as she realizes how desperately Lorelai wanted to escape from her home. Therefore, Lorelai uses her role as mother as a means to emancipate herself from the life of the upper class that her parents have carved out for her.

> Becoming a mother in her own turn, the woman in a sense takes the place of her own mother: it means complete emancipation for her. If she sincerely desires it, she will be delighted with her pregnancy and will have the courage to go through with it by herself; but if she is still under maternal domination, and willingly, she on the contrary, puts herself in her mother's hands; her newborn child will seem like her own brother and sister rather than her own offspring [De Beauvoir 494].

In rejecting her mother's place and her parents' house, Lorelai is able to forge a new identity for herself. Although the pregnancy was clearly unplanned, Lorelai is pregnant at a time in which women have choices regarding their bodies, and though abortion is not mentioned, one can assume that, with Lorelai's feistiness and feminist ideals, she would have sought an abortion if the pregnancy were completely unwanted.

In choosing motherhood Lorelai does take on what would traditionally be seen as a "good girl" role, but the fact that she chooses an untraditional time in her life to take on this role may negate anything good, as society overall clearly has negative attitudes regarding unwed mothers as "bad girls."

Nonetheless, fulfillment and purpose of womanhood is still linked very much to the ability to conceive: "Woman's proof that she is somebody is furnished when she makes a deposit, for everybody comes from somebody, one cannot have a nonentity for a mother" (Boone). Although clearly Lorelai had a strong sense of self before pregnancy (otherwise she would not have been able to run away and start a new life), she definitely redefines the traditional perceptions of motherhood in the way in which she performs motherhood.

Lorelai's mothering is juxtaposed against a background of other mothers on the show, particularly her own mother and Mrs. Kim, the mother of Rory's best friend, Lane, who is representative of the ultra conservative, ultra-strict mother Lorelai is not. This draws criticism from Ms. Kim as she notes that Lorelai should be paying more attention to Rory's actions: "You could keep your daughter from running around kissing boys" (1.07, "Kiss and Tell").[12] Mrs. Kim is critical of Lorelai as a mother and is cautionary regarding her unwed status, and as a result is less than receptive regarding Lane's friendship with Rory and subsequent associations with Lorelai. To Mrs. Kim, Lorelai is a "bad" mother in spite of the fact that her daughter turns to Lorelai for support and that Lorelai is more aware of the actions of both Rory and Lane than Mrs. Kim. Lorelai is also contrasted to her own mother who is still attempting to control Lorelai, as evidenced by the stipulation of a weekly dinner to secure a loan.

In one episode, memories of Lorelai's childhood come flooding back as she and Rory watch a mother chastise a little girl wearing a white frilly dress during a wedding reception (1.03, "Kill Me Now"). Her mother instructs her to "cross her legs and act like a lady." Lorelai wears a pained expression on her face as she tells Rory that she had many dresses like that as a child. As they look on at the little girl's expression of discontent Rory says to Lorelai, "Thanks for never putting me in a dress like that." The dress comes to symbolize the absurdity of telling a little girl to "act like a lady" and condemns the restrictions placed on little girls for the sake of conforming to expectations of beauty and decorum. By inculcating this ideology of being good from an early age and reigning in any behavior seeming to be socially unacceptable, mothers unwittingly perpetuate the rules of the patriarchy. Lorelai's refusal to dress and treat Rory as a dress-up doll breaks the pattern of imposing standards of beauty and decorum on little girls and enables Rory to break free from these standards. The distinction between Lorelai and Emily as mothers also occurs when Emily challenges Lorelai's mothering style when Rory and Dean fall asleep and, thus, inadvertently, stay out all night (1.09, "Rory's Dance"). Emily expresses concerns that Rory will end up pregnant just like Lorelai. Lorelai makes the distinction between herself and Rory by noting: "Rory is a good kid; she's not me." This separates Rory as a good girl, whereas, Lorelai's pregnancy and defiance of her parents situates her in the role of the "bad girl." In this episode, the "bad girl" becomes the bad mother as Emily asks Lorelai: "What kind of mother are you?"

Lorelai fires the same question back at her mother. Clearly, Emily feels that she was a "good mother" and Lorelai still ended up pregnant; yet, Lorelai is quick to point out that pregnancy or not, she and Emily would have never have had a good relationship: "I had nothing in that house; I had no life, no air. You strangled me. I don't strangle Rory." For Emily, good mothering consists of providing monetary items and opportunities that can be secured through money. For Lorelai, it is a foundation of a relationship built upon communication and trust. Ironically, Lorelai violates this when Emily leaves by accusing Rory of the same type of actions she had just defended her from, thus illustrating the tensions between the types of mothering and the commonality of concerns that plague most mothers. However, unlike Lorelai and Emily, Lorelai and Rory are able to communicate and rebound from an incident that would have left a schism between Lorelai and Emily, thus repositioning Lorelai in the role of a "good mother."

Yet, despite the closeness of relationship between Rory and Lorelai, Lorelai does not always put Rory's needs ahead of her own. Lorelai does not fulfill the role of the typical "self-sacrificing" mother, although it is clear that she has made sacrifices along the way, one of which is the forcible Friday night dinner that she must endure in exchange for the loan for Rory's Chilton admission. However, in some areas, Lorelai is not completely self-sacrificing and that is when it comes to dating. This is best exemplified when she dates Rory's English teacher, Max Medina. Although Rory insists that it is okay with her, it is still problematic given the nature of her own connection to Max. This raises a problem often confronted by children of feminists: "Philosophically, we want our mothers to be liberated except of course, when we want them to be home after school making the meals, intuiting our pains and needs and listening to our problems. In other words we set them up to be martyrs to sacrifice their own needs for ours" (Baumgardner and Richards 212). Rory wants Lorelai to feel free to live her own life provided that it doesn't complicate Lorelai's role as mother as well as their mother/daughter relationship; she expects Lorelai to make certain sacrifices. Even though Lorelai recognizes both the problem of being with Max and Rory's reluctance, she goes ahead with the relationship and defies one of the rules of the house by allowing Max to sleep over (1.08, "Love and War and Snow"). Lorelai's refusal to deny her sexuality could be seen by some viewers as "bad mothering" or others as "good feminism" as she challenges the norms regarding self-sacrifice; either way it illustrates the problem of negotiating the dual roles and highlights the subjectivity of determining what is "good" and what is "bad." Lorelai does not allow her role as a mother to interfere with her identity as a woman and a sexual being; she is not completely willing to sacrifice that part of herself, which is important from a feminist perspective that advocates maintaining both an identity separate from a mother.

One of the most obvious ways in which Lorelai defies the stereotypical roles of female domesticity is in her approach to cooking and housework. When she initially takes Dean on a tour of their home during his first visit she refers to the stove as a "place for storing shoes" (1.07, "Kiss and Tell"). Rory and Lorelai are constantly seen partaking in junk food together and their suppers consist mostly of take-out and eating at the dinner. Even Luke comments upon this when he serves them at the diner and tries to persuade Rory not to drink coffee like her mother. Mrs. Kim also warns against the horrors of junk food as she calls sweets "chocolate covered death" and gives Lane snacks of rice cakes unaware that Lane sneaks junk food in the Gilmore home. Even Emily views the weekly dinners as the only time in which Rory gets a decent meal (1.08, "Love and War and Snow"), even though she is not the one cooking it. The formal atmosphere at the dinner table at the weekly dinners is also an extreme contrast to the genuine enjoyment of Lorelai and Rory as they chow down on their hamburgers at Luke's. Lorelai's lack of domestic ability or inclination is in clear opposition to the values that one expects to have as a mother. In addition, food is an integral part of a family gathering and preparing meals together is often viewed as an opportunity for mothers and daughters to bond with one another. As a result, one would think that Rory and Lorelai may be missing a valuable experience, and they, in fact, may be. I know I have fond memories of working in the kitchen with my own mother. However, Lorelai and Rory still have the bonding experience of having a nightly dinner together and the fact that they do not have to clean up allows time for them to focus on talking to one another. In an in-depth study of mothers and daughters, Miriam Meyers examines the significance of food and the preparation of food in the relationships between women.[13] Meyers even acknowledges the role of dining out in her work: "Dining out as mother and daughter provides an opportunity to practice what anthropologists Farb and Armmelgos assert as the primary way of maintaining relationships in all society — eating together" (47). In fact, unlike many families, viewers also see Lorelai and Rory sitting down together for breakfast (at the diner, of course). Ultimately, the dining habits of Rory and Lorelai challenge perceptions that women should be responsible for cooking and serving the meals, perhaps overlooking the significance of the experience of just sitting down together.

As briefly mentioned earlier, Lorelai and Rory also challenge perceptions in terms of how much they consume and the type of food that they consume. In a society that favors thinness in women and the self-sacrificing habits of denying oneself food in order to achieve the ideal figure, Lorelai and Rory gorge themselves on junk food in numerous episodes. Yet, despite this approach to eating, unrealistically neither of them ever gains weight and both are able to maintain attractive figures and still adhere to standards of beauty. So, while Lorelai and Rory challenge the eating habits of women by refusing to diet or even watch what they eat, *Gilmore Girls* does not go so far as to realistically challenge these standards by showing either of the main characters as overweight or unattractive. Nonetheless, they do defy the expectations of women as never being able to achieve satisfaction with their bodies or their lives. Courtney E. Martin examines what she dubs "the starving daughter mentality," which plagues women who can never achieve perfection either bodily or within the realm that extends beyond the body. She notes that "These perfect girls feel we could always lose five more pounds" (34). In a survey of women Martin sought to explore the problems of eating disorders and the ways in which women connect their bodies to their overall happiness and power: "In my informal e-mail survey, not one woman said that she was ever satisfied with how much she thought about her diet or workout regime everyday" (52). Yet, neither Lorelai nor Rory seem plagued by these insecurities. In some ways the characters seem to be exempt from this pressure of perfection felt by most women who feel that to look good is to be good. Yet, the depiction of their relationship with food serves as an open feminist defiance of a culture that calls for women to deny themselves in order to achieve or maintain impossible standards.

Along with the other mothers shown on *Gilmore Girls*, Lorelai's unorthodox type of mothering is also juxtaposed against that of one of the traditional fictional mothers discussed in the beginning of the paper, the incomparable Donna Reed. In "That Damn Donna Reed" (1.14), both Rory and Lorelai watch the *Donna Reed Show* and profess feminist backlash against the 1950s roles that Donna must fulfill. This episode is significant in highlighting the feminist message of *Gilmore Girls* and, as a result, warrants an in-depth discussion. In one scene Donna and her daughter are washing windows together and Rory facetiously suggests that she and Lorelai do that, as well. Lorelai responds, "Mother daughter window-washing right after mother daughter shock treatment." Dean, who is also in the room, does not seem to understand Lorelai and Rory's reaction and professes that he thinks Donna's penchant for caring for her family is "nice." He protests that the character Donna Stone doesn't seem unhappy and Lorelai quips, "She's medicated." The contrasting viewpoints of Dean and Lorelai and Rory highlight the difference between a feminist and a patriarchal view of the duties of wives and mothers. To Dean this image of Donna Reed is "good," while to Rory and Lorelai it is "bad." This leads to a misunderstanding the next day because of Rory's concern that Dean viewed the show favorably. This prompts Rory to dress up later that night like a 50s housewife complete with pearls and heels and serve Dean dinner. He comes to admit that he prefers the usual Rory to the Donna Reed Rory. But Rory must also acknowledge that upon conducting some research on Donna Reed, she learned that she was a producer and groundbreaking in regards to the roles that women played on television. Indeed, many in the television industry have characterized Donna Reed as a feminist.[14] In recognizing this, Rory challenges the previous notions presented by both she and Lorelai that the women on these past shows could easily be dismissed as succumbing to the culture of the patriarchy. This is significant as the characters pay homage to other female characters that came before them and serves to highlight the blur between concepts of feminism and non-feminism, and good and bad.

Lorelai and Rory have their tense moments just as all mothers and daughters experience in real life. And I'll admit that the show may be a bit unbelievable at times. After all, nothing bad ever happens in Stars Hollow. Nonetheless, the character of Lorelai Gilmore has been a significant presence on television in representing two largely underrepresented groups, unwed mothers and feminists. The relationships between the characters and the ideals presented on the show represent feminism in a positive light, which is especially important during this time of liberal and feminist backlash. So whether viewers think that Lorelai is "good" or "bad," one thing is certain, unlike the girl with the little curl, *Gilmore Girls* could certainly never be considered horrid.

Notes

1. 19th century American poet known most famously for his poems "Hiawatha" and "Paul Revere's Ride."

2. Betty Friedan's ground-breaking book is considered to be responsible for launching the second wave of feminism. Published in 1963, *The Feminist Mystique* challenged the traditional domestic roles assigned to women and advocated choices beyond the home.

3. *Leave It to Beaver* was a situational 50s comedy which aired on CBS from October of 1957 to July of 1963. Despite its short time on the air, it has gained iconic status.

4. For discussion of Donna Reed please see Lynn Spangler's *Television Women from Lucy to Friends.* Westport, CT: Praeger, 2003. pp. 49–51.

5. *The Brady Bunch* aired on ABC from 1969–1974 and offered a different view of the traditional family. It exemplified the melding of two families due to second marriages. Nonetheless, the mother stayed at home and performed various roles in the house aided by a housekeeper, Alice.

6. For more on the tensions between Lucy and Ricky, please see Lynn Spangler's *Television Women from Lucy to Friends.* Westport, CT: Praeger, 2003. pp. 31–36.

7. For a thorough discussion of the impact of television in the lives of children and the images of single mothers, please see Juffer, pp. 45–75.

8. This is discussed during 1.01 ("Pilot") at the first weekly dinner that Lorelai and Rory attend. In this scene Lorelai's parents praise Christopher and the conversation ends with Lorelai leaving the table upset.

9. This occurs at Rory's birthday party given by Emily. The acquaintance greets Lorelai by saying "Lorelai Gilmore, scandal girl!"

10. *The Wild One.* Dir. Laszlo Benedek. 1953, Stanley Kramer. In this film Marlon Brando plays the rebellious Johnny Strabler who attracts the "good girl" Kathie Bleeker. This film is considered to have started the fashion trend of jeans and t-shirts.

11. The 1899 Tenement Reform Act outlawed bathrooms that were not enclosed by walls. The potting shed had an unenclosed bathroom area that Lorelai enclosed with a curtain.

12. Miss Patty sees Dean and Rory share their first kiss and gossips about it across town, thus prompting Mrs. Kim to make this comment to an unsuspecting Lorelai.

13. For more regarding this study and an in-depth discussion of individual interviews and the significance of food please see Meyers.

14. For discussion of Donna Reed please see Spangler, pp. 49–51.

Works Cited

Bathrick, Serafina. "*The Mary Tyler Moore Show:* Women at Home and at Work." *Critiquing the Sitcom*. Ed. Joanne Morreale. New York: Syracuse UP, 2003. 155–86.

Baumgardner Jennifer and Amy Richards. *Manifesta: Young Women, Feminism and the Future*. New York: Farrar, Strauss and Giroux, 2000.

Boone, Rebecca. *From the Mind of a Mother: Essays for the 21st Century and Beyond*. San Francisco: International Scholars, 1996.

Center for Disease Control. *National Center for Health Statistics*. CDC, 2004.

De Beauvoir, Simone. *The Second Sex*. New York: Vintage, 1989.

Dow, Bonnie J. *Prime-Time Feminism: Television, Media Culture, and the Women's Movement Since 1970*. Philadelphia: University of Pennsylvania Press, 1996.

Gamber, Frankie. "Wavelengths." *Bitch* Spring 2007: 42–47.

Heide, Margaret J. *Television Culture and Women's Lives:* thirtysomething *and the Contradictions in Gender*. Philadelphia: University of Pennsylvania Press, 1995.

Irigaray, Luce. *The Sex Which Is Not One*. Ithaca, NY: Cornell University Press, 1985.

Juffer, Jane. *Single Mother: The Emergence of the Domestic Intellectual*. New York: New York UP, 2006.

Martin, Courtney E. "Perfect Girls, Starving Daughters." *Bitch* Spring 2007: 48–55.

Mellencamp, Patricia. "Situation Comedy, Feminism, and Freud: Discourses of Gracie and Lucy." *Critiquing the Sitcom*. Ed. Joanne Morreale. New York: Syracuse University Press, 2003. 41–55

Meyers, Miriam. *A Bite Off Mama's Plate: Mothers' and Daughters' Connections through Food*. West Port, CT: Bergin and Garvey, 2001.

Norton, Eleanor Holmes. "Notes of a Feminist Long-Distance Runner." *Sisterhood Is Forever: The Women's Anthology for a New Millennium*. Ed. Robin Morgan. New York: Washington Square Press, 2003. 141–51.

Spangler, Lynn. *Television Women from* Lucy *to* Friends. Westport, CT: Praeger, 2003.

Got MILF?

Losing Lorelai in Season Seven

Tiffany Aldrich MacBain
and Mita Mahato

Watching the last episodes of a television series that we've grown attached to over the years can be a difficult experience, particularly in cases in which we've come to sympathize and identify with the characters on the show. In such situations, sitting in front of the TV for the final season can be much like saying a 22-hour goodbye to a set of friends who, for years, have had no small impact on our daily lives. Like we often do with our closest friends, we've begun to dress like them (has watching Carry Bradshaw at least made you *think* about buying a pair of Minolo Blahniks?), or we wear our hair the same way (remember the Jennifer Aniston 'do?), or, occasionally, we gossip about them ("Would *you* date a vampire, even if he had a soul?").

Given the influence that a favorite show can have on our lives, it makes sense that we would be emotionally invested in how the series ties up its loose ends and says its goodbyes. After all, we've spent six, seven, eight years sharing in the births, break-ups, and bad decisions of these complex, albeit fictional, personae. Our final view of our favorite characters thus becomes of central importance as we consider what we take away from the show. Will they get married to the "right" people? Will they get married at all? Will they end up in New York or Paris — in an apartment in the city or a house in the suburbs? Most importantly, will the final episodes encourage us to voice a meaningful goodbye or to grumble a resigned good riddance? If the answers to these questions are at odds with those that we hope for, then we can't help but feel betrayed — we thought we knew them!

Such a betrayal was in the cards for loyal viewers of *Gilmore Girls*, the hit CW series known for the quick and culturally savvy exchanges between Lorelai Gilmore (Lauren Graham) and her daughter, Rory (Alexis Bledel). With the departure of creator and lead writer Amy Sherman-Palladino at the completion of the show's sixth season in 2006, fans both anticipated and worried that the seventh installment would not only sound the show's death knell, but also disrupt the affection that they had developed for the characters over the years.[1] These anxieties would be confirmed; the Lorelai and Rory we encounter in the final episodes of *Gilmore Girls* contrast sharply with their earlier manifestations. Gone are the days when Lorelai wore her Daisy Dukes to her first meeting with Headmaster Charleston, or when Rory's hair seemed fashioned after Wednesday Adams's rather than coiffed with layers and side-swept bangs. Sherman-Palladino, responding to viewer complaints about the direction the show took back in 2004, suggests that this kind of nostalgia is a dangerous way for viewers to measure their sympathy with characters. She explains that she "understand[s] that viewers get attached to something and then it changes and throws you.... But that is the way *life* goes. I liked Rory in her little plaid school skirt too, but this girl has to grow and find out what kind of woman she wants to be" (qtd. in Press). Sherman-Palladino makes a good point. In spite of the qualities that draw viewers to the Gilmore Girls, characters as dynamic and intelligent as Lorelai and Rory need to be able to develop and grow; after all, that forward motion, consistent and sensible, is what kept viewers faithfully glued to *Gilmore Girls* through its first six seasons. In the show's seventh cycle, however, character development turns toward the inconsistent and unconvincing, leaving loyal viewers disappointed and a bit befuddled.

Rory's long-lost plaid skirt and plain-Jane hair are not the problem. Viewers have long been accustomed to seeing Rory as a grown woman; as Lorelai adjusted to her daughter's move to Hartford and move-in with Logan, so did we. Instead, at issue is the writers' treatment of Lorelai,[2] particularly in her relationships with Luke and Christopher. During most of the series these two men (and a few others) are satellites orbiting planet Lorelai — Lorelai is their (and the show's) sexy center, their rock, their gravitational pull. Season seven reverses that relationship, subsuming Lorelai's narrative into that of the men in her life and threatening to suck in viewers, as well. A lot is at stake in this narratological shift. Over the years fans have tuned in to *Gilmore Girls* because they are drawn to the type of single motherhood Lorelai models. Undoubtedly a "single mother by choice"[3] (Mattes qtd. in Silbergleid 1), she has maintained the right to raise her child by carving out meaningful and fulfilled existences for mother and daughter alike. We viewers, like the townspeople of Stars Hollow and Lorelai's assorted male suitors, are drawn to Lorelai precisely because of her distinctive ability to marry responsible motherhood to gratifying single womanhood. This unexpected union between mother and woman is in fact the only type of marriage the first six seasons of *Gilmore Girls* delivers for Lorelai; the role of wife is unnecessary, and even undesirable, as it would deprive her of the availability that renders her attractive. As much as we might root for Luke or Christopher or even Max to win Lorelai's hand, we are perhaps more compelled by that resolution's deferral, for it allows Lorelai's single motherhood to remain the central focus of the show.

Lorelai and Christopher's season seven marriage — short-lived though it is — signals a change in the show's intentions and impact. The sudden positioning of Rory's father as caretaker of the Gilmore Girls effectively changes the point-of-view through which we understand the issues surrounding family relations dealt with by the series. As if to suggest that Lorelai's struggles with motherhood are completed with the onset of married life, the first several episodes of the season turn our attention away from motherhood and onto the struggles of the patriarch. Christopher's presence registers as odd and even intrusive at times, and once the two are married, the narrative effectively channels our identification with Lorelai through her husband. In creating such a perspectival shift, the show's writers ask us to consider what kind of father Christopher will be, and what kind of husband for someone like Lorelai. Such questions about the place of the male in a show dominated by women are further invited by Luke's custody struggle over daughter April and by Richard's heart attack and distinctly self–centered and self–indulgent road to recovery. (Just eat the fish, Richard!) It's not that these aren't legitimate avenues for the show to venture down — they are. But the centrality of the men's struggles undermines and overshadows the refreshingly unconventional presentation of motherhood that made *Gilmore Girls* so appealing to its audience. In resituating Lorelai's function and position on the show, season seven also resituates its viewers, returning them from a narrative that understood patriarchy, for once, as an aside, to one that codifies traditional and male-centered conceptions of family.

Sex and the Model Mother

This isn't to say that marriage — even with Christopher — hasn't been a tempting possibility for Lorelai or her fans. In the years preceding Lorelai's marriage to Rory's father, we got something of a thrill in seeing the two reconnect, making out on the balcony at her parents' home, snuggling at the inn, getting drunk on tequila. Such moments between Lorelai and Christopher contain elements of innocence, intimacy, and fun reminiscent (for many of us) of sneaking off as teenagers and doing something they (we) ought not to be doing. But perhaps because of their history, the times when they come together as adults are not entirely carefree; their first experience with love, after all, produced a child and a dramatic family rift. Burdened by this complicated past, the encounters between Lorelai and Christopher take on a certain narrative weight, for they call on Lorelai, along with the viewers who sympathize with her, to consider acting in what prevailing opinion maintains are the best interests of herself and her daughter. Christopher is the favorite mate of conventional wisdom — the person who can make an honest woman out of Lorelai; he is Rory's father, approved of and endorsed by Lorelai's parents and, not incidentally, the heir to an enormous fortune. Yet, despite the temptation offered by Christopher's many returns during the first six seasons, what is crucial to note is that any future potential that might be nurtured in these passionate encounters is always nipped in the bud by something as trivial as a disagreement about Metallica (1.15, "Christopher Returns") or as significant as the news of Sherry's pregnancy (2.22, "I Can't Get Started"). Such narrative derailments do not register as postponements to an inevitable "happily ever after" for Christopher, Lorelai, and Rory, but rather as signposts that lead viewers to understand, again and again, why it makes more sense for Lorelai to remain single than to marry Christopher. The constant shelving of Lorelai's union with the father of her daughter effectively highlights and legitimates Lorelai's capacity to raise a family on her own — to be a mother without being a wife. In this sense, Sherman-Palladino's show answers critic E. Ann Kaplan's indictment against television and film's inability to "produce...images of sexual women, who are also mothers, and who, in addition, have fulfilling careers" (183). The basic premise that began *Gilmore Girls* unsettles the long legacy of clichéd representations of motherhood by having at its heart an affirming and positive presentation of a mother who is characterized by not only her sex drive and career, but also her single status.

Lorelai's unorthodox approach to single motherhood and family is underscored by her relationship with Rory throughout the series — a connection brought into focus as early as the pilot episode. Notably, the episode's only reference to Christopher comes toward the end of the hour, when Richard (Lorelai's father) mentions his name at dinner. Lorelai responds by asking her mother, "Why would he bring up Christopher? Was that really necessary?" Indeed, except for exposition, it *isn't* necessary, for the episode focuses on introducing viewers to a Lorelai Gilmore who is a sexually available and desirable woman, attached only, though ardently, to her daughter. The opening scene establishes this identity most pointedly when Lorelai and then Rory are hit on in Luke's diner by a twenty-something-year-old named Joey. Lorelai rebuffs both advances made by this "regular Jack Kerouac"— the first on the grounds of her obligation to spend time with Rory, and the second with a pointed, "She's sixteen!" Joyce Millman has suggested that this exchange between Lorelai and Joey calls attention to the interchangeability between mother and daughter: "The boisterous Lorelai is 32 going on 16[,] the serious Rory is 16 going on 32," and the young Casanova, situated between their ages, finds them both attractive. This early assessment of the mother-daughter relationship echoes the perception viewers have tended to have of the Gilmore Girls throughout the show's run.[4] But given that we never take Lorelai actually to be Rory's daughter (nor do we ever mistake Rory for the mother), we might reconsider how we understand the nature of the pair's allure. Lorelai's double rejection, together with the young man's interest in landing both of the Gilmores ("You know I *am* traveling with a friend..."), demonstrate that Lorelai gains capital in the young man's eyes not because she is youthful, but because she is part of a mother-daughter set. In other words, Lorelai is one hot mama. Amy Benfer, in her discussion of the same scene, also finds that motherhood gives Lorelai a certain amount of sexual currency: "Next to the idea that one will be picked up by two gorgeous, identical-twin nymphomaniacs, ...the idea of meeting a gorgeous mother-daughter duo ranks high on the list of male masturbation fantasies." More so than highlighting Rory and Lorelai's generational interchangeability, the early exchange in Luke's diner designates that Joey's attraction to Lorelai rests in the balance she is able to strike between her sexuality and her mother status.[5]

While Joey was doomed to get back "on the road," never to show his face in Stars Hollow again, his particular interest in Lorelai's maternal sexuality (or sexy maternity) would stick with viewers and keep them coming back for more. A quick Google search reveals, in fact, that Lorelai fans of all ages, genders, and backgrounds, characterize her as a "Mom I'd Like to Fuck," or MILF. Blogger "Mighty Jimbo," for instance, calls Lorelai "a serious MILF"; likewise, in a synopsis of the season seven premiere, *Portland Mercury* columnist Wm. Steven Humphrey refers to her as "hot MILF Lorelai"; *The Lumière Reader*, a New Zealand on-line journal, is a little more thoughtful on the matter: "Lorelai makes for a sly crossbreed of best friend, maternal dominatrix and universal MILF" (Wong). While the ubiquity of the acronym, MILF, makes its etymology difficult, if not impossible, to pin down, its popularity can be traced to the film *American Pie*— released the same year, 1999, that *Gilmore Girls* premiered. Of course, the fantasy of the MILF predates the turn of the twenty-first century. Perhaps most famously, Mrs. Robinson was a MILF before the term existed, though in a radically different sense than is Lorelai. While watching *The Graduate* (1967), we were never really asked to understand that adulterating and older temptress, clad in her predatory leopard print, as a viable option for Benjamin. Sexy and seductive, certainly. Wily and willing, of course. But as a married and noticeably older woman, Mrs. Robinson was set against her daughter's idealized youthfulness rather than characterized by it. Her primary function as a MILF was to represent the dysfunctional adulthood Benjamin feared would define his post–college world. Benjamin's decision to carry on with Mrs. Robinson reflected his poor judgment and, by extension, viewers who wished for or wanted to be Mrs. Robinson reflected *their* poor judgment.

Not so with the modern-day MILF from *American Pie*, known only as "Stifler's mom." While desire for Mrs. Robinson fuels Benjamin's angst and alienation, desire for Stifler's mom encourages a communal and socially sanctioned sexual desire amongst young men within and without the later film. The desire for the new MILF is met with approval and applause largely because it is structured on fantasy rather than on realization. Stifler's mom, much like Lorelai, does not pretend to be a realistic option for the young men whom she attracts; while Mrs. Robinson can be had, the new MILF is characterized by the impossibility she poses to the young men who desire her. Moreover, this unattainability is not the result of wifehood, but of motherhood. Thus, while Benjamin identifies Mrs. Robinson in terms of her husband, Stifler's mom is linked to her children; although she *is* married, her son's friends give her the moniker of Stifler's *mom*, not *Mrs.* Stifler. The 2003 Fountains of Wayne song, "Stacy's Mom," suggests a similar shared fantasy of the mother. The chorus, simply repeating "Stacy's mom has got it goin' on" (Schlesinger and Collingwood), calls its listeners to share in the fantasy of the mother with fellow listeners. The appeal of Stacy's mom is directly linked to her maternal connection with the less desirable "Stacy," rather than to a connection with a spouse. In fact, singer Chris Collingwood reveals that Stacy's mom "could use a guy like me" because Stacy's "dad walked out," leaving her mom alone, available, and, judging by the video starring model Rachel Hunter as the mom, partial to pole-dancing in the kitchen. If Mrs. Robinson was an active threat, prowling about in her leopard print, today's MILF is one whose motherhood allows her to be wildly alluring, but just out of reach.

While the standard MILF represented by the moms of both Stifler and Stacy are no longer simply the foils of young, male desire, they are nevertheless still the objects of it. "MILF" has yet to make it into the *OED*, but definitions of and opinions about the type abound in popular forums, particularly, as one might intuit, amongst teenaged boys and young men in their twenties. One Wiktionary contributor describes the term in detail, explaining that "the moniker MILF is a group decision.... When the (male) speaker calls the female a MILF, he needs no further validation, verification or empirical evidence.... It's his internal observation and desire, irrespective of what the MILF thinks, does, or says. By definition, if you're termed a MILF, you are a MILF. Of course the MILF can reject advances or be offended by the term, but that's irrelevant to the definition" (Keller). Notable in this definition, of course, is the complete lack of agency of the MILF herself, an important distinction supported by the inclusion in the acronym of the words "I'd like to." The emphasis is on the male "I" and his desire, not, as Keller notes, on the mom's thoughts, actions, or words. If this impulse to label the mother were to extend beyond fantasy (what "I'd *like* to" do) into action, it would certainly approach the realm of rape in its assertion of unchecked masculine power — a disturbing component of the term that compromises its otherwise comedic aspects.

Perhaps what makes the character of Lorelai Gilmore so appealing to viewers (many of them MILFs themselves[6]) is that she upends the standard definition of the term by resisting our compulsion and limiting our ability to objectify her. While the pilot episode presents us with a young man's assessment and pursuit of Lorelai, it also challenges the assumed authority and subject status of this desiring male by way of Lorelai's double rejection of him. Indeed, unlike the moms of Stifler and Stacy, who are, in a manner of speaking, "spoken for" by the males who observe them, Lorelai has a voice all her own — one that is strong, savvy, and impossible to ignore. When Lorelai responds to Joey's initial approach with her sharp and rapid one-liners, it leaves him looking silly, deflated, childlike. For instance, when she calls him a "regular Jack Kerouac," he takes it as a compliment. Also significant in curbing the usual objectification that accompanies MILF status is that the show's writers never again tread so closely to presenting young male desire for the mother as they do in the pilot.[7] While Paris Geller is permitted to have an affair with a much older, and decidedly paternal, male professor (season four), not one of Rory's boyfriends shows so much as a passing sexual interest in Lorelai. And Lorelai isn't remotely attracted to any of them, either; in fact, she actively dislikes Jess, is sorely disappointed in Dean, and is at best emotionally removed from Logan. Lorelai remains a MILF throughout the first six seasons of *Gilmore Girls*, then, not because she fulfills the fantasy of the young men with whom she interacts on the show, but because she encourages a shared fantasy of the (mostly female) viewers who identify with her. Moreover, in conferring a powerful subject status on Lorelai, this shared fantasy upsets Laura Mulvey's longstanding argument that the objectifying male gaze structures the gaze of female viewers; so long as Lorelai invites viewers to participate in her MILF fantasy, *Gilmore Girls* is able to reverse the logic in the assertion that "pleasure in looking [is] split between active/male and passive/female" (Mulvey 178). Without a man to rein her in or tie her down, Lorelai is always already active, dating men not boys, making risqué remarks, dressing provocatively, having sex while single, supporting herself and her daughter — and getting away with all of it, her reputation intact. Such presentation is not made for Dean, or Jess, or Logan (or even for the older Max, Christopher, or Luke), but for a television audience that eagerly takes pleasure in this new type of onscreen motherhood that confirms and sanctions off-screen experiences in ways that other available models cannot and do not.

Daddy's Home!

Of course, as Stifler's mom demonstrates, a MILF can be married; the question for Lorelai, whose MILF status entails much more than the sexual arousal at play in *American Pie*, is how she might maintain her subject positioning (and influence ours) even as she relinquishes her role as a single mother. Indeed, what viewers learn as they follow Lorelai through seven years of dating is that her approach to motherhood is not dependent on her remaining single forever, but on her ability to maintain the intimate relationship she has with her daughter in spite of the men in her life. By presenting Lorelai with several opportunities to marry (Max, Christopher, Christopher again, Luke, Christopher again), the series encourages its audience to explore actively what kind of a marriage (and what kind of a man) might nurture or, conversely, threaten the type of motherhood that attracts viewers to her. For example, Max triggers in Lorelai the impulse to defend her connection with Rory: "This is a family, Rory and I. You've walked into a family" (1.11, "Paris Is Burning"). By defining family exclusively as mother and daughter (the demonstrative suggests that family *is* "Rory and I"), Lorelai eliminates and even voids the possibility for a husband/father to enter into the Gilmore Girls' relationship. What is important to note is that Lorelai's exclusion of Max is not an exclusion of men per se — Lorelai accepts that men (Dean, Jess, Luke) will enter into their lives. Instead, Lorelai rejects the nuclear family paradigm that Max espouses. Max's idealized sense that marriage "means taking two separate lives and melding them together" (2.03, "Red Light on the Wedding Night") threatens Lorelai's exclusive relationship with Rory, for it calls upon wife and husband to relinquish their prenuptial understandings of self in exchange for new and shared identities. In leaving Max, Lorelai asserts that "family values" (i.e. what she values in a family) are generated through the interaction of unique individuals (on-screen and off), not through some easy fusion of husband and wife. While the preservation of her subject identity is a painful experience for Lorelai, it allows her to maintain her relationship with Rory, confirming for viewers the viability and appeal of her unconventional approach to family and motherhood.

Conventional conceptions of marriage are not the only ones the show presents and, in fact, in the same episode in which Lorelai leaves Max, Luke suggests a model that would allow Lorelai to maintain and nurture her bond with Rory. Luke's articulation is twofold, beginning early in the episode with a presentation of "wedded bliss" that is decidedly iconoclastic. He argues that marriage is "a bureaucratic civil service and a pretty pointless one.... The moment you say 'I do' you're sticking yourself in a tiny little box" (2.03, "Red Light"). In connecting marriage with regulation and custom, Luke's assessment empties marriage of the romantic associations Max's language of "melding" gives it. Marriage is a limiting and restrictive "service," associated in Luke's mind with legality more than with dynamic love. Of course, just as the other Stars Hollow denizens ignore Luke's pronouncements, we viewers also believe that he is missing something in his "civilizing" description of marriage. However, perhaps Luke, standing markedly outside of conventional thought, has the best vantage point from which to identify the redeeming qualities of matrimony. By removing the customary trappings associated with marriage, he invites viewers to evaluate, realistically, what kind of husband would be suitable for the uncustomary and untrapped Lorelai. Indeed, later in the episode, he adds a footnote to his vitriolic oratory. Confronted with Lorelai's distress over the end of her engagement to Max, Luke softens his position, stating, "If you can find that one person who's willing to put up with all your crap and doesn't want to change you or dress you or make you eat French food then marriage can be all right." In straightforward terms, Luke challenges convention by resisting the sappily idealistic, blindly nostalgic, and distinctly nuclear model of marriage envisioned by Max. Moreover, by presenting marriage as a conditional decision ("*if* you can find that one person") and not as a declarative statement ("marriage means..."), Luke allows for autonomy in the choice to marry, enabling the individuals involved to retain their separate identities and, thus, to avoid being stuck "in a tiny little box."

Fans could not possibly foresee the significance of Luke's off-hand remark about French food, but sure enough, in season seven, Christopher takes Lorelai to France and asks her to marry him over *un dîner Parisien*. Quicker than we could say "escargot," when senior writer David Rosenthal allowed Lorelai to accede, he shifted our focus from the possibility of Lorelai's continued autonomy, even within marriage, to her sudden and unconvincing submission to conventional gender roles.[8] Lorelai marries Rory's father and leaves the realm of sexual possibility to become fixed, settled, known, even neutered, all of which crushes our longstanding enthusiasm for her character. Her refusal to take Christopher's surname does not fool us; the autonomy and charisma that characterized her for so many years are exchanged for a complacency and docility that renders her complex MILF status defunct. Lorelai's marriage to Christopher thus supports critic Robin Silbergleid's claim that mainstream television narrative is constructed with a heteronormative agenda in mind, for the choice involved in becoming a single mother is "undercut...by resituating the threatened patriarch at the head of the family" (3). Examples of resituated fathers abound in popular television. After all, if the desires of viewers are generated out of what Silbergleid equates with "sentimentalized longing for heterosexual romance and domestic bliss," then it makes sense that Rachel would end up with Ross (*Friends*) and Miranda would end up with Steve (*Sex and the City*) for the respective sakes of babies Emma and Brady. Our expectations fulfilled, we love the shows' finales. However, the resituating of *Gilmore Girls'* particular patriarch is not fueled by the legitimate "longing" that is a requisite part of the pattern Silbergleid identifies. Instead, viewers are hard-pressed to find the allure of Lorelai's new role as wife: Lorelai herself is tentative about the change; Rory feels angry and hurt; and the Stars Hollow townies voice skepticism and disappointment. To a degree, audience members are *supposed* to respond to these cues and reject the marriage, and we do, but that response is problematized by competing, mixed signals. When Christopher says, "You're it for me, and I can't pretend to feel any less than I do," if we shout a collective "No!" toward our televisions, we do so because we recognize that Lorelai responds to the romance of the moment and, on some level, we swoon, too (7.03 "Lorelai's First Cotillion"). The second half of the season attempts to redirect Lorelai's trajectory, but the divorce does not vindicate her character. The scripts of the final episodes combine to form a sort of palimpsest, a new (and improved!) plot written atop the still- and ever-visible mistake of Lorelai's marriage to Christopher. From the moment writers flirt with the possibility of that union in season seven, the show "suppor[ts] the man's role as the active one that advance[s] the story, making things happen" (Mulvey 180); and viewers assume a passive position, gazing resignedly, apathetically upon Christopher's Lorelai even once we are assured she is ours again.

What we discover as we watch the first half of season seven, trying to make the most out of Lorelai's situation, is that the writers bookend, even corral, her longstanding empowerment and agency — on the one end with her youthful relationship with Christopher and, on the other, with her perplexing marriage to him. The life and vitality that have identified Lorelai for so many years are bartered for sluggish morning banter about bowling and moving furniture (both iconically masculine activities). Even Lorelai's determination to celebrate Christmas in January to reestablish her connection with Rory — the two have never before been apart over the holidays — is curbed by the presence of Christopher and Gigi, both interlopers and intruders in the Gilmore home. Gigi, for instance, parrots to her father what she has heard Lorelai tell Rory in confidence (definitely not Gilmore girl behavior), and Christopher searches through Lorelai's bedroom drawers, in search of a tool, of all things, and instead finds a private letter. The problem, then, is not only that unsatisfying "heterosexual romance and domestic bliss" have displaced Lorelai's vital single motherhood, but also that this state of affairs is anything but blissful and indicates a shift from a dynamic gynocentric narrative established through Lorelai's relationship with Rory to one that is customary and phallocentric. The marriage to Christopher irrevocably diverts our interest away from Lorelai's unconventional approach to motherhood and sexuality and onto her husband's place in her life. Her transition from single mother to wife effectively disables Lorelai's MILF status and, moreover, redefines that status as a problem to be resolved by the "right" man.

However, marriage, in and of itself, is not to blame. The show asks us to share Rory's sentiments as she expresses, again and again, her concern for her mother's happiness. Since Rory often expresses such sentiments in relation to her mother's various romances, it's safe to assume that happiness and marriage (or, at the very least, happiness and a sexually monogamous relationship) are linked in her (and likely our) minds. Silbergleid argues that "our cultural imaginary does not envision the [single mother by choice] family as anything other than second best" (8), and Rory seems to follow suit, at one point stating, "it's every kid's dream, right, parents back together?" (7.08, "Introducing Lorelai Planetarium"). Silbergleid goes on to posit that "[u]nless we can create narratives that operate under a non–heterosexual metaphor, the stories that we tell about the family will continue to reproduce, rather than challenge, dominant ideas about the family" (16). Certainly Stars Hollow is filled with the kinds of happily married couples, from Sookie and Jackson, to Babette and Morey, to Lane and Zack, that partake in this reproduction of dominant ideas about the family. (Lane and Sookie, both pregnant in season seven, literally reproduce these ideas.) However, these married couples keep company with single characters (Liz and Anna) who, like Lorelai, have raised children (Jess and April) largely without the help of a husband.[9] Thus, while *Gilmore Girls* may not fulfill Silbergleid's vision for narrative reform, it spends six years actively thwarting Rory's slightly sarcastic yet nonetheless idealized vision of "every kid's dream." Moreover, by positioning itself between the two polar visions of family, the bulk of the show's narrative is engaged in a reflective and critical conversation with both the traditional paradigm and the postnuclear reverie. Thus, Lorelai's love life is undeniably of interest to us, as it is to her Stars Hollow friends and her parents in Hartford, but it is an interest that, up until her marriage to Christopher, is second to the plotting that deals specifically with her ongoing status as a single MILF by choice.

Because no proposal but Christopher's eventuates in marriage, season seven asks viewers to consider whether Christopher could be "that one person"—Lorelai's soul mate, if you will. But given Luke's articulation of a workable marriage, together with the role Christopher has played in the first six seasons, it cannot be the case that he is (despite his own assurances). The news of Lorelai's marriage to Christopher is as hard for viewers to swallow as it is for Rory, who balks at the hastiness and inconsiderateness of her mother's decision. Christopher, after all, has never been a serious contender for Lorelai's lasting affections; Rory knows this, and so do we. No Mr. Big, rescuing Carrie from a disastrous move to Paris when Miranda charges him to "Go get our girl," Christopher propels Lorelai—*our* girl—in a direction that leaves us disoriented and disappointed. He brings her back to Stars Hollow from France, but as she sits on her couch regarding her gold wedding band, we share the shock and misgivings evident on her face. On the one hand, the act of marrying Christopher feels dangerously impetuous, like her earlier decisions to sleep with him. But on the other hand, perhaps the one with the ring on it, the act smacks of convention. Lorelai's quickie marriage is quite distinct from past "quickies" with Christopher: this one flips a switch, rendering defunct the tensions and relationships that have long sustained the series and Lorelai's viability as a twenty-first-century MILF.

Underscoring the tension between the marriage and Lorelai's prenuptial trajectory is a comment Sookie makes: "If there were no Luke...would it be Christopher? I mean, would he be 'the one'?" (7.14, "Farewell, My Pet"). Lorelai's answer is implicit in her downcast eyes and, later, in her tearful confession to Christopher: "You're the man I *want* to want." The revelation suggests that the marriage to Christopher moves the series toward an unexpected and unwanted resolution by disrupting the mother-daughter bond and reconnecting Lorelai with a past she has spent upwards of twenty years (and six seasons) trying to shake. The fact that the marriage ends in divorce does not nullify these effects, so the quick and predictable dissolution of the union feels always like the back-peddling of authors who misread their characters and viewers but do not have enough time (or motivation) to correct the mistake. Acknowledged too late is that Christopher, like the "old" Lorelai, is pedigreed, wealthy, privileged — but he is distinctly unlike the "new" her. This difference is evident throughout the seasons but is foregrounded when Christopher inherits an enormous amount of money from his father. Christopher's easy adaptation to extreme wealth highlights Lorelai's lack of interest in it. She is a Stars Hollow girl, content with a lifestyle just indulgent enough to allow her to afford take-out food and killer clothes. Christopher is harder to please and makes for an awkward addition to Stars Hollow. He tells Lorelai, "Look, I'm all for small-town charm. I'm happy to move here, sit on the front porch, and give the mailman a real chipper, 'Howdy-doo'"; but in the remark and his general demeanor there's a note, if not a symphony, of condescension (7.08, "Introducing Lorelai Planetarium"). Christopher's snobbishness manifests itself in faux pas after faux pas, as when he brings an abrupt halt to the knitting marathon by donating the entire amount of money the town has gathered to raise. The moment is as uncomfortable as that in the Parisian restaurant he buys out so that he and Lorelai can have dinner at an hour when every eatery in the city is closed. The gesture is magnanimous but also conventionally romantic — the sort of thing designed to sweep a woman off her feet. But a woman like Lorelai? Although she seems impressed, her show of appreciation lacks authenticity. The Lorelai we know would be more comfortable eating a three a.m. burger at Luke's diner than being responsible for an entire wait and kitchen staff's losing sleep in order to cater to her. This difference in Christopher and Lorelai spotlights the central crux of Lorelai's being — the incompatibilities of submission and rebellion, convenience and love, her past life and the new one she has forged on her own. The relentless push and pull between these opposing forces informs a central theme of *Gilmore Girls*. We see it in Lorelai's romances, in her vexed relationship with her parents, and even in her struggle to understand Rory, that countercultural and independent daughter who nonetheless wears her Daughters of the American Revolution membership as comfortably as she does her cardigans from Anthropologie. As if to accentuate his connection to Lorelai's past and her consignment to the position of object, Christopher represents the elder Gilmores' values in clear contrast to the younger Lorelai's. Emphasizing this fact is how comfortable Christopher is in the presence of Lorelai's parents (especially as contrasted to Luke, who never loses his jumpiness or, at best, amused impatience, around Emily) and how willing Christopher is to defer to their opinions. For example, in season five he conspires with Mrs. Gilmore to win Lorelai away from Luke: "Lorelai and I belong together," he tells his rival. "Everyone knows it. I know it, Emily knows it.... Emily told me it wasn't too late" (5.13, "Wedding Bell Blues").

Marrying Christopher amounts to sleeping with the enemy, at least metaphorically so, and the collateral damage of the act is immediately evident. Rory is out once her father is in the game; not only is she absent for the wedding, but her former bedroom is converted into a space for Gigi. Rory and her mom recover from these moments of division — sort of. But it seems to be no accident that Rory leaves home for Christmas this year for the first time ever and, we are left to imagine now that Christopher is in the picture, it might not be her last missed holiday. Dissociated from her daughter, Lorelai is also dissociated from her MILF status. She is wife more than mother, "unsexed" but no Lady Macbeth. The dynamics of her marriage are notably different from those of past relationships, including the one she's had with Christopher. In contrast to their heated hook-ups of years gone by, Christopher and Lorelai's latest union seems passionless, sexless. Throughout their marriage, Lorelai and Christopher are shown in neither pre– nor post–coital married bliss. The biggest idea Christopher has while he is upstairs is to put a flat-screen TV in the bedroom.[10] No longer the mom boys and men would "Like to Fuck," Lorelai is the wife who has been fucked — past tense and in more ways than one — by her husband.

The marriage seems inexplicable and prompts us to wonder how the writers could have been insensitive to this fact, until we regard the turn of plot as a social and ideological correction. Important to remember is that *Gilmore Girls* started in response to the WB's search for Family Friendly programming.[11] Silbergleid observes in popular television a "profound anxiety about female sexuality and reproduction that take place outside the confines of the normative family unit" (8), an anxiety that one might certainly bring to the first six seasons of a show about a single mother who repeatedly chooses not to marry the father of her child. According to Silbergleid, "[t]he threat" posed by these women is often "recontained within a dominant structure of both narrative and family." As we suggest above, Christopher aligns himself with status quo culture throughout the series. The plotting of season seven, despite its eleventh-hour revision, suggests that all along, *Gilmore Girls* engages in a losing battle of the culture wars, destined to wrap its forward-thinking worldview snugly within a cloak of family values and call it a night.

There Goes the Bride

If Christopher is Lorelai's Mr. Right, it is only as opposed to her Mr. Left, Luke, a man who is more right for her than is Christopher. Luke does not threaten the recontainment Silbergleid describes for he adamantly rejects the kind of "tiny little box" in which Lorelai finds herself after marriage. Longtime fans may be tempted, then, to assert that a marriage to Luke would be different, that once she divorces Christopher, were she to end the series by marrying Luke or even just rekindling their romance, "things around here" *wouldn't* have to change. To an extent, this assertion is true: if Christopher fits the "old" Lorelai, then Luke corresponds with the new. He is "the one" in a way that Christopher or even Max could never be, for he alone has been a constant presence in Lorelai's preferred life, and he alone understands Lorelai and Rory as mutually constitutive and whole. Both Max and Christopher try to insert themselves into the mother-daughter union, as if the paternal presence were integral to its functioning. But Luke eschews that wedge position; he sees himself as a father-figure to Rory and a partner to Lorelai and, more importantly, he can reconcile those two roles with the mother and daughter's shared identity, as demonstrated when he observes to Lorelai, "Her life *is* your life" (5.14, "Say Something"). In acknowledging that the two women are inextricably linked, Luke contents himself with being with the Gilmore Girls rather than co–opting them. As a result, Lorelai, when with Luke, remains in the realm of the desired-but-not-"had," arguably her rightful place, established and defended in episode upon episode of the first six seasons and gestured toward at the close of season seven.

However, even Luke's suitability as a mate is called into question as, in the new writers' hands, the show's perspective shifts from that of the Gilmore Girls to that of the Gilmores' guys—or, perhaps more aptly, boys. Lorelai can no longer resist the "Joeys" hitting on her in Luke's diner and, as a result, renders her subjectivity defunct. She actively slides into passivity. For instance, Christopher behaves like a jealous and impetuous teenager upon reading Lorelai's letter, a defense of Luke, and overreacts, leaving his new wife with no idea of where he is or when he'll be back. When the two finally try to clear the air, Lorelai takes responsibility for the demise of their marriage, and Christopher forgives her for making him leave. The Stars Hollow of season seven seems to be plagued by a male puerility that's hard to ignore: Luke and Christopher trade blows in a schoolyard scuffle; Richard pouts over his health food; Jackson refuses to have a vasectomy; Logan impulsively blows his fortune in Vegas; and Zack hits the road solo with his (and Lane's!) band. In emphasizing the regression to boyhood of its male characters, *Gilmore Girls* shirks its commitment to representing powerful femininity in a general sense. For each of these men-become-boys is connected to a woman whose needs he subordinates to his own. Even viewers who object to this inversion have no choice but to do the same; protest as we might against Jackson's selfishness, Sookie remains pregnant, so what can we do but join her in trying to see things from Jackson's perspective? Continuing to watch—if, indeed, most viewers still were—we are complicit in the show's shift to conventional iterations of male-female relationships, the lot of us following Lorelai's lead as she rationalizes that "babies are more than diapers...right?" (7.12 "To Whom It May Concern"). While Lorelai's identity has always hinged on her willing maternity, the scene in which she encourages Sookie to relish an unplanned and unwanted pregnancy demonstrates how far a-field season seven gets from how it histor-ically imagines Lorelai's allure. Here, now, she embodies a masculine ideal — still perhaps a MILF but of the sort that satisfies the likes of Stifler's friends and Mighty Jimbo. Figuratively, the *Gilmore* boys move beyond wanting and finally "get" Lorelai (and all female viewers who held her in high regard). For in elbow-ing to the forefront of the show's stage, the boys disrupt the complex set of stan-dards that has heretofore defined Lorelai and single motherhood, and consign us all to the played-out paradigm of the virgin and the whore.

The problem is that the dichotomy forced upon our protagonist is incon-sistent with her character development and out of place in any realistic rendi-tion of modern womanhood. As Kaplan notes, "One of the characteristics of the postmodern moment is the proliferation of subject positions that histori-cal individuals occupy. Whereas 'woman' was [once] congruent with 'mother' (the only other possibilities were the 'virgin' (nun–figure) or the unacceptable 'whore'), things are now more complex" (182). The reversion, in season seven of *Gilmore Girls*, to this outdated set of expectations begins to explain viewers' sense of loss. In apologizing to Christopher, in catering to her father, in reunit-ing (yet again) with Luke, Lorelai cedes to these men/boys the control she has taken over her life and allows herself to be defined — and simplistically so — by them. Because her story is no longer of her own devising, she seems weak and vulnerable — no longer the same easy-going, smart, strong woman whom we have long admired. Written into a plotline that she originally sought to evade, she falls into a prescribed story (or any number of stories) about a husband, wife, and kids. She ceases to be a rebel, and those around her — Christopher, Luke, Rory, the viewers — lose interest and set their sights elsewhere, too. The season ends with a cameo appearance by Christiane Amanpour, certainly a MILF herself. As Rory aligns herself with this hero of modern womanhood we, too, look elsewhere for inspiration, reluctantly leaving behind Stars Hollow and, with it, the Lorelai Gilmore we felt we knew and knew we desired, but now only dimly recognize.

Notes

1. In an April 7, 2007 entry, Maureen Ryan, web logger for the *Chicago Tribune*, recalls just such a sense of dread: "Speaking as a viewer who's stuck by the show through thick and thin, I think the comedy-drama should end its run in May. It's already gone on for one season too long. Not that I would have ended things with the scene that closed the previous season. Creator Amy Sherman-Palladino drove the show straight into a ditch last May, when she ended the season with Lorelai in bed with Christopher (David Sutcliffe) ... Fans had waited for years for Luke and Lorelai to get together, but breaking them up and putting Lorelai back with the callow Christopher-yet again-was going too far. We had already been there and done that, and I was thoroughly sick of those two as a couple."

2. According to Dawn Ostroff, Entertainment president of the CW, "With the loss of Amy (Sherman-Palladino, series creator), we wanted to maintain the quality of the

show. We brought in David Rosenthal, who was hand-picked by Amy" (qtd. in Kronke). That Sherman-Palladino chose Rosenthal as *Gilmore Girls'* head writer is somewhat perplexing given Rosenthal's decidedly controversial past. Hollywood's wunderkind of TV sitcom writing in the early to mid 1990s, Rosenthal unexpectedly quit a lucrative job at Fox, left his wife, and moved to New York City to produce the NC-17-rated play he wrote about his desire to bed model Heidi Klum. His behavior caused his agents to drop him, the industry to dismiss him, and his rabbi father to commit him briefly for psychiatric evaluation. In 2002, in the wake of his break from the industry, Rosenthal told Janet Reitman of *L.A. Times Magazine* that he is committed to exposing Hollywood as a misogynistic, white boys' club (hardly breaking news) and giving opportunities to minorities and women so that they "feel that the system is open to them." Perhaps Sherman-Palladino responded to the latter commitment in passing the *Gilmore Girls* torch to Rosenthal. But season seven of the show is so off the mark, particularly in how its female characters are sketched, that one has to wonder whether Rosenthal is committed to giving airtime to real women's issues and experiences or to those of women as fantastical as was his off-Broadway Heidi Klum.

　　3. Silbergleid borrows Jane Mattes's term "single mother by choice," or SMC, a sociological marker for single mothers who "tend to be well-educated, financially secure heterosexual women in their mid-thirties" but also "represent a real [ethnic, political, and religious] cross section of women in this country" (qtd. in Silbergleid 3). Silbergleid uses the term to refer to "the new single mother" as popularly represented in American culture and takes issue with the predominant view that women are SMCs only as a "Plan B"-"Plan A" being to marry and then have children (3-4). According to Mattes's definition, Lorelai is an SMC, but she also takes Silbergleid's assessment of the type in a more promising direction, for while getting pregnant at age sixteen was certainly not Lorelai's "Plan A," neither was marrying Christopher. Hers is a character who chose to raise a daughter on her own and was comfortable with the choice-a distinction only undercut by the show's troubling seventh season.

　　4. The interchangeability, often coded sexually, of both mother and daughter seems to have become the hallmark of the series. In an episode ("The Wrap Party") of Aaron Sorkin's *Studio 60 on the Sunset Strip*, Matt Albie (Matthew Perry), at the urging of best friend and show's producer Danny Tripp (Bradley Whitford), attempts to heal a broken heart by hitting on any attractive woman he can find. He impulsively targets the show's current guest host, *Gilmore Girls'* Lauren Graham, who plays herself. Upon running into Graham, Albie scribbles a note and says, "This is my number if you ever feel like coffee or a basketball game or something. And would you give a copy of this to the girl who plays your kid on the show, too?"

　　5. Rory, too, becomes interesting if seen on her own terms rather than in terms of her interchangeability with her mother. In some ways, Rory's identity is more multifaceted than is Lorelai's. Through the seasons, Rory juggles a variety of roles, including (bastard) daughter, young adult, prep school student, virgin, adulteress, college student, and even housewife (1.14, "That Damn Donna Reed Show"). While mother and daughter are superficially interchangeable, the show suggests that both "mother" and "daughter" are complicated and knotty categories.

　　6. James Poniewozik notes that "The WB's slogan this year [2005] is 'Be Young,' which is ironic.... [N]o sooner had the slogan appeared on screen than WB executives immediately noted that they are now trying to attract older viewers along with their traditional 12 to 34 year-old target audience" ("The WB: Is 'Be Young' Getting Old?").

　　7. Season five contains a moment reminiscent of the pilot's diner scene but less adamant about Lorelai's sexual attractiveness to younger men. Logan Huntzberger's friends Colin and Finn encounter Lorelai in a police station after Rory and Logan are arrested for stealing a yacht. When the young men realize that Lorelai is there to retrieve

Rory, Colin makes introductions: "I'm Colin, this is Finn, and you are...." Not amused by Colin's forwardness and Finn's rather lascivious stare, Lorelai responds, "Her *mother*." The debauched, socially privileged Finn merely comments, "My God, those are good genes," and the moment ends. Rory appears, and as her mother ushers her out of the police station, the guys drop to the floor and wave their arms at Rory's feet-not Lorelai's-in mock adoration of the more suitably aged daughter for playing "99" to Logan's "Maxwell Smart" (5.22, "A House Is Not a Home").

    8. Sherman-Palladino might have foreseen this implausibility, for she has admitted that much of the success of *Gilmore Girls* relies on the consistency in writing she and her husband were able to achieve in the first six years they were with the show. "Between the two of us," she said in an interview, "every draft either I write, or it passes through my hands, or passes through my hands and his hands, so that there is a consistency of tone. It's very important that it feel like the same show every week, because it is so verbal. It's not about car crashes or vampires or monsters or suspense. It's really about people talking to each other and the way they talk to each other, which is very specific" ("*Gilmore Girls* ... a Love Letter").

    9. Mrs. Kim is another such figure. Despite references to Lane's "parents" and a "Mr. Kim" (in episodes 2.01, "Sadie, Sadie," and 6.18, "The Real Paul Anka," respectively), Lane's father remains elusive throughout the series and plays no discernible role in the development of his daughter. Mrs. Kim, then, is at the very least a *de facto* single parent.

    10. The appearance of celibacy is mirrored by Rory and Logan's relationship: the two times Logan surprises Rory with a visit from London and once when he arrives from New York, they enter into rigorous conversation ("So, what's going on? Why are you here?") rather than vigorous sex-a far cry from the Logan and Rory of the pool house days (7.08, "Introducing Lorelai Planetarium").

    11. While *Gilmore Girls* demonstrated for so many years that being "family friendly" didn't have to mean buying into normative understandings of family, season seven conforms to the dark underbelly of the stipulations laid out by ANA's Family Friendly Programming Forum. The Association of National Advertisers, composed of companies including Ameritech, AT&T, General Motors, IBM, Johnson and Johnson, Pfizer, and Wendy's International, created the Family Friendly Programming Forum with the purpose of "support[ing] and promot[ing] the development and scheduling of family friendly programs that air during key prime-time hours when adults and children in a household are most likely to watch key television together" (http://www.ana. net/family/default.htm). ANA defines "family-friendly" in "purposefully broad [terms]: it is relevant to today's TV viewer, has generational appeal, depicts real life and is appropriate in theme, content and language for a broad family audience. Family friendly programs also embody a responsible resolution." Yet, while the forum might claim to uphold "broad" subject matter, treatment of issues that are common for and "relevant to" all targeted groups will inevitably be limited. What is meant by "responsible resolution" is also up for debate. *Gilmore Girls* was the first series created by the FFPF.

Works Cited

Benfer, Amy. "Knocked Up Like Me: What's Cooler than Bring a Middle-Class Teenage Mother? Having a TV Show All about You." *Salon.com*. 2 Nov. 2000. 27 Oct 2006 <http://archive.salon.com/mwt/feature/2000/11/02/gilmore_girls/index.html>.
"Family Friendly Programming Forum." 2007. Association of National Advertisers, Inc. 1 Feb 2007 <http://www.ana.net/family/default.htm>.

"*Gilmore Girls* ... a Love Letter." *Theage.com.au* 1 Feb. 2007. 1 Feb. 2007 <http://www.theage.com.au/news/tv--radio/unreal-girls/2007/02/02/1169919527754.html>.

"Gilmore Girls season one." 1998-2006. *Montreal Film Journal* 10 April 2007 <http://www.montrealfilmjournal.com/article.asp?A=A0000132>.

Humphrey, Wm. Steven. "I Love Television." *Portland Mercury* 21 Sept. 2006. 6 Oct. 2007 <http://www.orlandoweekly.com/columns/story.asp?id=10995>.

Kaplan, E. Ann. *Motherhood and Representation: The Mother in Popular Culture and Melodrama.* New York: Routledge, 1992.

Keller, Robert. *Wiktionary: A Multilingual Free Encyclopedia.* 7 June 2006. 27 Oct. 2006 <http://en.wiktionary.org/wiki/Talk:MILF>.

Kronke, David. "CW Exec Satisfied with Modest Improvement." *Dailynews.com.* 19 Jan 2007. 31 Jan 2007 <http://www.dailynews.com/tv/ci_5047653>.

Mighty Jimbo. *Digital Catharsis.com.* 11 Dec. 2002. 11 April 2007 <http://www.digitalcatharsis.com/archive/2002_12_08_archives.htm>.

Millman, Joyce. "The Parent Trap." *Salon.com.* 15 Nov. 2000. 27 Oct. 2006 <http://archive.salon.com/ent/col/mill/2000/11/14/gilmore_girls/index.html>.

Mulvey, Laura. "Visual Pleasure and Narrative Cinema." *The Narrative Reader.* Ed. Martin Mcquillan. New York: Routledge, 2005. 177-81.

Poniewozik, James. "Postnuclear Explosion: So Long, Huxtables and Nelsons. The Non-Normal Family Is the Norm in the New Domestic Comedies." *TIME Magazine.* 6 Nov. 2000. 3 Nov. 2006 <http://www.time.com/time/magazine/article/0,9171,998412,00.html>.

_____. "The WB: Is 'Be Young' Getting Old?" *TIME Magazine.* 17 May 2005. 3 Nov. 2006 <http://www.time.com/time/columnist/printout/0,8816,1062620,00.html>.

Press, Joy. "The Sunshine Girls: *Gilmore Girls* Creator Amy Sherman-Palladino Keeps the Chick Factor Sweet and Low." *Villagevoice.com* 25 Oct. 2004. 3 Nov. 2006 <http://www.villagevoice.com/arts/0443,tv,57816,27.html>.

Reitman, Janet. "The Loneliness of the Long-Distance Ranter: Self-Exiled Hollywood Whiz Kid David Rosenthal Thinks He Knows the Truth. The Question Is, Does Anyone Care?" *Los Angeles Times Magazine.* 5 May 2002.

Ryan, Maureen. "For the Love of Stars Hollow, Will Someone Please Cancel Gilmore Girls?" *Chicagotribune.com.* 7 April 2007. 10 April 2007 <http://featuresblogs.chicagotribune.com/entertainment_tv/2007/04/for_the_love_of.html>.

Schlesinger, Adam and Chris Collingwood. "Stacy's Mom." Fountains of Wayne. "*Welcome Interstate Managers.*" Virgin Records U.S., 2003.

Silbergleid, Robin. "'Oh Baby!': Representations of Single Mothers in American Popular Culture." *Americana: The Journal of American Popular Culture (1900–present)* 1.2 (Fall 2002). <http://www.americanpopculture.com/journal/articles/fall_2002/silbergleid.htm>.

Wong, Tim. "*Gilmore Girls*: The Complete first & second seasons." *The Lumière Reader: Film and Arts Crit.* April 2006. 10 April 2007 <http://www.lumiere.net.nz/reader/item/463>.

Wheat Balls, Gravlax, Pop Tarts

Mothering and Power

Melanie Haupt

Anthropological studies of women's control of domestic foodways focus on the mother as "gatekeeper" of the family's food (Lewin). A family's relationship with food is often a direct reflection of its class status, and the mechanics of its consumption and distribution in the home speaks to the gender hierarchy within the family. Carole Counihan states that,"[c]lass, caste, race, and gender hierarchies are maintained, in part, through differential control over and access to food" (8). The various familial hierarchies depicted on the network series *Gilmore Girls* offer a compelling portrayal of how women, as represented in popular culture, use food as a means of negotiating their gendered and class performances, as well as enacting minor disruptions of those hierarchies. Viewed through the lens of a feminist critique of the concept of the mother as the "gatekeeper" of the family's food, *Gilmore Girls* can be understood as a commentary on "correct" consumption and how that consumption informs one's mothering performance. For the purposes of this discussion, I am defining mothering as the essentialized idea of the person in the household who controls the foodways, particularly because nurturance and mothering via feeding are so closely linked in the collective cultural imagination.

Procurement of food and commensality are a defining feature of the *Gilmore Girls'* narrative (and the titular Girls' relationship). Lorelai Gilmore (Lauren Graham) directs her maternal love through consumption of processed (mass-produced, disposable) food, which serves to shift the image of the ideal mother as producer to mother as consumer. In Stars Hollow, Connecticut, to mother in the cultural mainstream is to consume. Therefore, within the context of the preparation and consumption of food, to read Lorelai against representations of other mothers in Stars Hollow is to realize that Lorelai is a pop-culture construction of the kind of mother young women should aspire to be: independent, liberal, and, most importantly, willing and able to keep abreast of popular culture and fashion trends and to spend, spend, spend. In short, Lorelai is an ideal consumer, and, within the logic of capitalism, the ideal mother; all other mothers in Stars Hollow, as we will see, are found wanting according to this rubric. However, as Counihan writes, "the commodification of women and their bodies is particularly prevalent in the United States through advertising, where women's bodies are routinely used to sell things and thus become things for sale" (200). As Lorelai enacts the shift from the image of the mother as producer to that of consumer under the auspices of extricating herself from the patriarchal hierarchy of her parents, she also enacts her own commodification. She does this by engaging in unabashed consumerism, feeding the economic and cultural structure that is engineered precisely to attract her dollars. The ideal mother is ultimately a product, and Lorelai is as much a package to be consumed as are the Pop Tarts she so voraciously devours. To understand Lorelai's portrayal as the perfect consuming mother who relies solely on mass-produced convenience foods, we must first examine her own mother, Emily Gilmore (Kelly Bishop). Emily represents the mother's traditional association with food, albeit within the context of the upper class.

According to Lewin (qtd. in Counihan 13), the mother is accepted as the controlling entity of the domestic sphere, especially in the domain of the kitchen and pantry: "Women are credited with control over the purchasing, storing, cooking, and serving of food. In addition, they are perceived as greatly influencing the food habits of family members" (McIntosh and Zey 126). William McIntosh and Mary Zey argue that despite the fact that women are seemingly in control of the food that comes into the house and is consumed by the family, men ultimately control the ways in which women procure and distribute food. While this may not be true on the surface of *Gilmore Girls*, particularly in the case of Lorelai and her daughter Rory, it is important to note that the Gilmore parents' class status is due to Richard Gilmore's (Edward Hermann) old-money pedigree, as well as his considerable success as an insurance executive. McIntosh and Zey state that, "in the United States, particularly today, the major source of the father-husband's ability to control the behavior of wives and children is the income he brings home" (133). Emily's domestic responsibility rests solely in the realm of managing staff (which includes the selection of meals and directing dinner service) and staging elaborate corporate parties for Richard's business associates and clients; all of her power as a gatekeeper derives from her husband's control of capital. Without her husband's substantial income, Emily would not be in a position of power, via the food she provides as a mother, over Lorelai and Rory. If the Gilmores were unable to bankroll Rory's prestigious private education, they would also be unable to require Lorelai and Rory to come to dinner on Friday night, the sole condition upon which the elder Gilmores agree to pay Rory's prep-school tuition (and, later, her Yale tuition until Christopher inherits his grandfather's fortune and takes over the financial burden). These dinners are emblematic of the parental and patriarchal control from which Lorelai has spent her adult life attempting to extricate herself.

The dinner table at the Gilmores' Friday night dinners is coded as a patriarchal space in order to communicate the ultimate control Richard holds over his wife, daughter, and granddaughter. The episode, "An Affair to Remember" (4.06), from the show's fourth season, offers a precise example of how Emily's use of the patriarchy to exert her power over Lorelai (and, by extension, Rory) via food and its consumption falls apart as the ascendant generation of the patriarchy encroaches. The opening shot pans down past a chandelier onto the dinner table, the primary site of the struggle between Emily and Lorelai. The chandelier itself is significant in that if it is not a phallic symbol per se, it is clearly a signifier of the old-money patriarchy. The table, too, is coded to create a patriarchal space. In the center of the table rests a low arrangement of roses flanked by two candlesticks; this particular table setting is a near-constant feature of the *mise-en-scène*. This marks the space as a site of feminine authority, one sanctioned by the patriarchal order. It also prohibits Lorelai and Rory's access to each other, which is understandable in light of the fact that they are allies in the struggle against the Gilmore regime. The family is dressed formally for dinner, with Richard clad in a suit and bowtie, Emily in a women's suit, and Rory and Lorelai wear feminine, youthful dresses; this manner of dress reinforces the official or ceremonial nature of the event, which signifies a formalization of the conflict between the Gilmore generations.

At the outset, Emily establishes her class standing and her concomitant values via a discussion of food and its distribution, as she explains that their neighbors, the Richmonds, are a disgrace because they handed out king-sized candy bars for Halloween, when the neighborhood had an established tradition of handing out full-sized bars. Lorelai is bemused, saying, "Two Halloweens ago, someone painted the Dupree's Chihuahua orange. No one went to the homeowners' association then." Emily's response is that "everybody hated Taco." The connotations here are obvious: a family that succeeds in upscale neighborhood one-upmanship in the form of Halloween treats is completely unacceptable. But a prankster who vandalizes a dog that represents the Other is, it seems, a hero. Clearly Mexicans, as represented by a dog named Taco, have no business in the gated communities of New Haven. Later, Emily announces that dessert is "mini lemon bundt cakes," and Lorelai clucks and says, "they're serving full-sized lemon bundt cakes at the Richmonds." Emily then declares that Lorelai is finished eating and instructs the housekeeper to remove Lorelai's plate. Because Lorelai has dared to mock the perceived disruption in the upper-class order of Emily's neighborhood, and, by extension, the elder

Gilmores' values, Emily retaliates by denying Lorelai the rest of her dinner. In this final shot of the scene, the frame includes the three Gilmore women, their faces visible to the camera. Richard is barely visible on the right-hand side of the screen, his back to the camera and his body in shadow. The patriarch literally looms over the scene, observing, but not participating in, the struggle between Emily and Lorelai. This particular shot encapsulates the problem of how the Gilmore women negotiate the patriarchy's stranglehold on their subjectivities; that it is couched in a discussion of king-sized candy bars and ends in Emily withholding food from her daughter supports MacIntosh and Zey's assertion that the woman as gatekeeper is merely a figurehead. It is the patriarch who holds the power because he brings in the money to purchase the full-sized candy bars and pays for the cook to bake the lemon bundt cakes. Emily's role is merely executive, and Richard sanctions the power that she exercises over Lorelai while at table.

Emily finds her self-worth not just in requiring Rory and Lorelai to come to a weekly dinner, but also in hosting social events for Richard's business. However, this particular episode finds Emily questioning her role in the patriarchy's new economy of eschewing traditional elegance in favor of (literal) flashiness. After the credits roll, the camera follows Emily as she carries a vase of roses into Richard's office, where he and his new business partner, Jason "Digger" Stiles (Chris Eigeman) pose for photographs. She must open the office door to get in, and the flower arrangement is the key with which she can enter this exclusively male space, as they are to be used as part of the *mise-en-scène* of the publicity photographs being taken to mark Richard and Jason's new partnership. This merging of the old guard with the new introduces a new tension into the Gilmore house, as Jason dismisses Emily's emphasis on taking photos of the signing as "a cute idea." "I learned long ago that when it comes to things like this, Emily is always right," says Richard, in a tone that suggests he is sincere in his acknowledgement of Emily's authority in such matters, trivial as that authority may ultimately be. Jason leaves, having refused Emily's invitation to stay for dinner, indicating his reluctance to participate in the type of nurturance her position within old school patriarchy represents and signaling his ultimate, overt rejection of her and her traditional role as corporate wife. Emily then asks Richard about the launch party she plans to host for the new business. "I'll leave that to your discretion. Just make sure it's dignified," is Richard's response (4.06, "An Affair to Remember"). She offers up a few ideas, to which he seems indifferent, as he has unspecified business to attend to elsewhere, and so she is left alone, gleefully pondering her Russian-themed party. She feels she is an autonomous entity planning a fabulous social event, while her husband, an "important man doing important things," views it as a mere triviality.

This dinner party creates another site for struggle between Emily and Lorelai within the context of food and its preparation and service. During this struggle, Lorelai symbolically castrates the system within which she must participate in order to bolster her bottom line while at the same time critiquing her mother's position in that same system; however, despite her efforts, she still finds herself subject to patriarchal control. Emily calls Lorelai's best friend, Sookie (Melissa McCarthy), who is a chef, and asks her to cater the event. Sookie and Lorelai are partners in a fledgling catering company to earn money before they open their inn, a fact that Lorelai has concealed from Emily. Lorelai is reluctant to agree to cater the party, but Sookie reminds her that they need the income to make the much-needed renovations to the Dragonfly. Lorelai grudgingly agrees and they go about the business of preparing for the party on the condition that her mother treat her professionally, to which Emily agrees; as a result, her demeanor during the pre-party run through is haughty and officious. Despite (or perhaps because of) the fact that they will be purchasing, preparing, and serving the food at Emily's party, she makes Lorelai and Sookie keenly aware of her class status and that she is in a position of financial power over them, primarily by making them use the servants' entrance to her home. Of course, it is Richard and his money that holds sway over this event and the women that organize it. Lorelai uses this space to undercut the patriarchy Emily represents, joking about the length of the tapers for the table setting. She says, "I cut those myself, so they can be adjusted either way ... Taller would be tougher once they're cut, but if they tell a lie, they'll shoot right back up." Emily responds, "I assume you'll instruct the servers to omit the Pinocchio jokes."

Despite Lorelai's awkward buffoonery, this scene reinforces her role as a rebel who constantly mocks and undercuts the patriarchy. While Emily succeeds in temporarily putting Lorelai in her place, her dominance within the space of the dining room is about to be undermined.

While this event functions as one of the defining factors of Emily's identity as a well-to-do corporate wife whose impeccable taste serves as a reflection of her husband's control over capital, it serves a different purpose to Richard and Jason. The party affords Richard and Jason the opportunity to network, to make their clients feel at ease, and to essentially brand themselves in their clients' minds as men who are worthy of their business. To Richard, this is just another aspect of doing business; it simply takes place inside of his home, rather than the office, which is why it is up to Emily to engineer and execute the details. To Jason, however, it is a stale holdover of a bygone era, which is what precipitates Emily's loss of power, her effective emasculation. Emily requests Jason's guest list for the launch party, which he did not know about. Emily asks Richard if he forgot to ask Jason to draw up a guest list, to which Richard gruffly replies, "Emily, I am a very busy man!" Jason is dubious about the launch party and the Gilmores explain to him the necessity of hosting such an affair for their clients. But because what was most important to Emily simply slipped Richard's mind, a moment of crisis for Emily emerges, as she faces the encroachment of the next generation's idea of what is an appropriate business function.

When Richard tells Jason that no one "can throw together a more elegant event at the drop of a hat than Emily Gilmore" she retorts, "and you still forgot to tell him." Jason counters that he thinks it might be better to get the clients away from "stuffy cocktail party music and floral arrangements.... Nothing bonds two businessmen together like one of them finding the other hung over with a hooker in his bed the next morning." Emily is horrified, and she protests that "there are mobsters in Atlantic City." Jason goes on to explain that dignified cocktail parties are a thing of the past and that their new insurance company should take a risk in order to get people talking.

It is important to note that Jason has a difficult relationship with his father, who is a successful businessman as well; in fact, he has entered into business with Richard Gilmore in an attempt to anger his father. In this way, his rebellion is parallel to Lorelai's; he, too, it is revealed later in the season, is subject to the whims of the patriarchy's old guard.

Despite Emily's brief attempt to convince Richard that a trip to Atlantic City is an inappropriate event for an insurance company, he asks if it is too late to cancel her party. She backs down immediately and says, "No, it's not too late to cancel." Here we see Richard, who controls the purse strings, overtly exerting his control over Emily in service to his own interests, leaving Emily free to, as Jason asserts, "hang out and relax," which leads her to question her place and her utility in this new regime. That questioning takes place during a surprise visit to Lorelai's house. Lorelai, who was not expecting Emily's call, is dressed in a Juicy Couture tracksuit, which Emily comments on upon entering the house: "You have the word 'juicy' on your rear end." Nonplussed, Lorelai assures her mother that she would have changed had she known she was coming over, to which Emily responds, "Into what, a brassiere with the word "tasty" on it?" (4.06).

This exchange brings Lorelai's awareness of current fashion trends into stark relief against Emily's traditionalism and adherence to upper-class elegance, as she is clad in a charcoal suit and pearls. We see Lorelai as a hip, consuming young mother unafraid to accentuate her assets in the face of a woman whose role in patriarchal hegemony is slipping. Despite their oppositional relationship to fashion and popular culture, they are united in their powerless positions after Richard and Jason assert their authority. Emily must inform Lorelai that the party has been cancelled and that Lorelai and Sookie's services are no longer needed. In the process, she explains the decline of her position as corporate wife and her acceptance of her subordinate role both in the past and in the face of the ascendant generation of the phallocracy. She tells Lorelai that "Things that were once considered proper and elegant are now considered stuffy and out of date," things like "canapés and cocktail parties and the people who plan them." She explains that Jason would prefer to take clients to Atlantic City. Lorelai comforts and defends her mother and the work she has put into the planning for the party, but Emily demurs, "It's really not important,

Lorelai. I do this for your father. I have done this for your father for the last thirty-six years. If he thinks that Jason's right, then it's fine with me" (4.06).

When Jason declares that the blueblood cocktail parties Emily devoted her life to hosting are obsolete, Emily interprets it as a statement of her own obsolescence and uselessness. She is little more than a stale canapé destined for the wastebasket. Emily has spent her entire married life upholding the patriarchy; when the patriarchy exerts its dominance over her, she is stripped of her power, which has a trickle-down effect on Lorelai and Sookie, who had planned to use the income from the party to support their business and families.

In a paradoxical move, Lorelai further distances herself from her mother (and, by extension, the old version of the patriarchy) by aligning herself with the new, non-traditional version of the patriarchy. Lorelai directly challenges the new patriarch and his authority over their lives. She confronts Jason and tells her that he not only made Emily feel obsolete and useless, but his actions also had damaging consequences for her. She asks him to cancel the Atlantic City trip and reinstate the party, but he refuses. Instead, Jason offers to take Lorelai out to dinner, arguing that she should go because Emily would hate it. This logic appeals to Lorelai and she accepts the invitation with a smiling, "You suck!" Like Lorelai, Jason will go to great lengths to distance himself from his blue-blooded parents. The difference between them, though, is that Jason controls capital and belongs to the new generation of the patriarchy; Lorelai is simply a woman trying to maintain her independence. This is why Lorelai must playfully chastise Jason before accepting his invitation to share a meal with him. While she does not appreciate his actions as the patriarchy's new guard, he does present her with an opportunity to irritate her mother. While this troubles her role as the rebel in a constant battle to buck the system, it is fitting that she would resort to the means available to her to achieve the ultimate goal of complete extrication from the Gilmores' grasp, which is ultimately impossible. Despite Lorelai's consistent subversion of patriarchal control in her life, she finds herself a victim of its pervasive effects on her. Indeed, as we will soon see, Lorelai's attempts to escape patriarchy's clutch merely causes her to enact her own commodification.

When Lorelai discovered, at age sixteen, that she was pregnant with Rory, she took the opportunity to leave her parents' home, distancing herself from the upper-class environment in which she was raised. She refused to marry Rory's father and instead got a housekeeping job at an inn in Stars Hollow. She and Rory lived in the gardener's shed for ten years; Lorelai then bought her house and became manager of the inn. Lorelai has raised her daughter as her best friend, her partner in adventures marked by copious coffee consumption and staggering amounts of junk food and takeaway meals; indeed, much of their bonding as a mother-daughter dyad is couched in the procurement and consumption of convenience foods, from the arrangement of Mallomars on the kitchen table to celebrate a birthday to eating biscotti bought in Italy while they watch two community members argue publicly. (Oddly, both women remain quite thin despite their shabby nutrition and lack of exercise.) At the end of the *Gilmore Girls'* third season, Lorelai and Sookie purchased the Dragonfly Inn and embarked in their career as owners of their own bed and breakfast. As the owner of a small business, Lorelai neither participates in the production of capital, neither does she control capital. While she possesses drive as a businesswoman, having earned a business degree at night school, her role as an entrepreneur rests firmly in the service industry. Her success is wholly dependent upon the happiness of her customers (i.e., the public, with all its concomitant fickleness); her father, on the other hand, need merely keep his board and shareholders happy. Where the old guard accumulates money, Lorelai is representative of the new economic reality: the businessperson as merely a conduit for currency. She is merely a consuming subject, as represented in her consumption of disposable convenience foods; that she is a hip, fashionable consumer of popular culture trends marks her as the mother every girl is made to think she wants via pop culture's interpellation. She never pushes vegetables on her child and is more interested in talking about the music of Sonic Youth or watching *Godfather* movie marathons than helping Rory with her science homework. She lies in stark contrast to her own mother, whose entire adult life has been subsumed in service to her wealthy husband.

This difference is laid bare in the episode "The Lorelais' First Day at Yale" (4.02), in which the imminent separation between mother and daughter precipitates a crisis that Lorelai must resolve. In doing so, she leaves an imprimatur of consumption that the young coeds assume and enact after she is gone. At the outset of the episode, Rory, frustrated at the enormous amounts of frivolous cosmetics she finds herself packing, exclaims to her mother, "You've inculcated into me a tolerance for rampant consumerism!" While this might be a valid criticism within the context of the impracticality of packing for a small dorm room, that same rampant consumerism is what helps to ease Rory's transition to college life. After Lorelai leaves the campus and returns home to Stars Hollow, she receives a text message from Rory imploring her to come back. When she arrives back to Rory's dorm room in New Haven, Rory unleashes a torrent of criticism, fed by her anxiety and homesickness, upon her mother.

She's upset that she hadn't been socialized "properly" so that she hates her mother and can't wait, like the others in her dorm, to be away from her mother. "It's going to be very hard to be Christiane Amanpour broadcasting live from a foxhole in Tehran with my mommy. I guess you're just going to have to learn how to operate a camera, because I'll need you there with me" (4.02).

Rory's separation anxiety and the attendant chafing at that anxiety provides Lorelai with the opportunity to enact the unique brand of mothering via consumption that is the hallmark of this mother-daughter relationship. She agrees to spend the night with Rory in her dorm room and facilitates a "local takeout test" so that Rory and her suitemates can get the lay of the land as to what New Haven has to offer in convenience foods (as well as the cuteness of delivery boys, which they rate on a scale of one to 10). The takeout sampling swells to beyond smorgasbord proportions, as Lorelai and the girls order every ethnic cuisine on offer in the city and organize the takeout menus geographically from global East to West. They order so much food that Lorelai invites all the girls on the first floor of the dorm to come partake in the feast. She then summarizes the information gleaned from the night's festivities. Lorelai notes that the Chinese food is popular, except for Freddy's Happy Tokyo Takeout, although "the delivery guy was a solid nine. If you're going to go to Baja Bill's you must get the cheese quesadilla and ask for Stan or Tommy. If you can't get Stan or Tommy, go to Paco's Tacos. The delivery guys are butt-ugly, but the food's better" (4.02).

What is interesting about this summary of the goods and services on offer is that it echoes Emily's attitudes toward ethnic Others and their role in the Gilmore women's lives, but their attitudes are informed by their class status. The Other has no place in Emily's world — even (most of) her maids are of European descent — and that unauthorized presence is simply unacceptable. For Lorelai, and, by extension, Rory, the ethnic male is appreciated because he is not only an object to be rated according to his looks, but he is also the delivery system for the convenience foods that bond them to each other. Not only do Lorelai and Rory hold economic power over these men, they hold the power of the gaze, as well. While the distance between Lorelai and Emily's attitudes toward the ethnic Other is not that great, that Lorelai assumes the gaze in relation to the delivery boys is an indicator that her brand of mothering is in some small part a subversion of patriarchal proscriptions for the ideal mother while at the same time reinforcing the stereotypical image of the young adult female as unapologetically boy crazy.

From a mothering standpoint, Lorelai's slumber party serves two purposes: not only does she ease Rory's social transition into college life, she ensures that her mothering, nurturing presence will be invoked every time Rory picks up the telephone to place an order for takeout food. In fact, Lorelai's strategy is so effective that the "Durfee girls" adopt her technique of sampling a wide swath of convenience foods in order to find the best possible product; that to enact this technique is to "Lorelai" the campus is significant. By adopting her policies, the girls not only invoke the nurturance that made their first night at Yale as perfect as possible, they also inherit the urge to mother via consumption, setting the mold for their own future parenting. One assumes that the girls in Rory's dorm see Lorelai as the perfect mother, wishing that their own mothers were cool enough to have hosted an impromptu shindig in their suites.

We have seen the ways in which Lorelai's attempts via her control over food to transcend her mother's subjection to the demands of patriarchy have served to figure her as an ideal mother, one who has broken from the domestic sphere and moves freely about her world and is an avid consumer of culture. Additionally, Lorelai's interactions with other mothers in Stars Hollow serve to underscore that portrayal. At the outset of *Gilmore Girls*' fourth season, Sookie is expecting her first child with her husband, Jackson (Jackson Douglas). Sookie is overdetermined in her bodily presentation; she is overweight (but pretty), desexualized (so much so that her fecundity is an ongoing joke/crisis in the series), and is always fully dressed from head to toe. While it is easy to believe that a chef would be heavyset, that Sookie is so disconnected from any sensuality reinforces the cultural understanding that heavy women are not sexual beings, even when they sport hugely pregnant bellies. Counihan writes, "The higher one's class, the thinner one is likely to be.... Fat is not only supremely unattractive in our culture, but it is a clear symbol of loss of control" (123). Because she is fat and she is a laborer, Sookie is not able to exercise the same control over situations that require her to encode food with emotion, unlike Lorelai. However, Sookie's incipient motherhood, coupled with her inability to nurture via food production, offers Lorelai the opportunity to help Sookie be a better mother via understanding what it is that children like to eat.

In the episode, "The Hobbit, the Sofa, and Digger Stiles" (4.03), Sookie and Lorelai are hired to plan and throw a child's *Lord of the Rings* birthday party. Sookie is, understandably, in charge of planning the menu, but signals her misdirection when she asks, "How many adults are going to be there?" Sookie has no sense of what is appropriate for children, questioning Lorelai's choice of paper tablecloths and plates and placing a chafing dish with an open flame within the reach of the young party guests. She is more concerned with what the adults want, rather than the children, setting out gravlax and brie with lavender honey and bourbon-glazed pecans for "the guests over the age of ten." It becomes increasingly clear that Sookie is only comfortable cooking for adults. When she cooks for profit for adults, she is successful. When she cooks for profit for children, she is inept at relating to/determining what children want and need, because for her, the food (i.e., the product) is what is of utmost importance. "I'm a great chef," she exclaims. "A great chef does not have the client decorate his own cupcakes!" At this point, a girl dressed as an elf enters the kitchen and asks for a juice box. Annoyed at the interruption, Sookie barks, "Hey! We're talking!"; the girl begins to cry and Lorelai soothes her with a juice box and sends her back out to watch the movie while the enormity of her incompetence with children dawns on Sookie: "I don't know how to talk to them, I don't know how to feed them. I cover up their party cloths and I set their fingers on fire. I make them eat jalapeño-chipotle cream sauce. I'm Mommy Dearest!" (4.03).

This moment of crisis leads Sookie to believe that not only can she not feed children the appropriate things, she is capable of using inappropriate foods as a weapon against them. Prior to this epiphany, food is the site of conflict between the reality of children's tastes and Sookie's expectations of how children should eat and behave. Ideally, women will channel their appetites and passions into culturally sanctioned avenues, primarily, motherhood. Susan Bordo writes:

> In the necessity to make such a division of labor appear natural we find another powerful ideological underpinning (perhaps the most important in the context of industrialized society) for the cultural containment of female appetite: the notion that women are most gratified by feeding and nourishing *others*, not themselves [118].

In other words, the ideal mother allows her own appetite to be subsumed by that of her family, and there is very much a right and wrong way to feed the family. Sookie's emotional crisis regarding her fitness to be a mother manifests itself in the kitchen, where she is made to understand that she has no inkling of what kinds of food children like. Lorelai must educate Sookie and guide her in the right direction as a mother. In this way, Lorelai is portrayed as the "ideal" mother because she knows what children want to eat. It is then up to Lorelai to reassure Sookie that she will indeed be a good mother to her child; because Lorelai has mothered a child and has a keen understanding of what it is that children like to eat, she is the perfect woman to bridge the gap that separates Sookie from the kind of idealized motherhood constructed by commodity culture.[1]

While Sookie is capable of being molded into the type of mother Lorelai is, Mrs. Kim (Emily Kuroda) is beyond help; all Lorelai can do is bridge the gap that between Mrs. Kim and her daughter, Lane (Keiko Agena). Whether it is to provide Lane with pizza before she must return home to Mrs. Kim's bizarre vegetarian cooking or calling Mrs. Kim on Lane's behalf when Lane sneaks out of the house to play a gig at CBGB and is afraid to go home, Lorelai creates a space where Lane can indulge in her pop culture obsessions and eat junk food. Mrs. Kim, a Korean immigrant, owns an antique business and is a devout Seventh Day Adventist so rigid in her beliefs and outside the cultural mainstream as to be absurd. Mrs. Kim is the gatekeeper for the foodways of her household, but her choices are likely so outlandish and disgusting to the show's intended audience that it there is no other way to read her than as a narrow-minded and inflexible mother who is seemingly unfamiliar with the concept of nurturance.

This aspect of her mothering is thrown into relief in the episode, "Die, Jerk" (4.08), in which Lane thinks that her mother is going to send Lane's socalled "marriage jug" to her boyfriend, which would indicate that Lane is ready for marriage. Lane confronts her mother about this issue in the kitchen, where her mother tells her, "Dinner is going to be a little late tonight. My gluten patties caught on fire, so we're switching to spaghetti and wheat balls." Mrs. Kim has no recollection of telling Lane anything about the mythical marriage jug and says, "I probably just told you that to stop crying. You always cried when you were little. Gave me a headache." This coldness and utter lack of empathy and rapport with her only daughter, coupled with the meal of wheat balls (which nearly catch fire, too) mark Mrs. Kim as irretrievably Other; not only is she a woman of color whose unappetizing food choices consistently self-destruct in her kitchen, but she is also a mother who will never adhere to the new meaning of "mother," which is to participate actively in mainstream culture. Indeed, Mrs. Kim eventually evicts Lane from the home when she discovers her participation in mainstream culture, which has been hidden under the floorboards and in the closet of her daughter's room for years.[2] For Mrs. Kim, to consume mainstream culture is to commit a cardinal sin; it is no surprise, then, that the natural place for Lane to stay after being ejected from her home is with Lorelai. Given that Lorelai is constructed as the ideal mother, one who nurtures her child, her child's best friend, and other people's children via Chinese takeout, Pop Tarts, and pizza, it is important to consider the implications of this construction, which is so widely celebrated and consumed in mainstream culture.

Gilmore Girls, and its host network, the CW (formerly the WB), are geared to a target demographic of white females aged 18–34 (Romano), who were represented in short-lived segments, during the first half of the show's seventh season, called "Aerie Girls," who dish "gossip, Gilmore style" during show's commercial breaks. The consumers of the pseudo-feminist product that is Lorelai Gilmore become products themselves, in that their *kaffeeklatsch* is nothing more than a "content wrap" purchased by American Eagle Outfitters in an attempt to market their line of undergarments and "dorm wear," dubbed "aerie," which is aimed at the clothing company's 15–25-year-old customer base. In other words, the girls' emulation of what they watch on the CW is a commercial for a clothing store. When we consider who was watching this show on Tuesday nights, an examination of the representations of contemporary mothers on *Gilmore Girls* reveals some startling truths. In a culture that values thinness, independence and power, it is hard to imagine that many young women want to be like Sookie, the pudgy, quirky chef-employee who is passionate about cooking and is as fertile as her husband's successful farm. Mrs. Kim is hardly an option. Not only is she frigid and lacking any empathy, she is a woman of color and therefore not a reflection of the show's target demographic. Likewise, they are probably not likely to identify with Emily, who is portrayed as joyless and haughty, and increasingly dissatisfied in her role as a thankless corporate wife.

The only other choice is to identify with Lorelai, who owns a business, eschews domestic chores, and stays abreast of pop-culture trends. She cannot be bothered to cook — in fact, she stores her pots and pans in her oven, where they remain unused — and opts instead to procure her meals outside of the home. If she and Rory do eat at home, it is out of boxes while sitting on the couch and watching movies. She has the means to have someone else do the cooking for her without resorting to mistreating staff, like her mother does. She displays a mastery of consumption of mass-produced goods and services and enjoys the leisure to read magazines, shop, and watch movies; the viewer rarely witnesses Lorelai stopping to think critically about the encoded messages about class, gender, and race that dwell within the media she consumes so rapaciously. To that end, Lorelai is the ideal postmodern subject within commodity culture, perfectly marketed to and marketable, an advertiser's dream of the mothers of tomorrow, Aerie Girls who will have abdicated all their maternal subjectivity in service to conspicuous consumption.

Notes

1. The fact that Lorelai is never seen preparing food for consumption and frequently seen eating, and that Sookie is frequently seen preparing and serving food but rarely eating, complicates a Susan Bordo-ian reading of this text.
2. A situation ripe for a queer reading.

Works Cited

Counihan, Carole M. *The Anthropology of Food and Body: Gender, Meaning and Power.* New York: Routledge, 1999.

Lewin, Kurt. "Forces behind Food Habits and Methods of Change." *The Problem of Changing Food Habits*, Bulletin no. 108. Washington, D.C.: National Academy of Sciences, 1943.

McIntosh, William Alex and Mary Zey. "Women as Gatekeepers of Food Consumption: A Sociological Critique." *Food and Gender: Identity and Power.* Ed. Carole Counihan and Steven Kaplan. Amsterdam: Gordon and Breach, 1998: 125–44.

Romano, Allison. "Dawn of a New Network." *Broadcasting and Cable.* 21 August 2006. 9 May 2007 <http://www.broadcastingcable.com/article/CA6364196.html>.

Generation Gap?
Mothers, Daughters and Music

FAYE WOODS

Gilmore Girls (WB 2000–2006, CW 2006–2007) represents a bridge between the overtly family-centric shows of the "old" WB, which linger in the continued presence of *7th Heaven* (WB 1996–2006, CW 2006–2007) and the post–*Dawson's Creek* (WB 1998–2003) teen shows the WB network (now the CW) cemented its network identity on. Centering on a mother and daughter, their small town community and their extended moneyed family, *Gilmore Girls* opens up space for viewer identification beyond the teen-centric dynamics of its contemporaries such as *One Tree Hill* (WB 2003–6, CW 2006–present) and *Smallville* (WB 2001–6, CW 2006–present). In doing so it demonstrates the extended viewership of teen-focused television beyond a teen demographic.

As both Clare Birchall and Rebecca Feasey argue in relation to *Dawson's Creek* and *Charmed* (WB 1998–2006), the audience for shows marked out as "teen television" by their protagonists' age and their appearance on the WB can reach beyond teenage demographics. The WB's internal audience research in 2005 suggested that "when viewers age 12–24 are asked if the WB is a network 'for people like me,' the responses are very favorable; when 'older' viewers 25–34 are asked the same question, the stats aren't as impressive" (Adalian). Yet Neilson media research suggests that despite such perceptions of the network as a youth station the network actually had a median audience age of 32.6 in late 2003, with *Gilmore Girls* registering as 32.4 (Livsey), illustrating the wider audience range of the network and one of its flagship dramas.

Focusing as it does on three generations of Gilmore women, Lorelai (Lauren Graham), her daughter Rory (Alexis Beldel), and Lorelai's mother Emily (Kelly Bishop), the show gains its narrative momentum from intergenerational bonding and conflict, while foregrounding female identity and ideology. Caryn

127

James from the *New York Times* suggests that "What makes 'Gilmore' distinctive is that viewers from all generations can find something to like, and not only in the characters they're apt to identify with." Because of its focus on generations of female protagonists, it draws its range of audience, and in its central protagonists illustrates the blurring of generational boundaries in culture as a whole, of which the appeal of teen-focused drama beyond a teen demographic is merely one symptom of. I argue that the show uses music — as a narrative element as well as part of the show's soundscape — to define these generational interactions as well as to configure and cement character identity and relationships. Within a larger conception of the way generational identity is constructed through music, this paper will examine how the show uses music and female voice to create its particular worldview, how it dramatizes the narrowing of the generational gap in society, how the characters utilize music as part of their cultural capital and taste distinctions and how the show's foregrounding of feminine identity problematizes stereotypes of music consumption in the form of Lane Kim (Keiko Agena).

Female Musical Voice

The female voice that permeates *Gilmore Girls*, with its proliferation of central and supporting female characters and its foregrounding of powerful female "talk" with Lorelai and Rory's fast-paced repartée, is extended to its soundtrack. Folk-tinged contemporary singer-songwriter Sam Phillips composes the incidental and emotional music cues as well as contributing songs to the soundtracks of early episodes. In doing so she contributes to a soundscape of female vocal dominance, as in comparison to other film and television scores which are purely instrumental, hers is dominated by an acoustic guitar and a sung refrain, the melody composed of "la-la-la"s. The female voice is never quietened in *Gilmore Girls*, as even in emotional moments, when Phillips' score supports or defines an unspoken moment, the female voice remains in the form of Phillips' la-la-la vocals. For example, when Rory's crush Dean surprises her with a kiss it silences her nervous banter, yet when she runs away in shock Phillips' wistfully romantic score retains the female voice in place of Rory's silence (1.07 "Kiss and Tell").

Sam Phillips and her music exist within the legacy of the female singer-songwriter tradition, and the connotations of emotional, confessional, female expression that the genre brings. A key predecessor in this legacy is Carole King, a former Brill Building songwriter and chronicler of sixties teen romance; writing hits such as "Will You Still Love Me Tomorrow," King became a defining singer-songwriter of the 1970s and beyond, with her 1971 album *Tapestry* ranked as the biggest selling album in history for almost 10 years (Cross). King cameos in *Gilmore Girls* as Sophie, the owner of the Stars Hollow record store. As such she acts as the metaphorical gatekeeper of the movement of Rory's friend Lane from (relatively) passive consumer of music to active performer of music, when Lane takes up a drum kit from the store. King's song "Where You Lead" from *Tapestry* is the title music for *Gilmore Girls*. Music scholar Claudia Gorbman suggests that title music defines the genre, sets a general mood and introduces musical themes (82). Significantly, King's track is reformulated as a duet for King and her daughter Louise Goffin with lyric changes to shift it from a song of romantic devotion, to one of devotional friendship. Following Gorbman's formulation, the lyrical expressions foretell Lorelai and Rory's relationship, with the mother and daughter duet literalizing this. The song works to suture us into the world of the *Gilmore Girls* as the folk tinged singer-songwriter style prefigures the sound of Phillip's score and the slightly nostalgic tone of using a classic song contributes to the patina of Stars Hollow as a utopian idyll little touched by contemporary life.

Generation Gap?

Lawrence Grossberg, writing in 1986, identified the impact of the Baby Boomer generation's refusal to "grow-up" on subsequent youth generations. He suggested that the Baby Boomers worked to redefine "youth" as an attitude, allowing them to both essentialize and appropriate it, arguing that

> As more and more people point to the increasingly troubled and adult-life qualities of young people, they are also observing the failure of the baby boomers to accept and arrive at traditional notions of adulthood [185].

Grossberg is using this moving of the metaphorical generational goalposts to argue for the reduced power of "rock and roll" for a contemporary youth audience, whose parental generation still claim it as their own and as such appropriate and enfold it into "official society" leaving youth to find other cultural outlets for their rebellion and enacting of "difference." This appropriation of youth and lack of defined parental generation that Grossberg identifies is continued as the following generation ages. To reduce what is quite a complex sociological argument to its bare bones, as Generation X[1] become parents, there is a concomitant reluctance to part with youth and what may be termed a generational narrowing between parent and child. *Gilmore Girls* can be seen as a realisation of this narrowing of the generation gap, through its presentation of mother and daughter as best friends, rather than opponents in generational warfare. Generational conflict is, instead, focused between Lorelai and her mother Emily, where any conception of the elder Gilmores as Baby Boomers is negated by class, with their situation as "old money" and members of the upper classes of society with all of its rules and strictures. As such, the generation gap, whilst deconstructed by Lorelai and Rory, is reconstructed between Lorelai and

Emily as predominantly one produced by class and Lorelai's rebellion against her position.

Two pieces of recent popular journalism outline a trend-based analysis of this reduction, even elision, of the generation gap. Although both articles look at parents older than Lorelai, they focus on parents who are within her age demographic and whose relationships with their children and their culture mirror hers. Sophie Radice in the London *Observer* quotes a 39-year-old parent who suggests of her relationship with her 13-year-old daughter, "There is much less of a distinction than there was for me and my mother's generation when I was a teenager." Sharing tastes in clothes and music, Radice's subjects evidence a close bond with their children leading her to question that "could it be that my generation, not quite willing to embrace middle age, has unwittingly hit upon a way of being able to communicate better with teenagers." Radice suggests that it is her generation's delayed parenthood, and its attendant extension of teenagehood, which allows them to better relate to their children. While Lorelai's own parenthood was not delayed, and it is her youth that allows her to be both mother and friend, we see here in Radice's account a general closing of the generation gap between parent and child along with a bid for friendship with ones child that marks out Generation X's parent-child relationship and a narrowing of generational taste differences that *Gilmore Girls* depicts.

Adam Sternbergh, in *New York* magazine, profiles the phenomenon of the "yupster," or "grup." His is a somewhat humorous piece focusing on the aging population of New York hipsters, but can be readily extended across that of Generation X. Sternbergh presents his piece as "an obituary for the generation gap. It is a story about 40-year-old men and women who look, talk, act, and dress like people who are 22 years old." He presents a generation of affluent, urban adults who are "evidence of the slow erosion of the long-held idea that in some fundamental way, you cross through a portal when you become an adult.... This cohort is not interested in putting away childish things." However, contrary to Grossberg's Baby Boomers retaining the culture of their own youth and dominating further generations representations, Sternbergh suggests that "[t]his cascade of pioneering immaturity is no longer a case of a generation's being stuck in its own youth. This generation is now, if you happen to be under 25, more interested in being stuck in *your* youth." This he illustrates through fashion and cultural choice — hoodies, jeans, snowboarding, messenger bags — and most prominently music. While previous generations were defined by parental and child musical taste barriers, this generation, brought up on eighties punk and electro and nineties indie and grunge, have no such taste barrier. "No wonder Grups like today's indie music: It sounds exactly like the indie music of their youth. Which, as it happens, is what kids today like, too, which is why today's new music all sounds like it's twenty years old. And thus the culture grinds to a halt, in a screech of guitar feedback" (Sternbergh).

Sternbergh ties this overall generational phenomenon of the Grup to a fear of the loss of passion in adulthood, suggesting that "it's also about rejecting a hand-me-down model of adulthood that asks, or even necessitates, that you let go of everything you ever felt passionate about." For Lorelai, becoming a parent means neither succumbing to her mother's conception of parenthood nor the end of youthful passions; she still wears band t-shirts, wakes up to a fluffy alarm clock and squeals with delight at the arrival of the latest XTC record.

As the generation gap narrows, music no longer becomes the defining difference that it once was. While in 1992 James Lull argued that "young people use music to resist authority at all levels.... A fundamental adolescent use of music is the 'need' to declare independence from parents" (27), I would argue that the changing parent/child relationships described by Radice and the movements in current music styles discussed by Sternbergh are evidence of a move away from this position. Dan Laughey, Sian Lincoln, and Christina Williams, in empirical studies of young music listeners, found an influence and continuity between parent and child. In particular, Lincoln elucidates the impact of parental taste on teenagers "musical biographies" and Williams found that her subjects "often liked the same music as their parents, did not feel that their parents' opinions were an issue, and did not seem to wish to appear rebellious" (235). This reduction of generational taste difference is demonstrated in the music relationships that play a significant role in *Gilmore Girls'* construction of character identity.

Musical Legacy and Continuities

Gilmore Girls is lauded for its fast paced dialogue and the diverse, often obscure cultural references that its characters— predominantly Lorelai and Rory, but also Sookie, Lane and Paris— exchange. Pop cultural referencing is a feature of contemporary teen texts such as *Dawson's Creek* and *Buffy the Vampire Slayer* (WB 1997–2001, UPN 2001–3), and Clare Birchall suggests that this referencing reaches beyond a teen audience, rewarding "those who understand these references— usually the young adult viewer — acknowledging their previous experiences" (178). However, *Gilmore Girls'* referencing is more free-ranging than its contemporaries, mixing pop culture, history, music, literature and politics and as a result allowing for a greater range of identification in range of its audience's ages and intellect. It rewards both music geeks and those with highbrow literature and cultural knowledge, reflecting the cultural construction of Lorelai and Rory as products of both high — Lorelai's pre-pregnancy private schooling and Rory's book-loving autodidact — and popular — they are avid consumers of junk food, television and old movies—culture. Its patchwork of references also works towards creating and sustaining its atypical worldview commensurate with its quirky small town fantasy. Birchall argues in relation to *Dawson's Creek*'s referencing of earlier teen texts, "[b]y the very virtue of its citation, its role in a particular tradition is established" (178). By drawing from both high and popular culture, *Gilmore Girls* places itself as "other" to mainstream, separating itself from its contemporary teen dramas and situating itself in a more "cultured" lineage. Much as Rory and Lorelai's access to Emily and Richard's money and social circle allow them to move beyond and acquire benefits beyond their own class and social status, whilst retaining their constructed "outsider" status, its references allow *Gilmore Girls* to vacillate between both an indie sensibility and a highbrow sensibility whilst retaining a populist demographic.

This is continued in its musical choices and referencing. For all its presentation of an "otherworldly" storybook New England utopia, its soundtrack music choices create an eclectic soundscape, combining the folk-inspired songs and score cues of Sam Phillips—whose whimsical tone reflects the quirky yet "safe" world of Stars Hollow—with a range of tracks which could problematize this worldview. *Gilmore Girls* features the music of 1980s-centric artists of Lorelai's youth such as XTC and the Jesus and Mary Chain, classic alternative nineties groups such as Mazzy Star and The La's and credible contemporary indie acts such as Yo La Tengo (who contribute the closing track of the pilot "My Little Corner of the World," figuring almost as Lorelai and Rory's ethos) and Wilco. Music artists ranging from contemporary indie band The Shins, quirky Seventies electro-pop duo Sparks and seminal Nineties alternative rock group Sonic Youth[2] appear in cameo performances and both singer-songwriter Carole King and eighties hair-rocker Sebastian Bach (of Skid Row) have recurring roles, the latter playfully undermining his hard-partying rock persona in the character of sandwich-selling, family-man Gil who joins Lane's band.

The music credibility offered by these acts and the music referencing that rock connoisseur[3] Lane contributes help to situate the show apart from the mainstream, constructing an "indie" sensibility, and to offset perceptions of conservatism or twee-ness that its storybook New England setting may induce. There is musical continuity through the range of acts, with a predominance of alternative and independent bands, constructing a musical lineage that is compounded by the music that characters use to create their taste distinctions and identities and in such a way this lineage works to reduce the music-based generation gap through the newer artists positions within this legacy or canon.

However, the tracks used of the contemporary artists are soft, acoustic-led numbers rather than the rawer-edged or experimental tracks of their repertoire, contributing to the comforting soundscape of the show. As such, these "edgy" choices could be seen to be recuperated into the "safe" worldview of the show, negating their power to present an alternative viewpoint or disrupt the show's aesthetic. Indeed, Sonic Youth's cameo is as a troubadour family, with Kim Gordon and Thurston Moore performing with their daughter Coco (6.22, "Partings") and together with Bach's Gil—whose comedic value is produced through the clash of his rock persona with his laid-back family persona — could present a enfolding of alternative lives into a family-focused worldview. Yet, I would suggest that these depictions extend the show's construction of "alternative" parental lifestyles, in the form of Lorelai. They are also presented with a degree of self-awareness and a "wink" to the audience with knowledge of the artists and in such a way function as an extension of the show's cultural referencing.

Creator Amy Sherman-Palladino tells a teenage anecdote on the sleeve notes on the *Gilmore Girls* soundtrack of trying to pass on her love of Prince to her father and failing. The show can be seen as presenting her fulfillment of this desire of intergenerational bonds forged though music. Kay Dickinson has argued that teen shows' use of non-contemporary music represents a parental baby boomer generation (figured as the shows' creators) imposing their tastes and worldview on the teenage audience (106–10). I would suggest that — aside from this cycle of teen television producers and showrunners belonging primarily to Generation X rather than that of the baby boomers — *Gilmore Girls* plays out what is an undeniable continuity in style and taste between generations of music. Rather than imposing, à la Grossberg's baby boomers, a previous definition of youth and music, *Gilmore Girls* — through its dissolving of generation boundaries — draws a musical timeline through the music of previous generations to contemporary music, illustrating similarities and demonstrating (and encouraging) the breadth of contemporary youth's taste.

Taste Distinctions and Cultural Capital

The idea of musical taste as something learned or passed down is strong in *Gilmore Girls*; just as Lorelai passes her tastes onto Rory — externalized in their cultural references — her father Christopher, although absent, is constructed as having the same taste distinctions as Lorelai and Rory, he shares some of their quick paced cultural references and has amassed a "legendary" CD collection (3.06, "Take the Deviled Eggs..."). Music aligns him with the "Girls" and against his new girlfriend Sherry, whose unsuitability is coded through her record collection of Billy Joel and "brunch Jazz" and who is accused by Lorelai of lacking the necessary reverence for Christopher's music: "To her, they're just identical, little metal discs full of annoying sounds you alphabetize like files in an office" (3.06, "Take the Deviled Eggs..."). Rory's second boyfriend Jess — who also prides himself on his music taste and uses it to differentiate himself against others, particularly Rory's first boyfriend Dean — is also shown to have his taste distinctions unconsciously handed down from his absent father. When they first meet at Luke's diner they sit quietly uncommunicative, yet both then unconsciously sing along to David Bowie's Seventies glam rock classic "Suffragette City" (3.20, "Say Goodnight, Gracie") that plays on Jess's stereo and when Jess visits his father's home in California he finds walls full of records and books reflecting Jess's own passion in literature and music (3.21, "Here Comes the Son").

It could be argued that music forms part of the particular kind of cultural capital that Lorelai passes onto Rory in the form of their system of cultural references. John Fiske, using the concepts of Pierre Bourdieu, argues that popular cultural capital, "produced by subordinate social formation ... can serve, in the subordinate, similar functions to those of official cultural capital in the dominant context" (33). Lorelai and Rory's cultural capital is a mix of popular culture with "official" culture, both inherited — in the official cultural knowledge of their upper-class social lineage, and Lorelai's passing of music and popular cultural knowledge to Rory — and learned — through Lorelai's populist tastes and Rory's autodidact intellectualism.

Fiske's ideas of fan cultural capital can be applied to the "Girls'" own cultural capital, as whilst they accumulate official cultural capital (their literary and historical references, Lorelai's inherited upper-class social manners and abilities which she utilises in her work environment[4]), like Fiske's young fans, they still desire to differentiate themselves "from the social values and cultural tastes ... of those who currently possess the cultural and economic capital" (33), (Richard and Emily, town mayor Taylor, "popular" mainstream teens such as Lindsay). This "social distinction" is expressed through their "accumulation of unofficial or popular cultural capital whose politics lie in its opposition to the official, dominant one" (33). Lorelai and Rory's cultural capital works in dual directions, excluding members of official culture through popular culture references and excluding members of popular and mainstream culture through official cultural references. This cultural capital functions as a bond between them and to exclude or include others through the taste distinctions that operate within this cultural capital. However, Rory's interest in and pursuit of a higher level of schooling and her personal advancement through her autodidact nature, in comparison to Lorelai's own rebellious teenage years, allows her access to a greater range of official cultural capital than her mother. As Rory enters further into the world of official cultural capital in her Yale education, relationship with Logan — who is also of a monied, high class family — and her dalliance with her grandmother's social circle when she drops out of Yale in season six, her relationship with Lorelai is tested. Their bond, usually cemented through their referencing system, is strained through Rory's unconscious use or conscious deployment of high cultural references that exclude Lorelai as a result of her unequal knowledge.

Jason Mittell, using Pierre Bourdieu, argues that "taste is not a universal component of aesthetics but rather an active cultural practice that works to both reproduce produce social systems and hierarchies." Through taste distinctions Lorelai and Rory define themselves against others and suture their own relationship. This system, as Clare Birchall argues in relation to references, allows the audience to feel superior and sutures them into the characters relationship when they too can understand the show's references. As such, this can be seen as a continuation of the show's integration and recuperation of less mainstream musical tastes I discussed in relation to Yo La Tengo and Wilco. Rory and Lorelai are constructed as edgy and different through their taste distinctions, but the very fact of their upbringing problematizes this. Their position of privilege (however critiqued by Lorelai) allows their ease of movement between different classes and areas of cultural capital and taste distinctions.

Their "'alternative' lifestyle is taken up and acknowledged, but safely negotiated and recuperated by the status quo and dominant structures are reinforced" (Gledhill 71). However, I do not wish to argue that this results in *Gilmore Girls* presenting a conservative ideology, or a reproduction of official cultural hegemony, merely that there are elements that problematize its, and its characters', own positioning as "other." Any construction of the show as "conservative" is countered by the central characters' relationships with musical taste, which continues the forging of generational identity yet problematizes Dickinson's conceptions of a conservative prioritizing of parental musical taste over contemporary youth.

Tia DeNora suggests that "[t]he sense of 'self' is locatable in music. Musical materials provide terms and templates for elaborating self-identity — for identity's identification" (145). Lorelai and Rory use music taste to define their bond and to differentiate themselves from others who may invade that bond. From the opening episode Lorelai and Rory's bonds are manifested through their musical tastes, with each borrowing CDs as well as clothing and make-up from each other — their "sameness" is awkwardly telegraphed through their retreating to their bedrooms, post-fight, both listening to Macy Gray's "I Try" (1.01, "Pilot"), a CD Lorelai had earlier borrowed from Rory. When Rory tries to reach out to a boy in the Yale University laundry room, commenting on his basket adorned with Smiths stickers, she talks of her mother passing on her love of them, in comparison to his mention of an older sibling. In such a way, Lorelai functions as both mother and older sibling, passing on musical knowledge and taste to a younger sister.

Rory is figured as closer to her mother than everyday youth — aside from Lane, who is cast as something of an outsider herself — and this is constructed through her musical taste. In "Rory's Dance" (1.09) Rory sets herself apart from her peers and their inferred music, suggesting the school dance will be "stuffy and boring and the music will suck" referencing cheesy boyband 98° as the music she expects, whereas Lorelai suggests it could be Rory's dream dance which is "All sparkly and exciting" where she will be listening to cult singer-songwriter Tom Waits on the dance floor. As such Rory's tastes are aligned with her mother against that of her peers. Lorelai's musical taste is constructed around the music of her youth — her childhood bedroom at her parent's house has posters of acts such as Echo and the Bunnymen placed over its ornate decoration — and its rebellious "outsider" connotations. In one of the few moments we see Lorelai reading. She is engrossed in the salacious biography of Eighties heavy metal band Mötley Crüe, inferring her rebellious youth and the choices she could have made if Rory was not there. However, there is the question of whether, like the Grups discussed by Sternbergh, the show and Lorelai present a fondness for contemporary music that sounds like the music of eighties and nineties youth, or whether the show privileges Lorelai's musical taste and influence over Rory's.

If the latter were true, this would present a nostalgia-infused musical reactionarism that Dickinson suggests occurs in *Dawson's Creek* (2004). In season one, Rory attempts to bond with Paris, Louise and Madeline by taking them to a Bangles concert with Lorelai and Sookie. Along with continuing the show's prominence of Eighties artists— and its prioritizing of the female voice through the Bangles' status as a rare all-female rock group — the concert serves to define Rory against her peers and towards her mother, as while Lorelai and Sookie, along with Rory, are excited, the more "normal" Louise and Madeline[5] are more interested in boys.

However, the knowledge learned from Lorelai in this way supports Rory's friendship with music autodidact Lane through a system of taste distinctions— who is figured as so vastly different from her own uptight religious mother that there is no inference her knowledge has been passed down. Through Lane's status as a musical connoisseur, Rory's music tastes are defined as authentic and classic. They talk of David Bowie, swear on the soul of Nico, the influential avant-garde and rock singer associated with Andy Warhol and The Velvet Underground and mourn the death of Joe Strummer, guitarist of iconic punk band The Clash. Yet these classic artists are also linked to credible contemporary artists such as Grandaddy and Beck are equally referenced, suggesting a rounded musical worldview (notably, *Gilmore Girls* was mentioned and praised by the ultimate rock-snob website *Pitchfork* at the time of Sonic Youth's appearance on the show [Phillips]) rather than imposing a previous generation's taste.

Although Rory shared cultural references and interests with her first boyfriend Dean — who was presented as a sensitive and a suitable match through his interest in musicians such as Seventies singer-songwriter Nick Drake and contemporary alternative rock artist Liz Phair — she finds a kindred spirit in Jess, and is attracted to him through his shared knowledge of books, music and culture. Jess defines himself against Dean, deriding his taste against Jess and Rory's shared taste distinctions and repeatedly suggesting Dean's inferiority due to his lack of the cultural capital he and Rory share, questioning what they talk about and framing their relationship as "teacher-student" (2.10, "The Bracebridge Dinner"). Where Dean is a good-natured and loyal boy-next-door, Jess's own identity is shaped by cultural definitions of the outsider, from books and popular culture. He is a combination of the archetypal fifties rebel and sixties beatnik, with a rolled up book tucked into his pocket rather than a comb. He mocks the populist elements of the "Girls'" cultural tastes, dividing himself into a higher bracket of taste distinction from them, yet both Rory and Lorelai mock Jess's stereotypical rebellious "youth" as a construction, through their knowledge of its cultural reference points. Rory has no need to rebel, as Lorelai has already constructed herself and her daughter within a limited position of rebellion in relation to her parents and the strictures of the town. However, when Rory breaks out of this "safe" area of rebellion with a criminal act in season five, she breaks from her mother.

Rory in turn defines herself against Dean's new girlfriend Lindsay, who likes popular mainstream acts Michelle Branch and Matchbox 20 (3.19, "Keg! Max!"), in comparison to Dean describing Rory as a "music freak," and Dean's construction in season one as a fan of alternative acts. As such Rory and her friends and immediate family situate themselves as above and apart from popular taste, reflecting the show's positioning of itself as hip-ly alternative through its soundtrack music. The show constructs a musical legacy of alternative, indie and rock music which positions the "classic" music of Lorelai's "parental" generation in line with a similarly valorized set of contemporary alternative artists which figure to situate Rory and her friends in a position of authority through their breadth of taste and cultural markers. Rather than imposing a reactionary parental taste in its musical choices, it figures a generational bridge through musical continuities, allowing shared tastes across generations.

Lane Kim, Female Rock Connoisseur

Continuing the show's prominent placing of alternative music and its centralizing of female voice and its foregrounding of music taste distinctions is the character of Rory's friend Lane. In contrast to Rory and Lorelai's closeness, Lane, a Korean-American, has an overbearing religious mother. Lane and Mrs. Kim's generational differences are also constructed through music, with Mrs. Kim's Christian music tastes, reflecting her own devout beliefs, constructed comedically as the total opposite of Lane's tastes. Mrs. Kim's music tastes are used by Lane to trick her into accepting Dave as Lane's boyfriend, when he masquerades as a Christian singer (3.09, "A Deep-Fried Korean Thanksgiving"). Lane herself undermines a set of stereotypes surrounding the rock connoisseur and record collector that appear throughout academia and popular culture, typified by music scholar Simon Frith, who suggests, "just to hear how girls listen to music ... they're not collectors like boys are. And that's something with a very long history and that goes across any number of cultures too. Being collectors and cognoscenti seems to be a very masculine attribute" (qtd. in Gross). Yet, Lane also plays out some key arguments surrounding male collectors, complicating gendered distinctions inherent in this field of discussion.

Mark Katz suggests that "[r]ecord collecting represents a relationship with music that helps us, in some part small or large, to articulate and in fact shape who we are" (11). Lane's musical knowledge and her CD collection provide essential markers of her identity and represent her autodidact persona. She constructs her own musical world, one which excludes her mother and peers, yet admits Rory and Lorelai through shared cultural capital, feminizing Roy Shuker's argument that "record collecting can represent a public display of male power and knowledge, serving as a form of cultural capital within the peer group" (314). Her music collection and knowledge provide her with cultural capital, and also allow her to eventually move her musical interest into a more social area, in the form of a band and a boyfriend who shares her interests.

Robynn J. Stilwell, when discussing the increasingly central role the feminine experience of records has taken in recent female coming-of-age cinema, highlights gendered distinctions between essentialism and socialization that tend to feature in discussions of record collectors, arguing that these are combined in such films, that "whether it is socialised at the level of expression to others (the classic male stereotype), or expression of the self to the self [the female stereotypes], this intimate relationship of girls and music, mediated by records, is often central to the cinematic articulation of the girl's self-discovery" (158). Stilwell argues that these films present an almost ritualistic ascription of the power of the record itself, along with the voice it contains and enacts, which does not continue over to the use of CDs in such films.

However, I would suggest that Lane has such a relationship with her CD collection, since it is central to her articulation of her self and instigator of her self-discovery, and she ritualizes their consumption and knowledge. Due to her mother's disapproval, she secretes them under her floorboards, imbuing them with a special power through their status as forbidden objects. Lane's spare and spartan bedroom evidences none of the personal identity decoration common to bedroom spaces. As Sian Lincoln argues, "a teenager's bedroom tells the story of their cultural interests and social lives. From CDs to posters, club flyers to gig tickets, each adds to the cultural history of that space" (411). Lane hides her "cultural history" and musical identity from her mother, under her floorboards and in a secret other "bedroom" of forbidden teenage items in her closet (rock posters, pink lights, lava lamps, patterned bedding, etc.) where she listens to her music on headphones. Will Straw highlights the conception of collections as fetishistic obsessions and argues that there are "competing images of the collection as cultural monument and private haven" (4). Lane segments her collection carefully ordered under different floorboards, divided into categories such as "Classic Rock, Progressive Rock, Pretty Boy Rock (Bon Jovi, Duran Duran, The Wallflowers, Bush)" and "New Wave, German Metal Bands, Broadway Soundtracks" (1.14, "That Damn Donna Reed"). For Lane, her collection is both private haven and a concealed, yet fanatically ordered monument.

Straw goes on to argue that "[r]ecord collections are seen as both public displays of power/knowledge and private refuges from the sexual or social world" (4). As discussed above, Lane's music collection and knowledge provide her with cultural capital that bonds her to Rory and Lorelai. However, she has little interaction with the wider sexual or social world due to the imposition of her mother's strict rules. Yet, in season two, with the involvement of Carole King's character Sophie and her record store, Lane finds her "calling" as a drummer, telling Rory "I am Keith Moon, I am Neil Peart, I am Rick Allen, with and without the arm, because I am rock 'n roll, baby!" (2.20, "Help Wanted"). In taking up the drums, Lane transgresses into another cultural space coded as masculine. As Mary Ann Clawson points out, drums "express the loudness and power that is central to rock music and to an occupation of sonic space coded as masculine" (201).

Her drumming and her music connoisseurship allow her to bridge the gap into the typically homosocial activity of musicianship. Will Straw highlights how, with the rise of alternative rock in the 1990s, "semiotic competence in reading the state of the musical field" came to attain greater capital than the raw power of the earlier rock scenes (15). Lane's connoisseurship — illustrated by the three single-spaced pages of musical influences she compiles for her band advertisement in season three — gives her the cultural capital, the "semiotic competence" to allow her entrance into the homosocial world that Straw characterizes as traditionally blocking females through shared knowledges (10).

Lane seeks to live out, romantically, Straw's conception of collecting allowing "rituals of homosocial interaction" in that "each man finds, in the similarity of his points of reference to those of his peers, confirmation of a shared universe of critical judgment" (15); she complicates this "homosocial" action through "heterosexualizing" its employment. On a date with a friend of Rory's boyfriend Dean, she tries to bond with him through her intense expressions of joy over Beck, Foo Fighters and The Velvet Underground and tries to reach out by referencing his Fugazi t-shirt; however, he has no interest and lacks any kind of music knowledge and her attempt fails (1.12, "Double Date"). However, the band allows her another chance at heterosexual interaction through her knowledge when Dave Rygalski responds to her "Drummer Wants Band" ad and they immediately bond over her Dead Kennedys t-shirt (3.06). Lane's status as the voice of the show's articulation of musical taste is compounded as the role music plays in their bond and attraction is literalized when it is reflected onto the show's non-diegetic soundtrack. Compared to Rory's romantic moments, which are generally soundtracked by Phillips's scored la-la-la cues, if at all, Lane and Dave's first kiss sparks the non-diegetic commencement of Bowie's "The Man Who Sold the World" (3.09, "A Deep-Fried Korean Thanksgiving"). The opening guitar riff (which Dave had briefly played as a private joke with Lane earlier in the episode) provides a romantic stinger to the kiss and the woosey electro of Bowie's voice mirrors Lane's teetering, shell-shocked reaction. Lane's music connoisseurship, contrary to its masculine, asocial stereotype, allows her to move into a feminine position of romance, without sacrificing her essential self.

Conclusions

Gilmore Girls reflects the narrowing generation gap in society as a whole, recognizing the spread of the "teen TV" audience beyond a teen demographic. Its address to its audiences of teens and beyond does not prioritize or declaim an older generational viewpoint, instead reflecting a movement between and collusion of tastes across any defined generational boundaries. *Gilmore Girls* presents a definition of generational identity in which music plays a foundational part.

The show sets up a system of elaborate references both to define its central protagonists against others and to position itself within a superior cultural legacy outside of "mainstream" teen TV and culture. It celebrates both knowledge and female voice and power, and these are extended to its soundtrack, where a female soundscape is created beyond its dialogue and a sense of alternative music's legacy is suggested in its range of popular song choices and references. *Gilmore Girls* uses music to elaborate characters' taste distinctions and their creation and manipulation of forms of cultural capital and undermines gendered assumptions in relation to musical knowledge. In doing so, it opens itself up to a range of audience positions, from young females, to broadsheet television critics and rock music aesthetes, each of whom can find elements of pleasure in the show.

Notes

1. Margaret Hornblower, writing in *Time* magazine, defines Generation X as those born between 1965 and 1977 (1997:58). As such Lorelai would be defined as Generation X, her parents as baby boomers and Rory as Generation M (for Millennium, those born between 1980 and 2000 [Israel])

2. I choose these decades to mark the groups' greatest mainstream success, but both Sparks and Sonic Youth have long and continuing careers, both releasing albums in 2006.

3. I choose this term over "fan," "record collector" or "audiophile" as Lane's music knowledge is demonstrated as wide ranging and essentialized, and these terms have negative or delimiting connotations.

4. Amy Benfer in *Salon*, while not mentioning Bourdieu, argues that the show subtly manipulates class distinctions to allow Lorelai the benefits of upper-classdom while positioning her in opposition to all it entails, suggesting that "she conflates two of the most pervasive American myths: She has the taste and pedigree of someone who was born knowing what to do with the silver spoon in her mouth *and* the independence of someone who has pulled herself up by her bootstraps." Benfer goes on to argue that "all of the skills that facilitated her rise from maid to manager are the skills that one acquires from undergoing 16 years of parental training in how to become a lady."

5. Paris functions as a more extreme version of Rory's intellectual and relatively solitary nature, naturalizing Rory's own "otherness."

Works Cited

Adalian, Josef. "WB Seeks Bigger Aud, Commits Frogicide." *Variety* (July 22, 2005). 26 July 2005 <http://www.variety.com/story.asp?l=story&a=VR1117926413&c=14>.

Benfer, Amy. "Knocked Up Like Me: What's Cooler than Bring a Middle-Class Teenage Mother? Having a TV Show All about You." *Salon.com.* 2 Nov. 2000. 22 January 2007 <http://archive.salon.com/mwt/feature/2000/11/02/gilmore_girls/index.html>.

Bennett, Andy, Barry Shank, and Jason Toynbee, eds. *The Popular Music Studies Reader* Routledge: London, 2006.

Birchall, Clare. "'Feels Like Home': *Dawson's Creek*, Nostalgia and the Young Adult Viewer." *Teen TV: Genre, Consumption, Identity.* Ed. Glyn Davis and Kay Dickinson. London: BFI, 2004. 176-89.

Clawson, Mary Ann. "When Women Play the Bass: Instrument Specialisation and Gender Interpretation in Alternative Rock Music." *Gender and Society.* 13.2 (April 1999): 193-210.

Corbett, John. *Extended Play: Sounding Off from John Cage to Dr. Funkenstein* Durham, NC: Duke UP, 1994.

Cross, Charles R. "Carole King." *Rolling Stone.* 2004. 9 May 2007 <http://www.ronllingstone.com/artists/caroleking/biography>.

Davis, Glyn and Kay Dickinson, eds. *Teen TV: Genre, Consumption, Identity.* London: BFI, 2004.

DeNora, Tia. "Music and Self-Identity." *The Popular Music Studies Reader.* Ed. Andy Bennett, Barry Shank, and Jason Toynbee. London: Routledge, 2006. 141-47.

Dickinson, Kay. "'My Generation': Popular Music, Age and Influence in Teen Dramas of the 1990s." *Teen TV: Genre, Consumption, Identity.* Ed. Glyn Davis and Kay Dickinson. London: BFI, 2004. 99-111.

Feasey, Rebecca. "Watching *Charmed*: Why Teen Television Appeals to Women." *Journal of Popular Film and Television* 3.1 (Spring 2006): 2-9.

Fiske, John. "The Cultural Economy of Fandom." *The Adoring Audiences.* Ed. Lisa Lewis. London: Routledge, 1992. 30-49

Gledhill, Christine. "Pleasurable Negotiations." *Female Spectators: Looking at Film and Television.* Ed. E. Deidre Pribram. London: Verso, 1988. 64-89.

Gorbman, Claudia. *Unheard Melodies: Narrative Film Music.* London: BFI, 1987.

Gross, Jason. "Simon Frith Interview." *Perfect Sound Forever* May 2002. March 19 2007 <http://www.furious.com/PERFECT/simonfrith.html>.

Grossberg, Lawrence. "The Deconstruction of Youth." *Cultural Theory and Popular Culture: A Reader.* Ed. John Storey. London: Harvester Wheatsheaf, 1994. 183-90.

Hornblower, Margot. "Great Xpectations." *Time* 9 June 1997: 58-65.

Israel, Betsy (2006) "The Overconnecteds." *New York Times* 5 November 2006. 21 March 2007 <http://www.nytimes.com/2006/11/05/education/edlife/connect.html?ex=1175400000&en=9d6bc1820226a603&ei=5070>.

James, Caryn (2001) "Home Sweet Home, but Not Saccharine." *New York Times* February 25 accessed January 22 2007.

Katz, Mark. *Capturing Sound: How Technology Has Changed Music.* Berkeley: University of California Press, 2004.

Laughey, Dan. *Music and Youth Culture.* Edinburgh: Edinburgh University Press, 2006.

Lewis, Lisa, ed. *The Adoring Audiences*. London: Routledge, 1992.

Lincoln, Sian. "Feeling the Noise: Teenagers, Bedrooms and Music." *Leisure Studies* 24.4 (October 2005): 399-414.

Livsey, A. J. "A Further Graying of Network Television." *Media Life Magazine* 15 January 2004. 9 March 2007 <http://www.medialifemagazine.com/news2004/jan04/jan 12/4_thurs/news3thursday.html>.

Lull, James, ed. "Popular Music and Communication: An Introduction. *Popular Music and Communication*. 2nd edition. Newbury Park, CA: Sage, 1992. 1-32.

Mittell, Jason (2003) "Television Talk Shows and Cultural Hierarchies: Audience Talking Genre." *Journal of Popular Film and Television* (Spring 2003). 23 March 2006 <http://findarticles.com/p/articles/mi_m0412/is_1_31/ai_101937867/print>.

Phillips, Amy. "Reminder: Sonic Youth on Gilmore Girls Tonight." *Pitchfork* 9 May 2006. 12 March 2007 <www.pitchforkmedia.com/page/news/35349/Reminder_ Sonic_Youth_on_Gilmore_Girls_Tonight#36349>.

Powrie, Phil and Robynn Jeananne Stilwell, eds. *Changing Tunes: The Use of Pre-existing Music in Film*. Aldershot, England: Ashgate, 2006.

Pribram, Deidre, ed. *Female Spectators: Looking at Film and Television*. London: Verso, 1998.

Radice, Sophie. "Generation Gap? So Not." *Observer* May 30 2004. 6 March 2007 <http://observer.guardian.co.uk/review/story/0,,1227544,00.html>.

Shuker, Roy. "Beyond the 'High Fidelity' Stereotype: Defining the (Contemporary) Record Collector." *Popular Music* Volume 23.3 (2004): 311-30.

Sternbergh, Adam. (2006) "Up with Grups." *New York* 3 April 2006. 24 April 2006 <http://newyorkmetro.com/news/features/16529/>.

Stilwell, Robynn J. "Vinyl Communion: The Record as Ritual Object in Girls' Rites-of-Passage Films." *Changing Tunes: The Use of Pre-existing Music in Film*. Ed. Phil Powrie and Robynn Jeananne Stilwell. Aldershot, England: Ashgate, 2006.152-66.

Storey, John, ed. *Cultural Theory and Popular Culture: A Reader*. London: Harvester Wheatsheaf, 1994.

Straw, Will. "Sizing Up Record Collections: Gender and Connoisseurship in Rock Music Culture." Ed. Sheila Whiteley. *Sexing the Groove: Popular Music and Gender*. London: Routledge, 1997. 3-16.

Whiteley, Sheila, ed. *Sexing the Groove: Popular Music and Gender*. London: Routledge, 1997.

Williams, Christina. "Does It Really Matter? Young People and Popular Music." *Popular Music* 20.2 (May 2001): 223-42.

Like Mother-Daughter, Like Daughter-Mother

Constructs of Motherhood in Three Generations

STACIA M. FLEEGAL

The WB's hit series *Gilmore Girls* is a unique and unconventional case study in women's lives. Fans of the show are undoubtedly drawn in by the witty verbal banter of the main characters and the compelling realism of small town life, but these are hallmarks of most successful sitcoms. What sets *Gilmore Girls* apart from the rest, and what is perhaps the most interesting reward of its analysis, is that the show is based entirely around a world in which women's experiences are at the forefront, and men's lives are secondary, considered only in how they factor into the happenings of the female main characters. Richard Gilmore's business and wealth are in the background of his wife Emily's socialite enterprises; Christopher, Rory's father, lives out of town and plays a minor and erratic role in her life; and Lorelai's relationships with men develop more in scenes in which she and Rory dissect the details of her dates than in time devoted to her actual romantic interactions with Luke, Max, or Chris. The world in *Gilmore Girls* is an inversion of patriarchal society, and Emily, Lorelai, and Rory are its matriarchs.

Nonetheless, the passing of the torch between generations occurs in societies both matriarchal and patriarchal, and in *Gilmore Girls*, viewers see three generations of women living, working, playing, and interacting amongst themselves and others in ways both vastly different and strikingly similar. Traditional roles are challenged, borders are crossed, mothers both bestow and glean wisdom from their daughters in relationships they construct within a matriarchal framework, so that all females, young and old, are essentially mothers in the sense that they impart knowledge back and forth to one another.

143

"No relationship is quite as primal as the one between a mother and her daughter," writes Gina Shaw in "Our Mothers, Ourselves: Mother-Daughter Relationships." Further, Shaw cites Lee Sharkey, director of the Women's Studies program at the University of Maine at Farmington: "It's the original relationship, and it's also a relationship that has been sentimentalized but not honored. Women grow up and our energy is largely turned toward men, but the original love relationship is with the mother." The women of *Gilmore Girls*— those with and without the Gilmore name, but essentially Emily (Kelly Bishop), Lorelai (Lauren Graham), and Rory (Alexis Bledel)—defy this proposed shift in energy from mother to man and, although it is sometimes hard coming, they succeed in honoring the mother-daughter relationship by redirecting all that they've learned back onto their "original love."

Motherhood on TV

In television culture, single mothers have about as much of a chance of being written good, forward-thinking, feminist parts as mothers in Disney movies have of survival. Take, for example, three women-oriented shows airing roughly at the same time as *Gilmore Girls*, and with the same target demographic (women aged, say, 15 to 35), which feature single mothers in one capacity or another: *Friends*, *Sex and the City*, and *Dawson's Creek*.

Rachel, Miranda, and Jen, respectively, give birth out of wedlock and before they are "ready." Rachel and Miranda both become pregnant by men with whom they've been previously involved, so the "young woman in trouble" stigma doesn't apply, especially if you fast-forward to the end of each series, when they both end up partnering with the fathers of their babies. Due to the magic of television, though, the stars of the *Creek* age five years between the last regular episode and the series finale, and Jen's daughter is already a year old. Basically, the whole messy business of her accidental pregnancy (Who is the father? Did she consider abortion?) is whitewashed, and the writers kill Jen off and give her baby to her gay — but partnered — best friend.

The message sent by each of these pop cultural pregnancies is that accidental single motherhood is not marketable. Rachel and Miranda simply must end up with the fathers of their children before their shows end, and while the Creek-watching society may have come far enough as to accept two gay men raising a baby, true "young women in trouble" ending up successful, let alone while remaining single, is still too far-fetched, too taboo.

Gilmore Girls, however, is possibly the first example of a show in which 1) the central character is a single mother who 2) "got into trouble" at age 16 and 3) resisted the pressure to "do the right thing" and marry the father, but 4) had the baby and 5) continued on to be a financially and emotionally self-sufficient woman who succeeds at both her chosen career and motherhood. True, the show starts when Rory is 16, not Lorelai, so the *Gilmore Girls* writers have effectively glossed over the struggles Lorelai underwent to secure her home and keep her daughter fed and clothed, but their innovation in presenting the ultimate success of a "young woman in trouble" is a step in the right direction: truth in presenting the diversity of the family unit, and praise for the strong women who live at the edges of what society deems traditionally proper.

It is important, for the purpose of this article, to draw a distinction between the "young woman in trouble" paradigm and other categories of single mothers. In a lengthy study in *Texas Journal of Women and the Law*, entitled "Single Motherhood by Choice, Libertarian Feminism, and the Uniform Parentage Act," Bernie D. Jones's primary focus is "women who have chosen motherhood when the traditional option of marriage and family seemed impossible," and notes that the social stigma regarding teenage pregnancy that it is "perceived to be the root of welfare dependence." She asserts that "federal and state policies continue to treat single mothers as irresponsible young women on the verge of becoming public charge," and that to the whole of society, "single mothers [lack] the legitimacy of marriage, and their status as mothers [makes] them suspect." Certainly, pop culture reflects these attitudes, but the very premise of *Gilmore Girls* seems to indicate forward progress. Motherhood, femininity, and female-to-female relationships are celebrated while men are distractions, even playthings (think of how much time Lorelai and Rory spend sitting in the diner tormenting Luke). The central relationships on the show are those between the three Gilmore women, and they are walking, talking examples of a humanism which embraces the women society is afraid of (either for their strength or their potential burden as "public charges") and a feminism which promotes the solidarity of female relations— mothers to daughters, and vice versa — and the wisdom born of it.

Emily-Lorelai

The pre-televised summary of the Emily-Lorelai relationship forms the basis for everything that comes after it, and in the spirit of women communing to impart knowledge, it is relevant to consider the findings of a psychological study by Leon Hoffman, published in *Psychoanalytic Inquiry*, entitled "When Daughter Becomes Mother: Inferences from Multiple Dyadic Parent-Child Groups." In this study, Hoffman assembles groups of new mothers to discuss the various people or resources from which they get advice on mothering. In summary, Hoffman declares that while these women gather information from a sort of motherhood network, rooted in oral tradition, of group discussions, parenting books, friends, and doctors, they focus primarily on "what their own mothers tell them" (635). The group leaders impress upon the new mothers the importance of synthesizing information from various sources and understanding that "*they*, as the mothers for *their* babies, are the only ones in a position to make the best decision for themselves, their children, and their families" (636). Lorelai instinctively knew this at age sixteen, when she fled, shortly after giving birth, the control of her overbearing mother.

Of course, the mother-daughter relationship may always be tedious, but Hoffman maintains that "[p]regnancy, and later, the new baby, reawaken or intensify in the new mother her feelings about her own mother." The new mother, he says, "may aspire to be a better mother than her own mother or may fear that she could never be as good a mother as her mother was or is" (630). It seems to hinge on the nature of the original relationship. If a woman had a good relationship with her mother prior to her own pregnancy, she may fear not measuring up, but if not, she may aim to be "better."

In every sense of the word, Lorelai is a born mother: she listens, protects, teaches, and nourishes. Does she do all of these things out of natural motherly instinct, or from a desire to continue her rebellion against her own mother by doing the opposite of what Emily did? Probably both. As Gina Shaw suggests, "the fear of growing up to be like one's mother has long been so common among Western women that it has a name: matrophobia."

The relationship between Emily and Lorelai is tenuous at best. If not for Rory, Lorelai might not speak to her mother, at all; as is, she screens her calls (2.17, "Dead Uncles and Vegetables"). When Lorelai needs a substantial amount of money to pay Rory's tuition at Chilton, the prep school that will help Rory get into Harvard, she swallows her pride, goes against every rule she's ever made for herself about living independent of her parents, and asks them for the money, insisting she'll pay them back. Emily manipulates her into promising the girls will come to dinner every Friday night from then on, thus securing a place not only in Rory's life, but in Lorelai's, as well (1.01, "Pilot"). Lest anyone disbelieve that Emily's intentions are to use Lorelai's financial struggles to gain a foothold in the lives of her daughter and granddaughter, they need only recall when Richard's mother, the original Lorelai, visits to offer Rory a trust fund to pay her tuition, and Emily worries that she'll lose all chances of staying in their lives if they become financially independent of her (1.18, "The Third Lorelai").

For Lorelai, her mother represents not only a *relationship* that is painful and oppressive, but a *lifestyle*. Lorelai loathes the lives of the elite, finding them boring, out of touch, and predictable. Her own life is self-made, not ordained by a group of cultured conservatives, and while it is imperfect and often difficult, she takes great pleasure in having built it on her own terms. Lorelai can have whichever friends she chooses, and certainly the bubbly Sookie, the sarcastic Michel, and the scruffy Luke are not friends Emily would have chosen for her. Her charming and earthly house, her Jeep, her collection of t-shirts with funny and explicit phrases, her love of junk food — are all evidence of Lorelai's personality, a personality she refuses to have stamped out by conforming to the standards of high society.

To Emily, Lorelai is still sixteen years old, frozen in time from the day she separated from her parents, stunted in her maturity by the absence of people who "know what's best for her." Emily sees her daughter as impractical and irresponsible every time Lorelai tries to maintain her independence in the midst of her mother's meddling. When Lorelai's house is infested with termites and she needs $15,000 for repairs to the foundation, she hits every bank in the area with her loan request while Emily sits back and rolls her eyes because she thinks her daughter is willing to jeopardize her home to spare her pride from having to ask for help (2.11, "Secrets and Loans"). In the end, a pained Lorelai accepts a bank's offer to grant her the loan if she gets her mother to cosign. Viewers and Lorelai wait with bated breath for the catch, and after Emily swears up and down that she "just wants to do something nice," Lorelai apologizes just before Emily flippantly adds that she'll now be having her Daughters of the American Revolution (D.A.R.) social meetings at the inn. Ta-da: the catch is another obligation to see her mother, this time at work! Emily's manipulation strikes again.

Overbearing mothers everywhere may say that Emily misses her daughter's presence in her life, that she was cheated out of Lorelai's last two years at home, and therefore has every right to be offended by what she perceives to be Lorelai's malicious bridge-burning. If any of this is true, then, at the very least, Emily is going about renewing a relationship with Lorelai in the wrong way.

There are instances, however, of displays of affection for Lorelai on Emily's part. While Rory is out at a school dance one night, Emily stays in Stars Hollow to watch over Lorelai, who has hurt her back. Doped on painkillers, in and out of consciousness, Lorelai murmurs, "Thank you, Mommy," when Emily drapes a blanket over her (1.09, "Rory's Dance"). Emily is first stunned, then moved when Lorelai drops her guard and allows Emily to take care of her. In one facial expression, we can see that Emily has longed for this moment, that she's missed mothering Lorelai. Similarly, when Emily meets Lorelai's surrogate mother — Mia, the woman who took in Lorelai and an infant Rory at the Independence Inn so many years ago— she manages to put her bitterness aside long enough to ask Mia for pictures of her daughter and granddaughter from a time when she didn't know them (2.08, "The Ins and Outs of Inns"). Hoffman's study verifies the likelihood that "new mothers can be preoccupied with their mothers and can replay their relationship with them transferentially with [people] who become surrogates for their mothers" (629), and Emily resents Mia for it, but not as much as she resents Lorelai.

Most of Emily's desire to mother Lorelai is misdirected, especially when she takes over the planning of Sookie's wedding as if it were her own daughter's (2.17, "Dead Uncles and Vegetables"). Once Lorelai points out what Emily is doing, Emily concedes, divulging her vision for Lorelai's own wedding as Emily always wanted it to be. On the surface, this would seem to be another near-loving moment between Emily and Lorelai ... except that every lavish detail is really just another example of how Emily is completely out of touch with who her daughter is. According to Laura Tracy, whose experience counseling mothers and daughters has led her to write books on the countless complexities of this fundamental relationship, declares that, "Storm clouds in the adult mother-daughter relationship most often arise over one very basic question: Will the mother accept the daughter as an adult?" (qtd. in Shaw). Not only does Emily not accept Lorelai as an adult, she doesn't even seem to see who the adult Lorelai is! It is as if Emily is stuck in a fantasy of what life with a dutiful, obedient daughter would be like, and only within that fantasy can she actually be affectionate with Lorelai.

For every instance of wistful motherly longing on Emily's part, though, there are two more disguised as her lashings out at Lorelai for what she believes are misguided life choices. When Rory is presented to society at a debutante event (which she only did to please her grandmother — more misdirected mothering), Emily and Lorelai are inches from sharing a tender, proud moment together before Emily says, "That should've been you up there. Nothing's turning out the way it's supposed to." A hurt Lorelai walks away feeling like all she's accomplished is negated, and the moment fizzles (2.06, "Presenting Lorelai Gilmore"). Again, when Lorelai is encouraged by Rory's headmaster to become more involved in school events, she joins the Boosters and directs a mother-daughter fashion show, of which she and Emily, in matching outfits, are the undisputed hit. Emily doesn't see that Lorelai moves through these events begrudgingly when she says to her, "Funny, isn't it? How nicely you seem to be fitting into the world you ran away from?" (2.07, "Like Mother, Like Daughter"). To Emily, this is an innocent observation, but to Lorelai, it's a dig, a biting reminder that to her mother, a real Gilmore is a high-class socialite, not an inn-keeper with an associate's degree.

Mostly, Emily's mothering of Lorelai takes a stern middle ground. When Christopher comes to the house during Friday night dinner and upsets Lorelai, Emily orders him out of her house (3.02, "Haunted Leg"), but continues to berate Lorelai's every move, as she does in nearly every episode. Quite simply, Emily doesn't understand Lorelai, and she may never understand her, or even try to, but she will not sever ties, and not just for Rory's sake. She does love her daughter, but, as the saying goes, she has a funny way of showing it.

Lorelai-Rory

To understand the kind of mother Lorelai is to Rory, it is first necessary to show the kind of mother she is not, and why. Emily's treatment of Lorelai is a large factor in Lorelai's mothering decisions; the most important thing to Lorelai is her relationship with Rory, and for the most part, she knows exactly what to do, and what not to do, in order to maintain it.

Lorelai and Rory respect and admire each other, and the lines of communication between the two of them are always open. Rory comes to her mother with problems large and small because Lorelai doesn't judge or belittle her when she makes a mistake. Rory's biggest advocate, in fact, is her mother, and Lorelai's most motherly act is her unconditional, even adamant support of Rory's dream (what Emily, as a mother, couldn't do for her). She knows how special her daughter is and won't tolerate anyone trying to keep her down. "Don't you go doubting who you are or how you should be," she says to Rory after Rory second-guesses herself when a guidance counselor derides her antisocial tendencies. "How dare that woman do this to you!" (2.07, "Like Mother, Like Daughter"). This strong support for her daughter comes in the same episode as the Boosters mother/daughter fashion show, in which Lorelai has the grace to turn from her mother's derision and offer praise and pep talks to her daughter.

Because Rory is "such a good kid," as her mother says, Lorelai is extremely protective of her, body and mind. When Rory calls from the emergency room after a car accident, Lorelai shows up frantic and, on having to ask the ER nurse a second time where Rory is, gives her an earful in a hissy fit worthy of Emily: "Hey, remember in *Terms of Endearment* that scene when Shirley McClaine is in the hospital and freaks out because they won't give her daughter a shot? She got that from me, and she toned it down a little." (2.19, "Teach Me Tonight"). In the same episode, Lorelai exhibits concern when Luke asks Rory if she'll tutor his nephew, Jess—concern not only for Rory becoming involved with a kid as angry and irreverent as Jess, but for the burden on her time, as well. She knows Rory is an inordinate studier, a determined and focused young woman, and she won't jeopardize either Rory's future or the hurt she knows Rory will suffer if she fails to achieve her goals.

Lorelai is not above punishing Rory when she deserves it, though. When Rory and Dean fall asleep and end up staying out all night after a school dance, Lorelai is livid and beside herself with worry (1.09, "Rory's Dance"). Later, as Rory goes back and forth between Dean and Jess and wonders who she should be with, Lorelai flat out tells her that she's treating Dean badly and lectures her on the importance of honesty and not leading him on (3.01, "Those Lazy-Hazy-Crazy Days"). Because Rory isn't a typical kid, even Lorelai is surprised when she acts out of character and messes up, but like a good mother, Lorelai brings her back to the right path by showing Rory where she strayed instead of cutting her down even further, like Emily does with Lorelai.

The main struggle that Lorelai undergoes in mothering Rory is contending with the possibility that, just as Lorelai was the author of her choose-your-own-adventure story, so too must Rory choose her own life — and what if she chooses the life Lorelai rejected? Because the pilot episode deals with Rory's acceptance to Chilton and Lorelai's financial distress, which results in her bridging the estrangement between her and her parents, the entire series is an examination of Rory's introduction into the world Lorelai ran away from.

In the series' third episode (1.03, "Kill Me Now"), Rory is bulldozed by Emily into learning to play golf (as part of her Chilton requirements) from her grandfather, and Lorelai is shaken when her daughter actually enjoys herself in the presence of socialites and money at the country club. The biggest fight that Lorelai and Rory ever have occurs when Rory is more than halfway finished at Yale and decides to quit. Rory walks away from their heated argument and right into Emily's world: she joins the D.A.R., hosts parties, and allows Emily to pick out her clothes, furniture, and friends while Lorelai publicly plans her wedding with Luke and privately sulks over the "loss" of her daughter. It would be pure speculation to suggest that Lorelai knew all along that The Great Divide was temporary and Rory would come back to her, and it would be inaccurate to propose that Lorelai handled the situation perfectly, but what she *did* do was sit back and allow Rory to try on the life of privilege and prestige which she herself balked at, and whether she knew it or not, it was the perfect plan to ensure the continuation, and even the strengthening, of her relationship with Rory, as a mother and a friend. As Tracy stipulates, "The best gift a mother can give a daughter — and, as she becomes an adult, that a daughter can give her mother — is permission to be herself. The daughter can be who she wants to be because the mother is who she wants to be" (qtd. in Shaw).

Rory-Lorelai

The most compelling argument concerning motherhood and *Gilmore Girls*, and all women, concerns the fact that all mothers are also daughters. Emily and Lorelai both mother and are mothered by their daughters. Motherhood can therefore be seen as a construct, and in truth, several constructs of motherhood exist in *Gilmore Girls*. The most notable exchange of mother/daughter roles is evident in the Rory-Lorelai relationship.

With regard once again to The Great Divide between Lorelai and Rory, viewers could see that not only did the situation present a mothering challenge for Lorelai, but it is also a very concrete instance of Rory mothering Lorelai. For example, Lorelai gets a taste of her own medicine when Rory moves into not only her grandparents' home, but into their elite world, as well. Lorelai's complex emotions at the time must include second-guessing her own choice from long ago to take the hard road to autonomy, but Lorelai sticks it out (just as her daughter does thirty miles away, in a life not her own). Remember the second part of Tracy's statement: "The best gift a mother can give a daughter — *and, as she becomes an adult, that a daughter can give her mother* — is permission to be herself" (emphasis added). Rory's actions force Lorelai to "grow up," in the sense of living up to her own measure of success, the one that spurred her rebellion at age sixteen: controlling your own destiny. For all Lorelai's bemoaning of Emily's not respecting her decisions, Lorelai has to step up and walk the walk of her own definition of good mothering when Rory, in a very Lorelai-like act, asserts her independence. When Rory reinforces Lorelai's parental ideology, she gives Lorelai the "gift" Tracy mentions, the gift of validation, which in itself is an instructional and nurturing act — a motherly act.

But The Great Divide is a rare and extreme instance of turmoil between Lorelai and Rory. The roles of mother and daughter between them seem to reverse in day-to-day, conflict-free life, as well. The two are incredibly close and take care of each other quite well in the absence of fathers and husbands. Rory lectures her mother on healthful eating, and even engages Luke, who takes her side against Lorelai and berates the older woman's bad eating habits (3.02, "Haunted Leg"). Even though Lorelai always does the right thing, she often despairs and needs Rory to remind her what that right thing is. She asks Rory for advice about men, and in the same episode in which she lectures Rory about her treatment of Dean, she calls her daughter in the middle of the night to be calmed down after a strange dream (3.01, "Those Lazy-Hazy-Crazy Days"). Rory often serves as the voice of reason for Lorelai, either because she's giving her advice, or because Lorelai is about to do something rash, such as date a Chilton teacher, and then thinks of her daughter and revises her plans.

While Rory's intelligence and talent are quite literally the basis of the show (Chilton, Yale, traveling abroad, the D.C. internship, the newspaper internship, high-profile journalism jobs), Lorelai's own wit and intellect are nothing to scoff at. She is the queen of wit and well-timed quips, sparring with people she knows, like Taylor and Kirk, and ribbing with service industry employees and her mother's endless string of housekeepers. She also single-handedly builds her career, working her way up from maid to manager at the Independence Inn, buying, renovating, and reopening the Dragonfly Inn with Sookie and Michel, and completing her associate's degree in business. Did raising such a precocious daughter spur Lorelai in her various endeavors? If so, we can credit Rory with yet another motherly act: setting an example of the relentless pursuit of one's dreams. How very like each other they are!

Lastly, when Lorelai graduates from business school, the one person she wants to attend the ceremony more than anyone else is Rory. When Rory doesn't show up because she cut school to visit Jess in New York City and doesn't make it back in time, Lorelai doesn't punish her, but is instead hurt at being neglected (2.21, "Lorelai's Graduation Day"). This obvious role reversal is symbolic not only of the flip-flopping of motherhood duties in the relationship between Rory and Lorelai, but of Lorelai's deep-rooted feelings of disregard by her own mother.

Lorelai-Emily

Rory is not the only daughter who sometimes mothers her mother. The reversal of the mother role between Lorelai and Emily is more subtle than between Rory and Lorelai, but it is evident nonetheless. Mostly through exam-ple, Lorelai instructs Emily about what a mother, and even a modern woman, can be (not *should* be). Time and time again, Emily is baffled by Lorelai's choices, but there is a trace of awe in her regard for Lorelai, as well. Juanita Johnson, a therapist in New York City who gives presentations on mother-daughter relationships with her own daughter, says, "One of the things that I observe quite frequently is that the mother knows so very little about her own self that she's placing way too much emphasis on how her daughter turns out rather than, 'What do I know about myself and how do I feel about myself'?" (qtd. in Shaw). Because Lorelai is so close to Rory, it would seem Emily could learn a thing or two about how to "keep" a daughter. Of course, Lorelai could teach her mother all kinds of things, if Emily would only listen — how to treat the maids, for example (Lorelai employs them at the Dragonfly) or how to use a DVD player (3.13, ""Dear Emily and Richard")— but the one thing she is most capable of teaching her, the one thing she won't allow Emily to interfere with, is parenting.

Actual instances of Lorelai mothering Emily are sparse, but I would argue that changes in Emily's attitude towards Lorelai's parenting skills are enough proof that she's seen the benefits of Lorelai's "let your daughter be who she will be" approach. For example, when Rory and Dean stay out all night after the school dance, ends as Lorelai orders Emily out of her house after Emily comes down hard on Lorelai for supposedly being a bad mother (1.09, "Rory's Dance"). She's convinced Rory will follow in her mother's footsteps— pregnant at six-teen, and no chance of going to Harvard — because, to Emily, turning into their mothers is what daughters do. Certainly, the grudge Emily holds against Lore-lai is because she didn't turn into mother's little socialite and thereby live up to the Gilmore name.

Later, though, when the four Gilmores unexpectedly visit the Yale cam-pus (Richard's alma mater), a button on Emily's skirt breaks and she is frantic and annoyed. A resourceful Lorelai takes her into the bathroom and fixes the skirt with a paper clip, something Emily never would have thought of, and the scene is reminiscent of a mother helping a daughter get ready for a dance or job interview, passing on little tricks of the primping trade. The two seem to be getting along well, until the women find out that Richard has set up a sur-prise meeting for Rory with the dean of admissions at Yale, and she freaks because she wasn't prepared for it. Lorelai is incensed; Rory is going to Har-vard! To her, this is another example of how her parents swoop in with their own plans and need to control everyone else while having no respect for the fact that people want different things than the elder Gilmores would have for them. For once, Emily agrees with her, though she doesn't say it out loud, only acts coldly toward Richard when Lorelai stalks off with Rory, the happy mother/daughter moment between the older women ending abruptly (3.08, "Let the Games Begin"). The Emily in season one, who called Lorelai a bad mother, would never have questioned her husband's motives out of respect for Lorelai. Perhaps she is beginning to see that, if you let your daughter grow, if you trust her and build her up instead of cut her down, she'll always want you in her life. Lorelai is teaching, through example, how to be a good mother, though Emily is a slow learner.

Besides fixing the button on her skirt and setting her up with the DVD player, something Emily believes she is too technologically inept to master, the roles memorably reverse in a more recent episode of the show (7.04, "'S Wonderful, 'S Marvelous") in which Emily throws a teenager-like fit when pulled over by a police officer and ends up in jail with no one to call to bail her out but Lorelai. Of course, Lorelai cannot contain her glee as she rides up front with Christopher while a sulking Emily rolls her eyes from the backseat. Rarely does she get an opportunity to sit in judgment of her mother's irresponsibility, like a mother over a naughty child.

A more touching Lorelai-mothering-Emily moment comes when a perceptive Lorelai pays an unexpected visit to her mother after she notices tension between Richard and Emily, especially when it escalates to a screaming match in front of all of their friends at Rory's debut. Emily's face — shock, then satisfaction — conveys what the audience knows; Lorelai must be truly worried about her mother to make an unsolicited visit. She assures Emily that she has no ulterior motive (of course, the manipulative Emily would think that way), just wants to "hang out," and that if Emily wants to talk about anything, now or ever, Lorelai will listen. Emily smiles, and the two sit in an atypically comfortable silence as Emily continues clipping daffodils in the garden; to her, Lorelai is being a dutiful daughter. Lorelai's act, though, is a motherly one (2.06, "Presenting Lorelai Gilmore"). She witnessed how her father treated Emily at the debut (and later reminded Rory how lucky she was that she always had someone to talk to). After removing herself from a lifestyle that often results in feelings of neglect in wives whose husbands build empires while they have nothing to do but plan parties, Lorelai returns to rescue her mother from those feelings, to protect her from that loneliness.

Rory-Emily

Just as most of Lorelai's mothering of her mother occurs by example, so does Rory's "mothering" of her grandmother. Purely didactic, Rory is a walking, talking result of effective parenting. Despite the fact that Emily often tries to "re-mother" Rory as she never got to with Lorelai (more on this later), her treatment of Rory is far more pleasant than her treatment of Lorelai. Emily may take advantage of Rory's eager-to-please demeanor by getting her to do things she might not normally do, like go golfing with her grandfather (1.03, "Kill Me Now") or attending a debutante ball (2.06, "Presenting Lorelai

Gilmore"), but through season five, she is usually supportive of Rory's dreams and desires—a stark contrast to her rampant disapproval of Lorelai's choices.

The exact moment when Emily becomes unsupportive of Rory's desires coincides with the moment that she becomes aware that she has taken advantage of Rory's vulnerability (upon leaving Yale and The Great Divide with her mother) and turned her into a younger version of herself, a surrogate daughter. Earlier episodes foreshadow this development, such as Rory's debut, at which Emily says to Lorelai, "That should've been you up there," or the portrait she has Rory sit for (2.08, "The Ins and Outs of Inns"), which is just like the one Lorelai didn't have the patience for. The Emily who fantasizes about getting a second chance at parenting, whether consciously or unconsciously, comes crashing back to reality when she realizes Rory is having sex with her boyfriend, Logan. For any parent, such a discovery is a turning point, a catalyst to the understanding that one's child is no longer *a child*. For Emily Gilmore, such a discovery plunges her into the fear that Rory will repeat Lorelai's heinous (in her opinion) mistakes, though it is her husband who voices such concerns: "We've failed." Emily, ever staunch, ever insistent that she have her way or else, responds, "We have not failed until that girl comes home pregnant, *then* we've failed!" Of course, she says this in Lorelai's presence (6.07, "Twenty-One Is the Loneliest Number"). Lest anyone believe Emily is acting well within her rights as an overprotective grandmother, they should recall the argument that took place when the tension between Rory and Emily finally comes to a head and Rory begins defending herself in a vocally abrasive manner, to which Emily spouts that she'll be in trouble "when [her] father gets home!" A stunned Rory takes a moment to respond, "You mean my grandfather" (6.08, "Let Me Hear You Roar"). Even the poised Emily can't recover from such a blatant Freudian slip.

Emily's desire to make Rory her surrogate daughter evinces two significant things. First, we can see that she feels cheated out of motherhood; Lorelai, her only child, ran away at sixteen, and even though the relationship between the two has been patched up somewhat, the old wounds are still there, and Lorelai is adamant about not letting Emily mother her. Second, it is clear that Emily has not yet completely internalized Lorelai's example of motherhood. She is the same mother to Rory that she was to her true daughter. That Emily is trying to validate her own life — the one she feels Lorelai, by rejecting it, deems shallow and meaningless— by trying to turn someone else into her is a distinct possibility. Just before the episode in which Rory asserts her independence from Emily and high society, Richard says to Emily that he wants more for Rory than a life of gossip and party-planning, and Emily is hurt when she realizes he doesn't want Rory to be like her.

The truth is, Emily is great at what she does, and there's nothing wrong with her lifestyle if it's what she chooses for herself. Lorelai knew the value of choice, and she waited for Rory to realize it, too. For Emily, the sting of making Rory her surrogate daughter and then "failing" for a second time to clone her after a D.A.R. socialite might be just enough to teach Emily once and for all that you can't control other people's lives. It is the job of a mother, or mothers, to teach such hard lessons, and Lorelai and Rory both take up the task of showing Emily that every woman is capable of walking a different path, and that success is relative to whichever path she chooses.

There seems to be a cyclic quality to the mothering that goes on between three generations of the Gilmore women. First, Emily mothers Lorelai "wrongly." Lorelai then rebels and mothers Rory in the opposite way. Rory internalizes from her mother (directly) and her grandmother (indirectly) about how and how not to mother and then mothers back to Lorelai in their co-dependent relationship, and to Emily as an example of how a daughter can turn out if you mother her "correctly" (Of course, mothering "wrongly" and "correctly" are relative terms; for the purpose of this article, again, I mean mothering as nurturing and teaching.). Throughout all of this, Lorelai acts as a sort of telescope through which one set of mothering ideals are passed and reflected (as opposites) to Rory, who interprets and passes them back through Lorelai to Emily. Lorelai is, therefore, both a creator of and a conduit or a sounding board for various constructs of motherhood, those both in the traditional (biological mother to daughter) and nontraditional (daughter assumes mother role) sense.

Surrogates, Other Mothers of Stars Hollow, and the Finale

The three Gilmore women share many qualities. They are all witty and talkative, neurotic, and easily excited. All are detail-oriented and want things done a certain way. It is no surprise that, out of three such stubborn and distinctive personalities, many complex constructs of motherhood would emerge.

But there are other female figures on the series whose mothering tactics are just as noteworthy. Paris seems eager to take on the surrogate daughter role when, shocked after The Great Divide and the apparent dissolution of a mother-daughter relationship she always admired and even coveted, she adopts Lorelai as her mother. Paris seems to be saying to Rory, I'll take her if you don't want her! She visits Lorelai at the Dragonfly, and they exchange cell phone numbers and begin having regular lunches. Of course, Paris' abrasive personality has always been more than Lorelai, or anyone, can take, and their intimacy doesn't last, but it is nonetheless another example of surrogacy.

An interesting development on the show is the introduction of Luke's daughter, April, which happens to occur in the same episode in which Rory returns to Lorelai after The Great Divide. Anna, April's mother, is a lot like Lorelai in the sense that she chose single motherhood rather than pressuring the father to step up to the plate ... or even telling him about April, at all. It is the young girl, in fact, who approaches her father first, and the ever-moral and dependable Luke does indeed step up, but he is yet another parent who doesn't want help; he keeps his relationships with Lorelai and April separate until the night April hosts a party at Luke's and he seeks Lorelai and her rapport with adolescent girls when the party starts to fail. When Anna finds out that Lorelai has interacted with April, she's livid. Anna won't let Lorelai be a surrogate mother to April, even knowing that her pending marriage to Luke will make her April's stepmother. Just as Rory and Lorelai show Emily how to lighten up, though, April's immediate attachment to Luke alleviates Anna's strict, over-protective manner.

Poor Lorelai; she tries to spread her successful mothering views and gets shut down, next by Christopher, who has a daughter, Gigi, with his girlfriend, Sherry. First, Lorelai must watch the pregnant Sherry get all the doting father-to-be attention she never got from Christopher. Then Lorelai baby-sits Gigi and is appalled at behavior she, as a mother, would never have tolerated, but is completely rebuffed by Christopher when she mentions how spoiled Gigi is; Christopher is another stubbornly self-reliant parent. When Sherry abandons both Gigi and Christopher, Lorelai becomes a kind of surrogate (again!) for Gigi when she and Christopher briefly reconcile, but the look on her face when Gigi screams her refusal to clean up her scribbles on Lorelai's hardwood floors is pure dismay (6.16, "Bridesmaid Revisited"). To anyone who believes Lorelai to be too lenient, too much of a best friend-type, to Rory, it should be obvious that Lorelai knows a good mother (i.e., one who knows when to play disciplinarian) will only ever have to endure one bad temper tantrum.

Abominable behavior abounds across town, though, in the House of Kim ... if purple hair dye, punk rock records, drum sets, missed prayer time, and dates with non–Korean boys are to be considered abominable. Certainly, Mrs. Kim would say so. The relationship between Lane Kim and her mother is one of two completely opposite lives converging at prayer circles and dinner tables, after Lane rushes home from band practice, ripping off sweatshirts with band names to reveal t-shirts sporting religious edicts underneath. Needless to say, the two women do not understand each other during early episodes.

The first truly touching moment between Lane and her mother two comes after Zack and Lane break up and Lane moves back home. Lane's extensive mourning period leads Mrs. Kim to do something drastic; she draws all the window-shades and pours them both a stiff drink. "Lane, it's been six weeks since you've come home," she says firmly, but softly. "You've grieved, and now we move on" (6.11, "The Perfect Dress"). Their relationship becomes much more mutually deferential at that point, so much so that when Zack and Lane finally reconcile, Mrs. Kim not only gives them permission to marry (a non–Korean guitar player who doesn't go to church!), but takes on a motherly sympathy and concern for Zack, as well. Just as Lorelai and Rory teach Emily through example that not all women must turn out exactly like their mothers, so does Lane show her mother that a life of rock and roll and loving a blonde-haired boy isn't a one-way ticket to eternal damnation.

This pattern of the younger generation reflecting their enlightened ideals about female diversity back onto the older generation plays out in nearly every mother-daughter relationship on the show, but it is perhaps no more clear than in the series finale, when the young women sit down to say goodbye after Rory lands an exciting job as a traveling correspondent for the Barack Obama presidential campaign. They are two 22-year-olds; one is a married mother of two who plays drums in a rock band and lives in her hometown, the other is a Yale graduate who just turned down a marriage proposal to travel the world and pursue her own passions. Their differences do not divide them, but foster respect for lives they don't lead or even necessarily understand.

The whole town of Stars Hollow has learned the lesson of respecting diversity from Lorelai and Rory. At first, they're shocked at Rory is leaving, but quickly congregate to throw her a surprise going-away party. We know life will go on in Stars Hollow much the same as it always has once she's gone, but all are inspired by having known the Gilmore Girls.

Even the elder Gilmores know it when they arrive at the party, although Richard is the only one who can swallow his pride to relay it: "I think this party is a testament to you, Lorelai, and the home you've created here.... It takes a remarkable person to inspire all of this" (7.22, "Bon Voyage"). And Emily doesn't refute it. She and her daughter are still more alike than they care to admit: both distract themselves with mundane details to keep from falling apart over Rory's departure. When Emily once more throws money at Lorelai (this time to update the Dragonfly with day spa amenities), Lorelai deciphers the code and assures her mother she'll still be attending Friday night dinners. Emily even musters the emotion to say to Rory, "It's an honor to be your grandmother." Surely, this is veiled praise for Lorelai's mothering.

Rory, who is never without such praise, offers it a final time in a speech to the entire town: "To my mom, who is just everything to me, and everything I am." And Rory *is* the living embodiment of Lorelai's strength and conviction, the product of her adamant self-reliance. Later, when Lorelai continues her distracted chatter in the form of last-minute advice about Rory's travels, Rory thanks her again: "You've given me everything I need" (7.22, "Bon Voyage").

What other validation does a mother need?

Works Cited

Gilmore Girls. 2007. <http://www.gilmoregirls.org>.

Hoffman, Leon. "When Daughter Becomes Mother: Inferences from Multiple Dyadic Parent-Child Groups." *Psychoanalytic Inquiry* 24.1 (Nov. 2004): 629–56.

Jones, Bernie D. "Single Motherhood by Choice: Libertarian Feminism and the Uniform Parentage Act." *Texas Journal of Women and the Law* 12.2 (Spring 2003): 419–49.

Shaw, Gina. "Our Mothers, Ourselves: Mother-Daughter Relationships." *Discovery Health* 2007. <http://health.discovery.com/centers/womens/daughter/daughter_print.html>.

Gender Lies in Stars Hollow

Brenda Boyle and Olivia Combe

It was about two years ago that Brenda's college-aged son (and Olivia's brother) subtly made *Gilmore Girls* a part of our family's weekly viewing habits. All five of us were entranced and amused by the quirky storyline, the rapid-fire delivery of lines, and Stars Hollow, which seemed so much like our own precious small town in the heart of Ohio. We could lose ourselves in that TV world, simultaneously feeling closely at home as we identified with all three Gilmore "girls"—Emily (Kelly Bishop), Lorelai (Lauren Graham), and Rory (Alexis Bledel)—and also distantly envious of the apparent charm of their lives. In becoming fans we longed for the reality of those lives, unconsciously recreating the (simulacra of the) warmth of their friendships and family as we sat together in front of the television set. No, we didn't want them to be real—we wanted their lives to be ours.

Gilmore Girls is the first television series "to make it to air supported by the Family Friendly Forum's script development fund" since "[t]he strong and loving mother-daughter relationship portrayed in *Gilmore Girls* reflects the growing reality of this new type of American family" ("Warner Brothers"). Our family's reaction is likely what the Family Friendly Programming Forum hopes for, as, in supporting the production of *Gilmore Girls*, it promotes "family friendly programming appropriate in theme, content and language for adults and children. It has cross-generational appeal, depicts real life and resolves issues responsibly" ("Family Friendly"). The trouble with this rhetoric, of course, is that it is subject to interpretation. What or who, for instance, determines what is "appropriate," the reality of "real" life, or the responsibility of "resolv[ing] issues responsibly"? This language alerts us to the agenda pursued by the show and its Family Friendly Forum support, and we have become attuned to what gender scholar R. W. Connell terms the "social effort to channel people's [sex role] behavior" (*Gender* 4) since "[g]ender difference is not something that simply exists; it is something that happens and must be made to happen" (*Gender* 14). What, in short, is *Gilmore Girls* advocating about the lives women can live now?

In the ensuing life of our fan-aticism, we have begun to think less long-ingly and more critically about the show. This alteration is especially in terms of the men with whom the two younger "girls," Lorelai and Rory, find them-selves or choose to be involved, and is most marked in another mother–daugh-ter pair from this Ohio family: Brenda, a gender scholar and the mother, and Olivia, a keen student and oldest daughter, readying herself to go to college. While our mother-daughter relationship is unlike Lorelai's and Rory's in that we are much further apart in age and Brenda is a generation older than Lore-lai, we believe our varying mother-daughter insights on what stories about gender the show attempts to tell can partly explain the appeal of *Gilmore Girls* to its American audience. What we find is, though the show purportedly is pro-gressive and campaigns for non–traditional relationships of all kinds, it nonetheless remains within the "appropriate" and strict confines of traditional gender dichotomy. Thus, a significant portion of the lives Lorelai and Rory lead is spent in preoccupation with men. What is surprising, however, is that while the conventional heterosexual mode pairs a masculine man with a feminine woman, this mother-daughter team represents their own dichotomous pair. They signify the perfect balance of opposites so idealized in traditional gender roles, with Lorelai performing the masculine role and Rory performing the feminine one. Thus, to maintain the illusion of bodily dichotomy, the women choose men, but to maintain gender dichotomy, Lorelai seeks feminine men and Rory seeks masculine ones.

Brenda argues that, while Lorelai's relationships might be interpreted as manifesting the freedoms that mature women now enjoy — they can speak about and act freely on their sexual desires, they can be fun and smart and articulate (without college), they can be attractive but not base their identities largely or solely on their appearances— the men with whom she involves herself are choices that do not endanger those freedoms. Though Max, Jason, and Luke may be regarded as intelligent rebounds from the erroneous choice Lorelai made when she was involved with Christopher in high school, thereby produc-ing Rory at the age of sixteen, Brenda sees all of them ultimately as ones who embody feminine traits that don't challenge masculine Lorelai. Contrarily, Olivia sees Rory as the more feminine of the mother-daughter pair, who lives vicariously through her super–masculine boyfriends. Though Dean initially is represented as a masculine rebel without a cause and Lorelai complains to Rory that he is so like Christopher, as Dean becomes more steadfast and predictable, he also becomes feminine, inadequate, then, as the necessary complement to Rory's femininity. Thus, Rory pursues a new rebel, Jess, who is unlike Dean in his dangerous unpredictability. Jess's disappearance and the distance evoked by college maturation make Logan, a smart but irresponsible and reckless son of a media mogul, look to Rory as the natural complement to her play-by-the-rules feminine propriety.

Traditional gender roles are by their nature reductive and bounded.

Nonetheless, it is important to estimate what they are so we can evaluate their consistency with Lorelai's and Rory's behaviors. To be masculine, then, is to be independent, dominant, intelligent, aggressive, forceful, competitive and often dangerous. To be feminine is to be dependent, submissive, nurturing/ collaborative, emotional, and selfless. Using these templates, we might argue that Lorelai is the aggressive, independent one and Rory is the collaborator of the mother-daughter pair. While their places in traditional dichotomous pairing is an important parallel to draw, though, we are also operating in our analyses under the influences of several theorists of sexuality and gender, discussed below, that complicate and even dismantle certain conceptions of gender.

Michel Foucault's *The History of Sexuality: Volume 1, An Introduction* (1978), has been instrumental in the development of gender theories. Foucault disrupts notions of history as stable and recordable as behavior, noting that history actually is a record of discourses, or the stories we tell about events. Moreover, contrary to the notion that social mores govern by limiting speech, Foucault asserts that societies govern more effectively when they multiply discourses, thereby normalizing what might have been seen as taboo. Foucault claims that, rather than modern Western society repressing discussions of sex as a way of governing it, the multiplication of discourses concerning sexuality govern that sexuality more effectively. As the discourse of "sex" is integrated into mainstream society, it is thus normalized and controlled. This control that Foucault describes indicates the relationship between truth and power, that truth is not an outcome but a determinant of power:

> This was the purpose for which the deployment of sexuality was first established, as a new distribution of pleasures, discourses, truths, and powers; it has to be seen as the self–affirmation of one class rather than the enslavement of another: a defense, a protection, a strengthening, and an exaltation that were eventually extended to others— at the cost of different transformations— as a means of social control and political subjugation [123].

Foucault helps us comprehend that assigning meaning to bodies through gender is an exercise in power, not "truth." This understanding makes it possible to see the two women, Lorelai and Rory, as opposites in a dichotomous pair, as we do not have to accept the "truth" that equates bodies and apparent physiology to gender behavior. Moreover, with Foucault's idea about discourse multiplication, we can see the normalizing effects of *Gilmore Girls* on the necessary "truth" of gender dichotomy.

Another writer whose ideas have been central to the development of gender theories is Judith Butler. In the Preface to the 1999 edition of *Gender Trouble*, Butler explains that "The view that gender is performative sought to show [in the original 1990 edition] that what we take to be an internal essence of gender is manufactured through a sustained set of acts, posited through the gendered stylization of the body" (xv). She further clarifies that with "what we take to be 'real,' what we invoke as the naturalized knowledge of gender is, in fact, a changeable and revisable reality" (xxiii). Thus, since the apparent biology of their bodies does not dictate their gender behaviors, what Lorelai, Rory and all of their mates do is *perform* gender, perhaps gender recognizable to and expected by the viewing audience. Neither Lorelai nor Rory essentially are masculine and feminine, but they perform their roles as parts of a pair required to be opposites by the "revisable reality" of the twenty-first century. While demonstrating the instability and consequent mutability of gender, Butler also emphasizes that gender as performance is rarely about consciously *choosing* gender, in the way one chooses a set of clothing to wear for the day; instead, gender is produced on and through subjects so that it is naturalized, both externally and psychically. To understand that Lorelai and Rory perform their genders in the way Butler describes, we must realize they each have internalized the form of gender suitable to the circumstances of their non–traditional family; they have not chosen their scripts from their "wardrobes" of gender identities nor does their choice extend in that direction. Instead, the viewing public and the mother and daughter both have internalized traditional gender roles and less conventional ones, choosing from them to accord with the American ethos of "appropriateness" and "reality." What seems to be appropriate in this case is a dichotomous pair, even one of two females.

In its current popular usage, "gender" is synonymous with the biology of the body; "gender" is used on employment applications to indicate whether one is male or female, when the biological term would be "sex." Robert Connell objects to this conflation of terms, arguing that to conjoin sex and gender is biologically essentialist, equating males to masculinity and females to femininity, and that "we must acknowledge that sometimes masculine conduct or masculine identity goes together with a female body" (*The Men and the Boys* 16). He further asserts that gender is a social practice that is related to the materiality of human bodies, but is not constituted by those bodies: "Masculinity *refers* to male bodies (sometimes directly, sometimes symbolically and indirectly), but it is not *determined* by male biology. It is, thus, perfectly logical to talk about masculine women or masculinity in women's lives, as well as masculinity in men's lives" (29).

The instability of gender might even be more apparent when it is performed by a body not traditionally expected to enact it, like masculinity in stylish and womanly Lorelai. In *Female Masculinity* (1998) Judith Halberstam argues that masculinity is most discernible when it is performed by female bodies. Her study examines drag kings, "tomboys," and butches in fiction and film, suggesting that these representations of masculinity in female bodies denaturalize the association between male bodies and masculinity. Moreover, she insists that "dominant masculinity" is identified — but illegible — in the white male body: "Masculinity ... becomes legible as masculinity where and when it leaves the white male middle-class body" (2). She further argues that while most studies claiming to de-center the white male body do that, she intends to examine the way "the shapes and forms of modern masculinity are best showcased within female masculinity" (3). Thus, in the New England Stars Hollow environment that celebrates tradition and heritage, binary opposites are still the rule of the day. Paradoxically, it also is a town that harbors few, if any, stereotypical heterosexual family units (and no overtly homosexual ones), thereby suggesting that traditional gender roles do not prevail. In this world, then, women ostensibly can safely enact any gender; the catch is that their partners had better be gender opposites.

Early in the series, Lorelai and Rory do not appear to be opposites; they even have matching names. The opening season argues that these two women are alike, if not identical. In the "Pilot" episode (1.01), when Rory meets Dean and then decides she does not, after all, want to go to Chilton, Lorelai remarks: "This is about a boy. Of course. After all, you're me... Someone willing to throw important life experiences out the window to be with a guy." Later at the diner, Luke exhorts Rory not to drink so much coffee since she will grow up to be like her mother. "Sorry, too late," Rory grinningly answers, proud of her similarity to her mother. While subsequent seasons occasionally draw these parallels between the two women — such as when Lorelai applies to them the names "ElectraWoman" and "DynaGirl" (2.03, "Red Light on the Wedding Night") — the episodes more often call attention to Lorelai's and Rory's differences, differences that can be attributable to gender behavior. As soon as the second season's debutante ball, Lorelai recognizes how Rory's desires track away from hers: "This [debutante ritual] is all the stuff I ran away from and I assumed you'd be running with me" (2.06, "Presenting Lorelai Gilmore"). Moreover, satirizes Lorelai, to be the lady a debutante must be, she must be entirely helpless, implying Lorelai would never deign to be the lady to which Rory aspires. By the end of season four when Rory sleeps with married Dean, Lorelai openly disapproves of Rory's decision, calling attention to how different these two females are.

Despite their apparent similarities and subtle differences, the two females live together happily enough. That they are able to coexist, we contend, is because they are gender opposites. What makes their gender opposition apparent, though, is in their couplings with men. While there are patent signs of Lorelai's masculinity — she drives a Jeep, she demands independence from her parents and Christopher at an early age, she works at the Independence Inn — the more subtle indicators are the genders of her men. The twenty-first century discourse of pairing normalizes, if not physiological opposition, gender opposition. Lorelai is masculine in her relationship with feminine Rory, and because dichotomy is traditionally required, she must seek opposites in the men with whom she is involved. To explore that discourse, Brenda examines four men in Lorelai's life: Max, Jason, Christopher, and Luke, followed by Olivia's analysis of Rory's three men, Dean, Jess, and Logan.

Brenda's Analysis of Lorelai

Max begins as a suitable mate to Lorelai's masculine gender, but his attempts to assert his dominance ultimately foil their partnership. Max is featured in season one, when Lorelai meets him through Rory at Chilton, and season two when they date and then become engaged. That Max is a teacher of literature and not math or even history already feminizes him. Once they've stopped seeing one another out of Lorelai's fear of how her dating a Chilton teacher affects Rory (2.11, "Secrets and Loans"), it is Lorelai who is in control as she initiates the resumption of their affair (2.17, "Dead Uncles and Vegetables"). At this point Max is satisfied with their gender arrangements, that Lorelai is dominant and in control. As soon as another male — Luke — vies for Lorelai's attention, however, Max behaves as though wakened from a dream; it is his traditional gender role as a masculine man to provide for the dependent and feminine woman. In "Love, Daisies, and Troubadours" (1.21), the three of them coincidentally meet at Lorelai's house, as Luke has come to retrieve his large toolbox — a quintessential sign of phallic masculinity — and Max has arrived to go on a date with Lorelai. Luke delays Max and Lorelai's departure with his dogged insistence that Lorelai depends on him for his handy-man abilities. Unable to match Luke's useful, manly skills, Max can only boast that he is the one dating Lorelai and belittle Luke's feminine provision of coffee to her. Luke counters with his reminder to Max that he is not an infrequent dater but a constant presence in Lorelai's life. As the verbal duel between the men concludes, Lorelai responds to Max's urging that they leave, "Uh, yeah. Just wanted to make sure you two were through swinging those things around. Someone's bound to lose an eye." His obtuse reply, "What are you talking about?" leads to Lorelai's exasperated, "Nothing. I'll get my purse."

There are several interesting elements in this scene. First, Max is challenged to be masculine only in the presence of another man, one who both fulfills the traditional gender role of a man as "handy" and carries a large toolbox, and also who domesticatedly provides the coffee that is Lorelai's lifeblood. Second, Max is aware of and accepts the challenge, but can only try to minimize the importance to Luke of his role in Lorelai's life; the ability to decipher literature appears not to be a sustaining provision Max can offer to Lorelai. Third, Lorelai also recognizes the skirmish in which the two men engage as one less over her attention than over the men's masculinity; she is the venue only for their "swinging those things around." In short, though Max attempts to assert a masculinity against Luke, it does not affect Lorelai's because she identifies the behaviors of both men as performances.

Lorelai contributes to her dominance over Max in her comment in season two's "Hammers and Veils" (2.02): "In this town [Stars Hollow] I am the queen. You are simply my jester." Nonetheless, in the third episode, "Red Light on the Wedding Night" (2.03), Max's attempts to usurp Lorelai's dominance result in her calling off the wedding. Though Max still shows evidence of his femininity—Luke teases him about his brown sweater but Max doesn't identify the compliment as a tease; Lorelai has to order Max to go to a strip club, as she has done—Max's demand that he have keys to Lorelai's home and that he have rights to discipline Rory are what persuade Lorelai that she should not marry him. So, when Lorelai explains to Rory during their road trip that she didn't want to marry Max "[b]ecause I didn't want to try on my wedding dress every night" as her mother had, Lorelai is equating the wedding dress with submission and dependence, both qualities of a femininity to which she will not succumb.

As the feminine opposite to Lorelai, Christopher is more problematic, especially since in season seven, Lorelai marries him. Early in the series, though, Christopher appears as a viable replacement for Max when he appears in "Presenting Lorelai Gilmore" (2.06). He arrives in a staid Volvo sedan, not the more dangerous motorcycle he'd previously been driving in season one (1.14, "That Damn Donna Reed"), and he appreciates the stability of his nine-to-five job. These elements appear to have feminized Christopher, which makes him more appealing to Lorelai. She seems conflicted about the gender implications of Christopher's changes, though, since she interprets his Volvo positively as "conservative on the outside, bad [meaning masculine] on the inside." Her attraction is moot, of course, since Christopher is involved with another woman, but later in the season they get together when this other relationship is failing. At that point, Lorelai says about Christopher, "Bossy ... and I like it" (1.22, "I Can't Get Started"). They are compatible for just a short period before Christopher opts to resume his relationship with the now-pregnant Sherry so that he can be the sensitive, attentive father he never was with Rory. As Lorelai explains to Luke when she is mourning losing Christopher, she is conflicted about her own gender performance interfering with her relationships with men: "I fancy myself Wonder Woman. [But] I really want the whole package [of love, comfort, and safety]" (3.01, "Lazy-Hazy-Crazy Days"). Christopher, then, in his new second season persona is a conundrum because he is performing both masculinity and femininity, "conservative on the outside, bad on the inside." Notably, Christopher is the only one of Lorelai's beaus who leaves her, taking from her her dominance and independence. That Christopher manages to compromise Lorelai's independence/masculinity is especially telling when they marry in season seven. Though he convinces her to elope when they deliver Christopher's daughter to her mother in Paris, Lorelai has not yet seemed fully persuaded that it was the right thing to do. All signs mid–way through the season pointed to Lorelai's reestablishing her dominance in the relationship, as she refuses to say vows with Christopher at the wedding party her mother was planning (7.10, "Merry Fisticuffs") and elects to remain in her home in Stars Hollow, a place where Christopher is feminized as the source of his power/masculinity, money, has little effect (7.09, "Knit, People, Knit"). Lorelai's separating from

Christopher in Episode 14, "Farewell My Pet" (7.14) reasserts her masculinity, her commitment to Stars Hollow, and her resurgent interest in Luke.

Like Christopher, Jason also relies on material wealth to perform masculinity and that reliance, too, ultimately is the downfall of their relationship. Though Lorelai confesses to Rory that Jason is "completely not my type," suggesting he is not complementary to her masculinity, she also admires Jason's masculine ability to manipulate other people, to, as he puts it, talk "other people into doing things they don't want to do" (4.09, "Ted Koppel's Big Night Out"). Her admiration extends especially to his manipulating her mother into inviting him to dinner (4.08, "Die, Jerk"). Jason is, to a great extent, performing masculinity as he drives a muscular Mercedes coupe and maintains an independent household. Those very signs of masculinity, though, cripple Jason and enable Lorelai's dominance; his car is inadequate to hauling the furniture he and Lorelai purchase, so she drives her Jeep (4.12, "A Family Matter"), and his living alone makes it impossible for him to sleep in the same bed with anyone (4.10, "The Nanny and the Professor"). In fact, Jason seems to be afraid of being found unmasculine, as apparent in the message he leaves on Lorelai's answering machine when she's been refusing to date him: "A better man, a smarter man, a different man would have gotten a clue," that clue being Lorelai does not go out with "the type" who performs masculinity (4.09, "Ted Koppel's Big Night Out"). Jason relies especially on his father for verification of his performance of masculinity. Only after his father opts to sue Jason and Richard Gilmore does Jason believe his father sees him as masculine: "In a weird way, my father trying to destroy me is the first time I've ever gotten any real respect out of him" (4.18, "Tick, Tick, Tick, Boom!").

Even before Jason's realization about the tenuousness of his gender disposition, Lorelai is not relinquishing hers. Not only do they take her car to go furniture shopping, but she drives. She is the one to sleep in, bathe, and come downstairs to a meal prepared by Jason. At her parents' home for dinner with Jason and his parents, Lorelai accepts Richard's invitation to a very masculine pursuit, smoking cigars in the study (4.18). "All right! Let's fire 'em up!" Lorelai declares, her father responding, "I meant the men, but would you like a cigar?" "No," Lorelai replies, "you guys go, circle the fire, pound your chests." Though Lorelai is joking, there is as much sincerity in her *Iron John* allusion as there is in her remark to Max about "swinging those things around" in the later part of season one. Lorelai recognizes the performance of masculinity being enacted, though she does not anticipate what is to come: Jason's father, Floyd, sues, Jason and Richard countersue, and in the resolution reached by Richard and Floyd, Jason loses his business. His efforts to regain his masculine stature in the world of business lead him to sue Richard Gilmore and to Lorelai's subsequently breaking up with him. While his other attempts to perform masculinity seemed harmless to Lorelai's, this one appears to be her breaking point.

Oddly, it is Luke's feminine insistence on selflessly parenting April, his newfound daughter, that leads to the demise of his and Lorelai's engagement, as his feminine need to nurture April conflicts with his feminine need to complement Lorelai. Early in the series when Luke and Lorelai are not involved, he strikes the perfect balance of masculine and feminine: he is independent and a force to be reckoned with in town politics and in opposition to Max, but he also selflessly nurtures by helping Lorelai and running the diner. Admittedly, it is Luke who initiates their relationship at the end of season four. One particular instance of their alternating performing genders is when Luke and Lorelai go on their first official date (5.03, "Written in the Stars"). Not only do they leave Stars Hollow, Lorelai's masculine domain, but also Luke reveals a secret part of his life, a restaurant where he usually goes three times a week. He also reveals that, unlike Lorelai, he remembers the exact date of their first meeting eight years earlier and even kept in his wallet the horoscope she'd written on then. His attention to the details of their relationship is what characterizes this behavior as feminine: emotional, selfless, and submissive. Later back in Stars Hollow, after they've spent the night together, Lorelai descends to the diner to get coffee, clad only in Luke's flannel shirt, a costume signifying her masculinity (flannel being Luke's trademark) and her femininity (with bare, vulnerable legs).

The best representation of their trading genders, though, is when Lorelai proposes to Luke (6.01, "A House Is Not a Home"). Lorelai assumes the masculine male role of proposing, but she also plays the giddy and emotional feminine role of wanting to mark the occasion officially: "We should do something official ... to commemorate the moment." After all, she quips, "Luke table-for-one Danes and Lorelai I'm-sorry-I-need-a-forklift-for-my-emotional-baggage Gilmore" are getting married. As they search for something with which to toast the occasion, Lorelai continues performing femininity and Luke does masculinity, remaining calm and rational in the face of Lorelai's overexcitement. Luke emphasizes his masculinity when they finally find an alcoholic beverage suitable to the occasion and he disdains it, saying "Men aren't supposed to drink Zima" because "it's chick beer." Later, however, after they've consummated their engagement and Lorelai is drifting off to sleep, Luke assumes the feminine role of wanting to discuss domestic issues, like having children and buying a home. Thus, despite the community's skepticism about the actual proposal — Babette and Miss Patty assume Luke has proposed to Lorelai and Kirk challenges Luke to buy the ring instead of Lorelai — Lorelai and Luke manage to find a complementary balance and sharing of gender roles that makes their relationship possible.

This sharing comes to a halt, though, when Lorelai asserts her uncompromising dominance and presents Luke with an ultimatum: marry me now or call off the engagement (6.22, "Partings"). While Lorelai is femininely emotional in the delivery of her challenge and Luke is masculinely rational when he answers that he needs to think about marrying, Lorelai is the one who wishes to act on her own desires and Luke wants to remain subject to his developing relationship with his daughter, April. This absolute demand and absolute refusal, then, cements Lorelai into her masculine and Luke into his feminine positions, thereby ending the possibility of their compromising on gender and, subsequently, their relationship.

Olivia's Analysis of Rory

My brother was the first of us to question how it was that so many guys were interested in Rory. What was so attractive about her? I answered that sure, she was pretty and intelligent, but what is appealing about Rory, in chest-pounding, let's-go-kill-and-eat-a-woolly-mammoth way, is how feminine she is. There are many characteristics about her that corroborate this. For example, Rory engages in basically no physical activity. She plays no organized sports, and has never been interested, or the tiniest bit talented, in them. When Richard takes her golfing, all she can manage to hit is the grass (1.03, "Kill Me Now"). She comes out into society at a debutante ball, and does not have the same horrified reaction to the white dress and pearls scene that her mother did (2.06, "Presenting Lorelai Gilmore"). Of course, there is her Chilton uniform. Plaid, pleated skirts and shrunken sweater combos scream femininity in that they have been integrated into the sexual fantasies of men worldwide, most recently thanks to the Naughty Catholic Schoolgirl incarnation of Britney Spears and her pompom-ed pigtails. And the most feminine aspect of Rory's character is just how dependent she is on the males in her life. Most big decisions or altercations that she undergoes are directly related to a man. In season five, for example, Logan's father tells Rory that she won't be able to cut it as a journalist, and she believes him (5.21, "Blame Booze and Melville"). There is no standing up for herself, no fighting against his claim — Rory crumples like wet paper. Her breakdown leads to her getting arrested with Logan for trying to steal a yacht and subsequently dropping out of Yale. (All of the legal matters, and even informing Lorelai of her decision, are, of course, handled by Richard rather than Rory). This emotional and submissive dependency is glaringly feminine, and what makes it even more so is that Rory accomplishes it all in flirty dresses. So when she cannot live aggressively or dangerously herself, Rory chooses the most masculine of men as boyfriends to live through instead.

When Dean is first introduced in season one, he is like James Dean back from the dead. He's the new kid from Chicago, the mysterious, leather-clad stranger, tall, dark, and handsome, who takes an interest in Rory and her intense concentration while reading. He is the first boy who has ever made her tongue-tied, an impressive feat. Rory is so overcome by girlish attraction to him that the very night of meeting Dean she wants to give up even Chilton, the elite prep-school she has just been accepted to, so that she can stay at Stars Hollow High and be closer to him. Lorelai, of course, is not pleased. "So who is he?" she demands. "Dark hair, romantic eyes, looks a little dangerous? Tattoos are good, too. Does he have a motorcycle?" (1.01, "Pilot"). Eventually things calm down, Rory goes to Chilton and gets the guy, and at first everything seems perfect. Unfortunately, all good things must come to an end, and in this case, the end is Dean becoming feminized and losing his masculine allure. The turning point is their three-month anniversary, when Dean is the one who remembers the occasion and plans a "whole big thing." While Dean declares his love for Rory, she claims she has "to think about it a bit" because "saying 'I love you' is a really difficult thing." Peeved that he could say it and she could not, Dean's tantrum ends with him muttering, "Whatever. It doesn't matter. Alright, let's go," and stalking away, and thus the transformation from mysterious and manly to whiny and feminine is complete (1.16, "Star-Crossed Lovers and Other Strangers").

Although Rory is on-again, off-again with Dean in seasons one, two, three four, and five, whenever Rory is with Dean, there is always some more masculine guy, someone more tantalizingly dangerous, lurking slightly off in the wings...

At first it's Tristin, the bad boy from Chilton; then it's Jess, the bad boy from New York; and then it's Logan, the bad boy from Yale. And all this time Dean remains domesticated and feminized by Stars Hollow. There is that brief stint during the summer at the end of season four when Dean and Rory finally sleep together (it is a testament to how boring and hormone-less Dean is that in two years of dating Rory the subject of sex never comes up) (4.22, "Raincoats and Recipes"), when Dean is dangerous in Rory's eyes. After all, he's a construction worker, a job that the Village People would agree is basically on par with the Brawny Paper Towel guy, and married — his and Rory's is a forbidden and secret love, how could that not be dangerous? But Dean splits up with his wife, Rory goes back to Yale, and suddenly he isn't so dangerous anymore; he is just a feminized guy left behind in Stars Hollow.

Jess. Ah, Jess — he is the one that never loses his masculine appeal (and my personal favorite... Do I sense a pattern for teenage girls?). Lane puts her finger on his appeal when Rory complains about his being "great one minute and then the next...." "It's a part of why he's cute," Lane explains, "— he's unpredictable.... Every girl has to fall for a bad boy. It's the rule" (4.22, "Raincoats and Recipes"). And a bad boy he is — Jess is a bad boy from the very second he steps off the bus into Stars Hollow near the beginning of season two. He is from New York, sent by his mother to live with his Uncle Luke and finish high school because he's "getting in trouble" and she can't handle him anymore. He smokes; he gets into fistfights at school; he steals beer from Lorelai's fridge; he plays tricks on the innocent town, stealing garden gnomes from Babette, taking the baseballs from the school team, drawing a chalk outline of a body on the sidewalk in front of Doose's Market; and he acts with barely restrained contempt for every-one — everyone, that is, except for Rory. From the second they meet, Jess is drawn to Rory, and Rory is drawn to him. He provides a stark contrast to Dean, who would never have read *Howl* or understood what Rory meant if she had called him Dodger (Jess: "*Oliver Twist!*") (2.5, "Nick & Nora, Sid & Nancy"). Therefore, Jess is new and intriguing, and made even more so when he pursues Rory at town events, from the Bracebridge Dinner at the Independence Inn to the Bid-a-Basket Festival to the 24-Hour Dance Marathon. Dean's femininity is trumped by Jess' masculinity in every way, and that's why Rory can't keep herself from finally kissing Jess at Sookie and Jackson's wedding at the end of season two. Then, unfortunately, she has to go off to Washington for the summer (2.22, "I Can't Get Started"). While in D.C., she receives a huge stack of letters from Dean, but it is revealed that the only letter she thinks about writing is one to Jess. At the beginning of season three, when Paris asks Rory when she'll know if a guy is right for her, Rory still has Jess on her mind when she claims that "probably when you're not looking, you'll find someone who ... complements you. Someone who likes what you like." Rory qualifies that sameness and predictability when she adds "Someone compatible — but not so compatible that they're boring... There's just something about not quite knowing what the other person is going to do at all times, it's just ... it's just ... really exciting" (3.01, "Lazy-Hazy-Crazy Days"). It's obvious that she's referring to Jess because Dean is so predictable at this point that there is not even the tiniest element of "not quite knowing" going on whatsoever. Jess, however, demonstrates his unpredictability even more when Rory comes back to Stars Hollow, gets all pretty in a little dress and matching mary-jane heels for her first face-to-face with Jess since the kiss, and then sees him engaging in some quality hormones flowing free and wild, open-mouthed tonsil hockey with some trashy blond girl up against a tree in the middle of town (effectively getting himself more action with her in five minutes than Rory and Dean have accomplished in two years). When Rory and Jess finally do run into each other in Doose's Market, Jess is not apologetic: "You kiss me. You tell me not to say anything — very flattering, by the way. You go off to Washington, then nothing. Then you come back here, all put-out because I didn't just sit around and wait for you like Dean would have done?" (3.2, "Haunted Leg").

Dean eventually breaks up with Rory when he can't take her obvious attraction to Jess any longer. Jess gets rid of the trashy blond, and for the majority of season three Rory and Jess are dating. For the first time in Rory's young love life, there is sexual tension — at one party, she and Jess end up kissing on a bed, his hand reaching for her belt, until she pushes him off (3.19, "Keg! Max!"). He isn't lecherous by any means, but Jess is aggressive, a very masculine characteristic that keeps Rory interested. He is still a jackass at school; he is moody and doesn't always open up to her about everything, thus remaining mysterious. Jess likes Rory a lot, more than anybody else, but he never completely gives in to the relationship, which is why Rory didn't end it or become interested in someone else while she is still with him. At the end of season three, it is actually Jess who leaves Rory when he unexpectedly goes to California (3.21, "Here Comes the Son"). This abrupt departure takes place when Rory "might have loved" him, so her feelings are never completely shut off, and Jess is ensured intriguing appearances in seasons four, five, and six. Jess has always been dangerous, has always been the Kerouacian rebel, and has never been feminized by Stars Hollow or, more importantly, by Rory.

Rory meets Logan at Yale, and initially finds him to be a cocky, spoiled, wealthy cad who treats other people like they're below him. Logan is a part of her grandparents' world, a blue-blooded baby whose adolescence was spent partying at New England boarding schools during the year and at his parent's mansion in the Hamptons during the summers with all of his equally rich, equally snobby, and equally inebriated friends. While his privileged wilding and stupid risk-taking behavior, perfectly epitomized by his participation in the Life and Death Brigade (*in omnia paratus!*), are at first a black mark against him, Rory finds herself growing more attracted to him as time passes. However, she is still too much of a "very good little girl," as one champagne-silly trollop at a Life and Death Brigade event puts it, to get Logan, the ultimate ladies' man. That is, until he starts making her take more risks. When Rory goes along with Logan to report on a Life and Death Brigade gathering (themed in a sort of Gatsby on Safari kind of way) in season five, Logan tries to get Rory to jump off a huge structure with him, where the participants are prevented from plummeting to their deaths only by pulleys and an umbrella.

Logan shames Rory into jumping, saying "You're just a little sheltered.... It'll be fun, it'll be a thrill... Just something different... It's your choice, Ace. People can live one hundred years without really living for a minute. You climb up here with me, it's one less minute you haven't lived." After they had jumped and Logan has not let go of her hand, an exhilarated Rory calls the leap a "once in a lifetime experience!" but Logan says, "only if you want it to be" (5.07, "You Jump, I Jump, Jack").

This conversation is allegorical; on the one hand, it is about hurling oneself off a platform, and on the other, it is about being with a guy like Logan. He is all about being young and taking risks simply to live, never taking into account what any of the consequences could be. He draws Rory into this world with him, taking her from a life of days spent studying and watching *Duck Soup* with her friend Marty to one of nights of dancing, exorbitantly expensive Chinese restaurants, and decadent parties. Logan is a man who doesn't lose his masculinity in the same easy way that Dean does, nor does he completely retain it in the style of Jess. For example, he cheats on Rory in season six, and even though she is furious with him for weeks, she doesn't leave him because his infidelity makes him even more masculine. But now, in season seven, Logan has a steady and responsible job working for his father, he wears suits and ties to work, he has business meetings—and, slowly, he is losing his wild ways that attracted Rory to him in the first place. Instead of ice cream/beer floats in bed, it is chaste kisses on the mouth as Logan goes off to work. Even Lorelai has warmed to Logan, which is never a good sign, because Lorelai only likes Rory's boyfriends when they have become feminized and predictable. (She doesn't like Dean at first, but loves him later; she always hates Jess; and she hates Logan at first, but he is growing on her). And now the end of season seven, and perhaps the end of the series, is drawing closer, and there are signs that say Logan is losing some of his masculine edge. First there was the reappearance of Marty, whose continued crush on Rory snapped her out of her Logan trance. Rory has also begun a little crush of her own, and on the older, but still young, man who is teaching Richard's class at Yale. (For academic Rory, there's nothing sexier than a professor—think Indiana Jones). Although it's obvious that this girlish crush isn't anything that will develop into a dramatic plot twist later on in the show, it's still relevant because it means that Rory isn't completely moony over Logan anymore. When she and Lorelai drive down to North Carolina and Logan follows Rory there, hoping to make up from a fight they'd had, she manages not to throw herself into his arms in the style of Scarlett O'Hara, even exclaiming that his "grand gestures" don't impress her anymore. And what is Logan, the rich and preppy quintessential Yale male, without his grand gestures? He's less of a man than he was before, that's for sure, and definitely not the same guy who drew Rory into the partying crowd that she has come to know and love. As Logan's mystique and masculinity fades, replaced by boring, responsible, and predictable femininity, the likelihood of a new man on campus for Rory increases. If only he looked like Jess, then the world would make sense again.

Conclusion

The Women's Liberation Movement of the 1960s and 70s promised to women of subsequent generations that, given the necessary social and political changes, women would have choices about many elements of their lives: whether and when to reproduce, whether and how to develop professional careers, whether and with whom to develop romantic relationships. The lives depicted in *Gilmore Girls* appear to fulfill that promise, as the two post–Liberation Movement women of the show, Lorelai and Rory, have options that Emily did not and does not. Lorelai, for instance, could choose to carry her child to term but also choose to remain unwed, an option presumably unavailable to mothers of Emily's generation and social status; regardless of financial straits, Rory can choose to attend one of the United States' most elite colleges, one that would have been forbidding if not forbidden to females of Emily's generation.[1] Yet if a legacy of the Movement and its era is that the roles these women must or are permitted to perform — their "sex roles" or gender — are "something that happens and must be made to happen," then it's imperative to examine *Gilmore Girls'* complicity in such a construction (Connell, *Gender* 14). This is especially so in light of some of the theories emanating from the era, many of which were discussed earlier in this paper. Michel Foucault's foundational theories that multiple discourses (i.e. a long-running series) are more restrictive than limited ones and that truth is not a transcendental signified but is in fact a by-product of power led to the gender theories we have used to investigate *Gilmore Girls*. These include Judith Butler's notion that gender is not an essence but a performance; R.W. Connell's distinction between gender as behavior and sex as physiology which facilitates men and women manifesting non–traditional gender behavior; and Judith Halberstam's contention that the performances of traditional gender behaviors are more visible in bodies not traditionally expected to manifest them. Using these lenses, what we discover is that, despite its liberal appearance, *Gilmore Girls* is limited, perhaps even reactionary, in the options it offers to women as it works to reify the dichotomous world of an earlier generation.

What our mother-daughter viewpoints reveal is that the *Gilmore Girls* series offers two options for women's gender behaviors. The older woman — Brenda/Lorelai — may opt to retain all the privileges won by the Woman's Liberation Movement of the 1960s and 70s only if she chooses men who don't challenge these perquisites with contending versions of masculinity. Men who do challenge them, such as the younger and older Christopher and an intransigent Luke, must be discarded. The younger woman — Olivia/Rory — may act out all of the privileges garnered by the Movement, but she must never endanger her (fundamental) femininity, a product of her being female. Thus, the show's basic premise is that women have choices but parenthetically those choices are restricted to a gendered mantra of "opposites attract." With Emily and Richard's traditional model of gender dichotomy as backdrop, the series *explicitly* says that women of subsequent generations may be whatever their hearts and bodies desire. The lives that Lorelai and Rory lead certainly seem to be very different from Emily's. However, the show's *implicit* options limit those roles to being in a dichotomous pair, requiring women find their gender opposites, thereby reinstituting binarism as the only model for romantic relationships. Ironically for women, perhaps that traditional model of gender is what the Family Friendly Programming Forum finds "appropriate."

Note

1. Harvard was opened to women in 1963. See "Women in Harvard History" at <http://www.hno.harvard.edu/guide/underst/under4.html> for the full story. Though Yale had accepted women into their graduate programs and a very few undergraduate ones, the entire university was not opened to women until 1969. See "Milestones in the

Education of Women at Yale" at <http://elsinore.cis.yale.edu/oir/book_numbers_updated/A9_Milestones_for_Yale_Women.pdf> for more details. Of course, it's only the largesse of the upper class— Emily and Richard or Christopher — that makes it possible for Rory to consider either college, a prototypically feminine/submissive position.

Works Cited

Butler, Judith. *Gender Trouble: Feminism and the Subversion of Identity*. New York: Routledge, 1999.

Connell, R. W. *Gender*. Malden, MA: Blackwell, 2003.

Connell, Robert. *The Men and the Boys*. Berkeley: University of California Press, 2000.

Family Friendly Programming Forum. 2007. 3 January 2007 <http://www.ana.net/family/default.htm>.

Foucault, Michel. 1978. *The History of Sexuality: Volume I, An Introduction*. New York: Vintage, 1990.

Halberstam, Judith. *Female Masculinity*. Durham: Duke University Press, 1998.

Gilmore Girls. 2006. The CW.com. 3 January 2007 <http://www.cwtv.com/shows/gilmore–girls/about>.

Warner Brothers. 2007. 3 January 2007 <http://www2.warnerbrothers.com>.

Food Fights

Food and Its Consumption as a Narrative Device

Lindsay Coleman

In the *Gilmore Girls* episode entitled, "That Damn Donna Reed" (1.14), Lorelai (Lauren Graham) and Rory (Alexis Bledel), the mother and daughter protagonists of the series, lounge on their couch in front of the television, and induct new boyfriend Dean into the metaphysics of *The Donna Reed Show* and television programs of its ilk. "My favorite episode," Rory chimes, "is when their son, Jeff, comes home from school and *nothing* happens." Their pleasure in this "nothing" is genuine, without a hint of sarcasm or irony, of the like a camp-obsessed audience might bring to a similar viewing. Indeed, what they share with the show is an affinity for its worldview, in which subtle degrees of what the action-minded brand "nothing" happens every day. The series *Gilmore Girls* is brimming with detail, be it the contents of a menu, or a complicated Lorelai popular culture analogy. However, scenarios which explicitly deal with the series foundational narrative drives—Lorelai's ongoing conflict with her parents, the two leads pursuits of romantic fulfillment—are more rare than might typically be found in most long-running series. Instead seemingly frivolous detail prevails. If *Seinfeld* is the show *about* nothing, then *Gilmore Girls* is a show in which degrees of "nothing" happen, a seeming absence of confrontational action and conflict embraced by its characters.

Yet what exactly is meant by this term, and, indeed, this school of television? *Gilmore Girls* offers a community in Stars Hollow in which a pair as witty and effervescent as the title characters would seem not the starry, charismatic individuals, but rather the natural product of their environment. As such they offer, with the exception of Rory's school experience, as among the most unjaded central characters on all of television in a series with dramatic elements. The girls may offer themselves with their quirks and foibles, yet they may face the

world unselfconsciously, confident in the knowledge that their eccentricities will
be nurtured and indulged by those around them. Lorelai's parents, Richard and
Emily, Luke, Dean, Jackson, Sookie: all are avowed oddballs residing in safe,
upper-middle class New England, replete with the consumer wherewithal and
puritanical souls to ensure an extended life of idiosyncratic indulgence and
whimsy for our protagonists. Sexual admiration and resentment may muddy
the waters occasionally, but rarely sex that is not of the closed-doors, lights-off
kind. Violence more frequently finds expression in hurtful verbal barbs than
anything physical. Economic and emotional pressures exist, but are easily
assuaged by the presence of Lorelai's rich parents and her benevolent father, in
particular. As such the scenarios of the series are a throwback, with updates in
tonality and cultural detail, to domestic series of the 50s in which character is
more or less constant, and manifestations of event and emotion are found in
the most domestic and white-bread of activities. In a dead-serious inversion of
the parody that was the 1998 film *Pleasantville*, details such as a yard sale may
contain crucial character detail, and precipitate emotional watersheds that will
form the central events of the episode. The minutiae of life for the quirky, comfortable, and untroubled form the dramatic points of development for the
Gilmore Girls.

This aspect, while comfortable, admittedly detracts from the realism of
the scenario. A critic of the series makes the following observations:

> In fact, Lorelai appears to be a happy single parent — something rarely seen on tele-
> vision drama and quite a switch from the days of Murphy Brown, who was vilified
> by politicians (most loudly, Dan Quayle) for her decision to rear her child on her
> own. I think the difference here is in the amount of apology offered. Murphy
> Brown offered no excuses and was unrepentant. While Lorelai Gilmore is plainly
> pleased to have Rory in her life, she does talk of having "thrown [her] life away"
> and things not going as she had "planned." Not that insisting that one's child be
> educated and aware of the consequences of sex is surely a bad thing, but in the case
> of *Gilmore Girls*, never-wed single parenting falls into the "mistakes were made"
> category, while Murphy Brown made an active choice.
>
> In addition, in both cases, the mothers are privileged, white, and have financial
> support on which to fall in case of emergency — Murphy through her career and
> Lorelai through her wealthy parents. I am still waiting for a show focusing on a
> non-white, content parent who is single by choice. The idealized New England set-
> ting also helps counter the non-traditional family in *Gilmore Girls*. This isn't a
> mother and child in anonymous suburbs — or worse, the city. What better place to
> raise a child than in a quaint, clean, Connecticut village in which everyone knows
> everyone else. Without a dad, I guess it does take a village to raise a child. Go
> ahead girls, don't have an abortion — have that baby at age 16. It will all work out
> just fine, right? If you are pretty and charming and live in Utopia, everything will
> be great [McLoone 1].

Effectively the controversial politics of teen pregnancy as an issue are ingen-
iously sidestepped, a major departure from *Murphy Brown*'s confrontational
stance. Yet, this highly imaginary, contrived space allows for an indulgence of

the conceptual, wherein the poetics of a scene may escape the banality of say, Kitchen Sink drama, and scale the grandly whimsical.

The exact nature of each event of minutiae may be described as multi-various and subject to increasingly subtle interrelation. The discovery of an old jacket of Luke's in "Concert Interruptus" (1.13) during a yard sale leads Lorelai to the shuddering discovery that her chum once had a girlfriend, and indeed that he may have had his heart broken. This exchange takes place in a living room crowded with detritus between three women of varying closeness to Luke. Yet, remarkably, the focus of their attention remains on the clothing, the sensations its tangible texture and heft exert, and indeed that of the objects around them, exerting as much influence on the scene as the conceptual and emotional meanderings of their conversation. While this mastery of the material, and its emotional memory, as minutiae might seem the exclusive provenance of the cash-flushed and fully matured Rory and pal Lane, they exhibit their own facility with the tangible and the ethereal alike. In "Double Date" (1.12), Lane spills her CD collection onto that hallowed domestic plane the kitchen table. While conversation hovers on the subject of music taste, Lane exposes her new taste, a yen for Dean's taciturn friend Todd. Remarkably this odd conversation transition finds apt poetic expression later in the episode during one of the titular double dates as Lane attempts to warm her crush up by quizzing him on his music tastes. Effectively the maneuverings of a new interpersonal connection are the expression of a tactile encounter with the surface of a compact disc and an emotional encounter of unpinned feelings and verbal static. The younglings note and understand the transition between forms and feelings not fitfully but with an uninhibited virtuosity that eludes their seniors, and might be more far-reaching were it not for their status of preciousness and the knee-jerk condescension it is met with. The story of Rory's development is thus not only of her dawning womanhood, but of her growing archness in the compartmentalizing of said variants, of a distancing from instinct through structured, one might even say mannered, repetition.

While an impromptu yard sale or shopping spree may provoke the least likely of connections within the narrative, as evidenced through the revelation of Luke's past and Lane's unusual segue into an attempted flirtation the consumption and preparation of food constitutes a far more persistent, ritualized aspect of Gilmore "nothing." The incidence of consumption and preparation of food occupies, in most instances, numerous points of an episode's running time. Obvious examples would doubtless be the meals at Emily and Richard's which begin episodes, or Rory and Lorelai shopping for food at episodes' beginnings. Another example would be situations, typically at an episode's twenty-minute mark, where the duo visit Luke's diner. These are frequently complemented by concluding scenes at the forty-minute mark where they return to Luke's diner. And naturally almost any conversation with obligatory best friend Sookie must entail the tasting of her latest dish. While it may be oblique to a scene's core emotional struggle, it nevertheless always provides the setting, or the context for any exchange to commence. Thus, food enjoys an unusual degree of narrative space. Where perhaps an HBO series would favor a sexual tryst as the sensual activity which might act as narrative catalyst, in *Gilmore Girls* it is the discussion, preparation, and consumption of food. Lorelei in fact chows down with her gourmand friend Sookie (Melissa McCarthy) while reminding her of a handsome acquaintance they had met at a bake sale, and off-handedly mentions her interest in allowing him to break her dry spell of celibacy. The setting of the conversation, a diner, the context of the conversation, a bake sale, and the activity in which the women partake, eating, all revolve around food. Their focus is, in fact, so singular that Sookie has difficulty keeping up with her friend's euphemistic references to sex. Indeed Lorelei's crush is further commended by his love of coffee. Sex hovers in the air as a subject, while food is the base foundation of repartée above which it levitates. Food, ironically, sets the template for many kinds of Gilmore consumption and desire.

Indeed a structured analysis of sex within the series, as determined by set parameters, early in its run resulted in findings consistent with this notion.

Number of instances	4/9	4/23
Sexual Humor	0	0
Female Sexual Objectification	0	0
Male Sexual Objectification	0	0
Sex in Commited Relationship	0	0
Sex in Casual Relationship	0	0
Abstinence	0	0
Reference to Protection	0	0

Number of instances	4/9	4/23
Sexual Humor	0	0
Female Sexual Objectification	0	0
Male Sexual Objectification	1	1
Sex in Commited Relationship	0	0
Sex in Casual Relationship	0	1
Abstinence	0	0
Reference to Protection	0	0

Gilmore Girls: "There's the Rub" Episode 2.16, April 9, 2002, and "Back in the Saddle Again" Episode 2. 18, April 23, 2002, 7:00–8:00 (Okey 29–30).

Sex, as an articulated quantity in the series, appears *verboten*.

As such, food is an essential expressive medium of character desire and frustration in the series. There is certainly cinematic precedence to this notion. *Big Night* is the tale of two Italian immigrant brothers, Primo and Secondo, running a family restaurant in Eisenhower America. Primo, the purist chef, refuses to compromise to the vulgar dictates of the marketplace, as symbolized by the brothers' boorish competitor (Ian Holm), a restaurateur for whom spaghetti and meatballs in thick sauce represents an admitted degradation of

Italian cuisine, but a populist one, nonetheless. In essence, much of the plot details the business and emotional struggles of the two brothers as the slicker Secondo struggles to maintain the books, and loner Primo attempts to maintain his dedication to his heritage through the traditional Italian food he creates. The exact skill and passion he brings to this venture, and indeed its artistic, philosophic legitimacy is information dramatically withheld until the film's final act, in which a feast is prepared for the brothers' friends. The manner in which this is presented is through an active camera, handheld, encircling the dinners, with joyous music played over their feasting, as one course follows another. The interpersonal connection, the physical abandon and looseness of the sequence, the exaggerated camerawork and complementary hamminess of the actors enthralled feasting assures that this is a banquet transcendent on almost all levels. Stylistically, filmically, Primo's prickly stance of defiance, his rigid standards, his belief in the importance of tradition, are entirely justified. Food, the audience learns, is a uniquely powerful substance, indeed worth losing social connection, economic standing, and even love over. A similar filmic experience is *Babbette's Feast,* in which a woman prepares a banquet for her friends and neighbors, in the process revealing the same magic of food, and the emotions which is preparation and perfection can stir, as does *Chocolat,* wherein the sensual wonders of a village *chocolaterie* transform dull 1950s France.

Yet, while dramatically the transcendence of food is withheld until the final act within these films, in which the revelation and justification of the philosophy of a character is found in the form of a single set-piece banquet, and its attendant preparation, the television format allows for an infinitely richer examination of food-as-character metaphor. In "The Lorelais' First Day at Chilton" (1.02), there are clearly seemingly bizarre interpersonal rumblings occurring in Sookie's hotel kitchen. She notes to Jackson, produce manager, on the subject of peaches, "they're smaller than the last batch. Smaller means watery." She then discovers an allegedly bruised peach. He neurotically protests his innocence, his exasperation clearly expressing a degree of ongoing frustration in their professional relationship which has surpassed civility, bypassed hostility, and landed in a terrain of semi-familiar joshing, semi-adversarial zeal. In "Kill Me Now" (1.03), Sookie's frustration at Jackson's (Jackson Douglas) inability to provide strawberries for her shortcake, instead supplementing blueberries which he feels less substandard, is in one respect a battle of contrasting standards and priorities. In other words, it is a conflict revolving around business, supply and demand, in this case the commodity of fresh produce. The scene is thus entirely appropriate to the business setting of the narrative. As in *Big Night,* where Primo refuses to compromise on the subject of his ingredients, while budget-conscious brother Secondo frets, so too is the incidence of vying business and service interpretations within a food industry setting entirely appropriate. In some respects this scene might even be judged to resemble a more sedate form of some of the battles Artie Bucco (Joe Ventimiglia) might undergo on issues such as pricing, preparation and ingredients in *The Sopranos* and might also share in conversation with his occasionally sympathetic mobster friend Tony. Yet the particular accents in the exchange of Sookie and Jackson, its verbose intensity, suggest an interaction based around more than the utility of business. More is at play here than keeping the diners happy. The confrontation has its own gravity, a specificity bordering on the myopic. On another level their fights constitute those of a married couple, counterparts with contrasting priorities for their shared provenance of produce. This notion is confirmed by Jackson's jealous, indignant rage when he discovers Sookie purchasing strawberries behind his back, tantamount to infidelity. Effectively, as is later proved by their courtship, the two are food-flirting, sublimating their passion and attraction for one another into the natural sensuality of food. Indeed, in season two, Sookie confesses that their now consummated relationship retains much of its verve through their now-choreographed food battles. From their beginning intimations of watery peaches, to their blueberry-strawberry wars, the two engage in a form of courtship through the most convenient semantic-tactile mode at hand, food. Once again *Big Night* is referenced as shy Primo seduces his crush (Allison Janney) against all expectations during the preparation of the final banquet in the film's last act. For Sookie and *her* crush, squeezing tomatoes, smelling baking, chasing one another around a fruit and vegetable store, all are physical, tactile expressions of a mutually sublimated sexuality, which inevitably surfaces and manifests in the very plain fact of her multiple pregnancies.

Indeed, the progression of their relationship seems to follow in this pattern, of an attraction alternately sublimated — later appropriately manifesting — and reinforced by the props and exercises in food preparation and consumption. On their first date, a double date in fact (1.12, "Double Date"), Jackson's whiny cousin Rune's (Max Perlich) complaints as to the restaurant of choice lead to a lull in which neither the presumptive couple's appetite for food or emotional consummation is satisfied. Mutually frustrated, the two couples relocate to Luke's, at which point Rune insists he and Sookie's crush, Jackson, leave. In a small voice Sookie expresses that the date has not yet started. It is surely no coincidence that the explicit ordering and consumption of food has not commenced, either. To begin their relationship, Sookie and Jackson must break bread together. Her desire for him is mediated by the notion that they first successfully dine together.

So it follows that the first minor battle within said relationship occurs around the further continuance in the breaking of bread. When Jackson attempts to prepare Sookie her first home-cooked meal as his girlfriend, a neatly choreographed battle is pitched by Sookie to gain access to the kitchen. Where it once had been strawberries/blueberries as the center of their struggles, it is now a parsnip. Yet the dynamic has changed. The vegetable is not the mutual focus of their projected desire for one another. It is a phallic symbol of power in the kitchen, and of Jackson's usurpation of Sookie's sacred matriarchal realm of her own cooking space. Jackson is, not so subtly, introducing his phallic symbol to said space, provocatively waving it under her nose. This is not the only instance of Jackson regarding his occupation of a virgin space with his phallic prop. In a town meeting he notes that his miniature proxy in a prospective model of town development proposed by the series busybody Taylor is holding a tiny zucchini, a phallic vegetable initially symbolic of his imprint on a new town landmark. In the earlier instance Sookie reaches for this new totem of the kitchen, penis-envy alternately confused with and supplanted by parsnip-envy. Yet, regardless of whether she claims the vegetable or not, Jackson has invested in the object a phallic overtone, a talismanic force which reconfigures Sookie's relationship and her ingredients. Her discomfort is over not Jackson's taste ruining their relationship, but that, like the aforementioned emotional consummation paralleling the breaking of bread, here the presumptive physical consummation of the relationship runs congruent to Jackson besieging of Sookie's other most private space, her kitchen. He is, according to the "nothing" stated in the episode "That Damn Donna Reed," not explicitly instigating any kind of obvious interpersonal dominance or manly prerogative. Yet, according to the interactions with items by Lorelai and Rory in the yard sale, within a simple act of tactile contact with a potent prop — this time of cooking implements and ingredients — of the sleepy New England bourgeoisie a revelation or transformation may occur. By fingering her pots, grasping her food, Jackson is imprinting his identity onto her kitchen, and effectively both her body and heart.

By season four of *Gilmore Girls*, Sookie is now pregnant with her first child. As her pregnant bulk now replaces her gourmand bulk, she navigates her kitchen, a further elaboration of the powerful food dynamic in her courtship and consummation with Jackson. Sookie's pregnancy, in practical terms, exists as a very literal manifestation of this former spinster allowing a man into her life. She has figuratively and literally allowed for Jackson's imprint in her most personal domestic and biological spaces. This notion of imprinting is further accented in the fifth season where she becomes a political wife and her selectman husband's most ardent supporter as he expands his, and in turn their, span of influence to the entirety of Stars Hollow. Is not his phallic model zucchini not also a quiet joke on Amy Sherman-Palladino's part of his eventual patriarchal, phallic domination of the town as its menschy selectman? Yet, beyond Jackson's imprint, there is also the presence of the young individual, later followed by a sibling, in her womb who now shares not only in her eating for two, but also through her conceptualizing, preparing and presenting the food she has baked. Effectively, she is sharing her food wisdom with the unborn, and happily so. Effectively food cognizance, as following on from food instigation — Sookie and Jackson's first date — food imprintation — their first cooked dinner as a couple — exists as a statement of their personal liberation from eccentricity and marginalism, eventuating ultimately in the advocacy and utility both exhibit as politicians. Through the breaking of bread, the banging of pans, the stirring of the mix, and finally the bearing of the child's weight, Sookie emerges from a process of revelation. Via her physical and tactile initiation, through the technical implements of food, through domestic ritual, she graduates to a new emotional realm, that of couplehood and family, and further to the maturity of a kind of statesmanship. In eating for two, she has now found the ultimate expression of her foodie soul, as a flowering of the superego.

Sookie's particular arc, however, despite its myriad transitions, is deceptively complex. Arguably, her character develops quicker than that of Lorelai's, absorbing much of the tension surround the latter's virtual regression throughout the series. Sookie is married and pregnant, and developing solid personal relationships with greater rapidity than her friend. However Sookie's arc, ironically, does not betray her early conversation with Lorelai on the topic of the handsome stranger at the bake sale. As a secondary character, Sookie's sex life is literally more consummative than that of her friend; yet, unlike the regressing Lorelai, it does not receive screen time. Sookie's pregnancies seem more the result of a fecund disposition and her and Jackson's articulations of family planning, as related to their food and political careers, rather than a sex life per se. Also, remarkably, Sherman-Palladino allows for every ritual manifestation of love, specifically marriage, in relation to Sookie to be dominated by food. Emily's interference with Sookie's wedding plans results an obscene sideshow in which the menu is fretted over more than the wedding vows. Likewise Sookie loses sleep as she obsesses over the florid wonder that is her wedding cake. Marriage to Jackson is a given, a trifle. Getting the cake right is not. Finally, comprehensively, there is Lorelai's broken engagement to Max. It is not the hurt of the two Lorelais' departing to Harvard without Sookie, nor the heartbreak Lorelai recounts to her friend that devastates Sookie. It is the immaculate cake she must now share with her staff, rather than give to her friend. Pregnancy, a manifestation of Jackson's phallic imprint, is her duty as a foodie. In her generosity with food, Sookie creates two new mouths to feed.

The flowering of the foodie soul is unique to Sookie's character arc. Yet elements of her initial struggles/flirtations with Jackson echo another essential food fight within the series, this time specifically that of the Gilmore family. What is striking is how almost completely this battle over food-as-child/lover parallels one of the series' central paternal struggles, that for the soul of Rory between her mother Lorelei and her grandparents. Food fights may parallel one another, and metaphorically complement, providing a poetic echo of each combat's muffled intensity. Rory's introduction to both audience and estranged grandparents might well be judged to resemble that of a glorious fruit platter. Her hair is glossy, her eyes luminous, cheeks rosy and fresh. Her gait might be called carelessly graceful. She is, in short, the visual approximation of some ideal of youth, her appeal more delectable, and easily digested, than spiky, tart, or smoldering. Effectively Sookie and Jackson's respective arguments on quality, freshness, and blooming potential seem entirely apt as a metaphor for the young Rory. So, too, is she entirely objectified by both her mother and grandparents and, equally, coveted. Rory, it might be said, is the ultimate tactile prop of sleepy New England, the dew-eyed, future Ivy Leaguer devoid of youths vices, and abundant in its charms.

In this respect she also comes to represent many of the notions of tyrannical youthful consumerism in the culture market, in particular those that swirl around the show.

> Aging talent complains it cannot find representation, much less work. A thirty-something writer who faked being eighteen to land a job on the TV series "Felicity" was summarily fired when her real age was discovered, and a number of writer friends have told me that forty is practically a death sentence in the television business. All of which leads to an inescapable and frightening conclusion: We live in a culture of the young, for the young and by the young, and anyone over 49 — the demographic of breakpoint of old age for most television advertisers— is tossed onto the trash heap of history, all eighty million of them [Gabler 3].

As such the sustained narrative prejudice against the older Emily and Richard Gilmore and their conservative worldview seems to bespeak an ageist consumer bias throughout the series.

Indeed the battles which develop between Lorelai and her parents on the subject of Rory gravitate entirely to matters of taste and consumption, be it the relative discrepancies of Yale over Harvard, or Europe via backpacker hostel or five-star hotel. Anxious that Rory will enjoy an afternoon of golf with her father at the Stars Hollow country club and, in my view, jealous of the potential emotional access she will have to her taciturn father, Lorelai is keen to disparage her daughter's bonding in "Kill Me Now" (1.03). Eager to trash the experience over Luke's diner food she asks her daughter what she would like to order. Rory replies, "I had a big lunch at the club"— she then adds with a gentile accent which annoys her mother —"which was *quite* good." Lorelai immediately assumes her daughter's lack of appetite, coupled with her new absorption of the patter of those who sidestep the reality of appetite as a life pleasure, the élite, is effectively a kind of repudiation of the life she has created for her daughter. It is a life populated with appetite-driven ejaculations, exaltations, and the girly-hip patter of which the recommendation "quite" may pass a stunning chill through the air. This anxiety only gains in strength, not only through the episode, but also the season. Upon perusing Rory's school uniform, the domestic item which will precipitate her groveling appeal for money from her mother, Lorelai notes that her daughter looks as though she were swallowed by a kilt. Similarly, when Rory is offered broadband by her grandmother in the season one episode, "The Lorelais' First Day at Chilton" (1.02), she counters: "Well, we like our Internet slow, okay? We can turn it on, walk around, do a little dance, make a sandwich. With DSL, there's no dancing, no walking, and we'd starve. It'd be all work and no play. Have you not seen *The Shining*, Mom?"

The speed of broadband, she counters, would necessitate perpetual motion, perpetual utility, and the pair would starve. Both scenes reveal Lorelai's essential fear of Rory adopting alternative modes of consumption. In the kilt comment she reveals her nerves as Rory enters a stimulating academic environment. Her daughter's heretofore absorption in their elliptical and witty conversations will be overtaken by a cogent engagement with her individual academic potential. The second scene supports this anxiety. Might Rory now, with the accelerated flow of information created by broadband, subsist completely on the similarly elliptical nature of the then relatively novel internet? Could, Lorelai perhaps wonders, Rory replace movie night with streaming videos? Given the intangible but palpable effects of élitism and intellectualism, will they curtail Rory's appetite for the solidity of sandwiches? And will this end the sisterly bond of the pair based in flexible domestic engagement and the ready sharing of secrets and recipes? Thus, food, that most tactile and domestic of items, may easily be superceded by the less subjective, more directly reciprocal returns of élitist utility. It may, in the mind of Lorelai, be suppressed by temptations that exceed the quirky charms of Stars Hollow. This tension is explicitly established in "The Lorelais' First Day at Chilton" (1.02) when the school's principal offers Rory the complete scope of opportunities the establishment will bring her — an Ivy League education and the connections to go with it — while noting her scant social engagements in her previous school. Rory replies that Stars Hollow as a community is a social engagement in itself. Her loyalty is clearly heartfelt, yet also the audience can perceive both her eagerness to assimilate into the consumptive attitudes of her new environment as well as her willingness to acquire its utilitarian intangibles, even at the cost of sacrificing what entails emotional and moral comfort food.

At this point it is useful to mention the dark influence that is Rory's erstwhile peer and friend Paris. The young woman exemplifies a notion of youth strangled in infancy, struggling to maintain a ghost of itself until full adulthood. Where Rory is idealized, Paris is needy, neurotic, transgressive. She also perfectly emphasizes this particular supplanting of food/sex with élitist knowledge. In the fifth season, during a presumptive wake for Paris's dead, near septuagenarian lover, Rory attempts to disperse copies of his final novel. Yet, mistaking the event for a kegger party, young men and women mill about in flirtatious conversation, an actual barrel of beer being introduced to the wake behind the back of an oblivious Paris. Rory, clearly, will never be as thwarted or dark as her friend. According to Amy Sherman-Palladino and her husband, Daniel Palladino, in "Commentary on 'You Jump, I Jump, Jack'," the fear of the audience may arise more from Rory's proximity to, and the ongoing flirtation with, an élitism that is the rich at their most toxic.

On a similar narrative track are the efforts of Luke (Scott Patterson) to exert an influence over Rory's diet. In the "Pilot" (1.01), the Gilmore Girls and presumptive father figure Luke exchange barbs on the choices the young women make in their orders. The over-caffeinated Lorelei and under-caffeinated Luke — ironically, the keeper of the coffee — are obvious antagonists in life attitude and philosophy. Where Luke is naturally stolid, Lorelei is flighty and kooky. Where he is intensely practical —fixing the pair's variously damaged and in-need-of-repair domestic implements and surfaces— she is whimsical. Ironically, this combination of personality, naturally complementary, precipitates an ideal fusion in the realm of food and the domestic. While Lorelai is certainly drawn to the domestic realm, she is not a domestic goddess of the order of Martha Stewart, nor is she a specific kitchen goddess as might be the pantry-bound Nigella Lawson. Famously she chooses not to cook, instead favoring to eat out. Rather she simultaneously indulges in food as a ritual to which she is subservient and a commodity in which she would rather be receiver than giver. Lorelai responds to the tactile and sensory, the essential experience of food, instinctively rather than instrumentally. It is a mystery to her, one she is eager to keep. Yet, in this experience, she is shallow. She lacks the fluid transitions, spanning time and context, the audience may note in Rory and Lane's experience of the same. Luke, while superficially inarticulate and emotionally constipated, instills in Rory by example an instrumental, tactile-yet-directed variation on domestic engagement, be it the preparation of his acclaimed recipes, or the sanding of Lorelai's porch. Effectively he demonstrates to her the potential physical force, or perhaps just distinct hint, of deliberate domestic engagement. In this respect he counters Lorelai's ellipses in favor of a demonstration the sensual may have an entirely utilitarian vector, if deployed with thought, and anti-verbal force. What this relationship effectively creates, the formation of counterparts that might best approximate Rory's parents, is a partnership which allows the particular central dynamic and tension of the series to exist. Indeed, in a confrontation with Rory's actual father at the second wedding of Lorelai's parents, Luke affirms how, in a million practical ways, he has been more of a male parent to Rory than his rival has. Where her mother gives Rory license to whimsy, particularly on matters of the domestic and food, her school and grandparents reinforces alternate means of consumption, namely prestige and knowledge. Where either side might be construed as extreme and coercive towards their young charge, Luke shows a potential middle path, one which might allow for the two strands of consumption to commingle. This allows for Rory to please both her grandparents, and mother, to succeed among the nations élite, while preserving her folksy roots and appetite-driven repartée. Yet, sadly for him, within this emotional tug of war, the presumed repressive case Luke is ultimately the loser, the expendable father figure, as evidenced by the sustained dismissal he suffers from Rory's grandparents, her real benefactors.

The audience can observe this in her strategic dismissal of his food, and food context advice. Naturally, as oppositional mentor to her mother, Luke attempts to discourage Rory from consuming coffee as might her mother, and thus embracing effervescent heedlessness. Caffeine, after all, is the least grounded of nature's legal substances. It suppresses appetite, cranks up the nervous system, artificially stimulates conversation and emotional engagement, and acts as a diuretic. Health-wise and even, arguably, on the front of social development, coffee is unwise for a teen to consume prodigiously. His disapproval clear, Rory blithely ignores him. He similarly often notes that Rory's unhealthy choices from the menu might hint at her emulating her mother's similarly unhealthy choices in life. Where he would have her exert refined taste she instead demonstrates her mother's brash vitality in her choice of chili fries. Chili may damage the digestive system, adding to the acidity of the stomach. Deep-fried chips contain oil and will do no favors for Rory's flawless complexion. Yet, Rory's palate, and her heart, is her mother's. Indeed the changeability of said shared palate, and the erratic life choices it springs from, are easily apparent in the first few seasons of *Gilmore Girls*. One moment Lorelai promotes chili fries and the like, the next sandwiches. As early as "The Lorelais' First Day at Chilton" (1.02), Lorelai considers a date with a slightly sleazy co-member of the PTA. She then proceeds to deliver Rory to a preparatory school wearing cut-offs and what appears a tie-dye t-shirt. After seducing/being seduced by Rory's teacher, she then proceeds to complicate her daughter's life at the school and her own by eventually breaking her engagement with said teacher. At each questionable conundrum, Luke's taciturn presence is always noted.

How Luke's character manifests precisely may be noted as similar to Sookie's entanglement of love, sex, and food. Just as Sookie makes her pregnancy — and the sex that went with it — a paean to her love for Jackson and to their empire built on sustained food flirting, so too does Luke direct his repressed desires for Lorelai, as proven in their fifth season consummation, into an uninvited paternal attitude towards Rory. Both characters deflect sex, an activity private and consummative, into social acts of largesse. The greater Luke's desire, the more actively he sublimates, frantically mending porches and cooking the finest and most obscure dishes for both mother and daughter. As he cannot appropriately shower the dating, therefore off-limits, Lorelai with gifts and treats, he transfers his generosity to her daughter and her peers in the form of Lane. Similarly aware that she has a father in Christopher, as least officially, he attempts to use his cooking as both a rewards system and a vehicle for paternal life lessons. By the fourth season, with Rory gone, and with it the awkwardness of his uninvited parenting, Luke's buffer is gone. So, too, is Lorelai's as she, in true Freudian fashion, dreams of Luke in her house and bed at season three's beginning. In this unique instance food now becomes the remaining buffer between them as a future couple, and the alternating offers and withdrawals of service at Luke's form a pattern from the fourth season. Yet, naturally, once the couple has connected physically, food becomes not a space of sex's sublimation but rather, as with Sookie, an expression of love. The *emotional* state of their relationship, provoked by Christopher's drunken insults of Luke, prompts Lorelai to not cheat with Christopher, but with eating at another diner. Eating may thus entail an act of emotional celebration, or betrayal, as Luke notes when he reconciles with Lorelai — she is has been drinking the coffee of another diner.

The structures that make this food-love parallel work so well in the series are through Sherman-Palladino's clear grounding of food talk and the domestic and emotional-domestic agenda. Lorelai and Rory talk food at their home, but they famously do not eat there. As such the scanning of Luke's menu mixes with gossip of the day and prioritizing of the day's events and home's chores. The two bond as intimately in this very public space as they might in one another's bedrooms. Likewise, the fact that Sookie and Lorelai's bed and breakfast, the Dragonfly Inn, is a corporate contrived version of the domestic, makes their many menu discussions, mixed with business debates and gossip on their partners, an epic metaphor for their burgeoning love affairs, and their love for each other. Sherman-Palladino's most potent structural development of this complex congregation is the dinners at Emily and Richard's. The minutiae of these dinners, with their debates on Emily's maids, Richard and Emily's faltering marriage, Lorelai and Emily's troubled relationship, Rory's future and the day's menu, are just as epically potent as those of the Dragonfly Inn. A slip in the *frission* of gourmand repartée, emotional grandstanding, and élitist whining might, after all, imperil Rory's future. Bad dinner conversation means a break in the structure of love and support that generates Rory's Yale education and Lorelai's compulsive resentment towards her parents. In short, remove the tensions of the élite's daily agenda, their palate's specifications, and their need to show love through money's use, and there is very little tension to sustain this "nothing" series. Sherman Palladino's structure is a triangle of dependencies.

Indeed, a structural choice of writer/creator Amy Sherman-Palladino is to place a congregation of Luke, Rory and Lorelai at his diner following some variation on a self-confessed questionable call by Lorelai. As such the scanning of the menu is a substitute/conduit for taking stock of the day. While Luke rarely engages in these discussions other than the odd wry/judgmental comment, or grunt, his masculine presence is so apparent in this estrogen-fest that his physical proximity may inspire strong sensations of disapproval and moral gravity in the free associating stretches of conversation in the mother-daughter foodies. He is the third wheel, as noted, who may bridge the gaps of an exchange, either through the bolstering of his acquiescence or the reverse psychology of his attempts at jocular condescension. Be his interjections welcome breaks in estrogen intensity, or opportunities for adversarial bonding on the subject of his masculine cluelessness, he is needed to break the escalating whimsy regardless. He thus appears roughly in every third or fourth scene, bookending each narrative act, never more so than through his droll/clueless interjections in the first anxious conversation on the subject of élitist consumption found in "Kill Me Now" (1.03), to which I have already referred in this essay. Rory engages with Luke in the diner as she awaits her mother. Upon learning that she went golfing with her grandfather, he lightly scolds, "Did you know golf courses are an environmental blight because of the chemicals they use to keep the grass green?" all the while pouring for her an ample cup of coffee. Effectively the moment is charged with a kind of transactional reprisal. He indulges her bad habit, softening her defenses, while simultaneously informing her of the life-and-universe changing effects of her new consumptive attitudes. She has hurt his values yet again, but he is willing to indulge her vices in the interests of preventing greater evil. In this moment Luke is tonally insensitive to a milder manifestation of the same conformist eagerness which could be noted in her earlier visit to the principal. His gesture is thus doubly defeated, both in delivery and reception, as she confirms to the wise proprietor that she was adequately aware, and again willing to abuse resources as only the entitled may. Luke once again ironically provides a tonal bridge upon Lorelai's entry. His justified, yet dependable grouchiness, complete with offhand comments on Rory's abuse of the natural world immediately eases the mother into a direct connection with her daughter's stimulated ambition for inherently greater consumption. Again, he is tone deaf to the inherent female tensions within the encounter and beats a retreat, yet he has more than served his purpose. In allowing the daughters to both join in fond reverse-condescension at his iracibility, he allows them to bond, along with the food and coffee he provides and its attendant elevations, in a place of mutual comfort. From this realm of equality and dotage, the battle lines may be drawn on the most genuinely level of playing fields, in this case made tangible by the flat dining table on which they sit, in turn equipped with the energizing stimulants of their brimming coffee cups. Luke may retire from this food-fueled engagement, yet his unconscious position of arbitrator of food and power cannot be lost on the audience. This ingenious dynamic formulated by Sherman-Palladino is further facilitated by Luke's socio-political status within the town.

While Luke exemplifies a masculine ideal — ruggedly handsome, cowboy taciturn, vulnerable yet manly, sensibly forceful — which, as has become clear by the fourth season, becomes irresistible to Lorelai, his importance in the realm of both food, and the Stars Hollow domestic realm becomes increasingly apparent. In the first season he is referred to as the keeper of the coffee. Indeed, ironically, it is from this position of power and respect that Lorelai repeatedly chooses to identify with and regard him. When asked who is he to her, she primarily identifies him as the provider of her food, then her friend — almost as an afterthought — and finally as a male who engages in her domestic space.

This jumbled, one might say kaleidoscopic, conception of Luke can only claim his coffeeness, his unending providence in the realm of food, which can define him in any stable sense among the vying tumble of references and blurring shades of emotion found in Lorelai's charming mind. Thus food, as with Sookie, is otherwise the most consistent conduit to Lorelai's heart, and the prevailing source of Luke as source of food and thus master of perhaps his presumptive girlfriend's happiest realm. Indeed the failure of connections with Max and Jason might be judged to derive from their whole-hearted embrace of knowledge and information consumption. Luke, she eventually realizes, is the sole bridge from her folksy, "nothing" community, to the realm of food-hunger free consumption she finds in the big words of Max's Proust novels, and Jason's polyglot struggles to tame the international market. Implicitly, Sherman-Palladino makes clear, in order to retain her roots and her daughter, Lorelai must make Luke a part of her life. Max and Jason are too far into the realms of sex, as evidenced by the former's romantic insistence, and information, as evidenced by the latter's remove, to completely facilitate the central relationship in her life, that of her daughter and Lorelai. Luke, in the parlance of a romantic comedy which might meld easily in the Gilmore universe, completes Lorelai inasmuch as he unites the disparate forces of attraction in her relationship with her best friend and soulmate Rory.

Indeed, Rory's reference to Luke as Hagrid is one of the more apt references/analogies which the series has formulated. Like the character in the Harry Potter books, Luke is sympathetic and "simple" enough to engage the "children" of *Gilmore Girls* and sufficiently well-formed and stoic to engage as an equal with both Stars Hollow's "adult" cultural arbitrators, and the equally attractive, skilled love-rivals he finds in Max and Jason. Never is this clearer than in the opening scenes of "Love and War and Snow" (1.08). Here a town meeting is called to reframe the notion of commerce in the domestic realm in Stars Hollow, and indeed the ongoing definition of the domestic itself. Effectively the permissibly tactile, and the uncensored engagement with such, and by association the freedom of the kitchen, is under implicit threat. The folksy nature of the town, with its cunchy lavalamps, unhindered parking, and homecooked menus, is threatened with the conversion to militancy, or at least a form of military nostalgia as the town mayor proposes a dedicated war reenactment. Effectively he hopes to introduce a celebration of an entirely new form of consumption, namely anti-consumption. In resurrecting a simulacrum of past generations, this celebrates neither the living word of powerful knowledge, as might be found in an élitist-yet-universalist work of Proust, nor the life- and contemporaneity-affirming experience of sensual engagement with transitory taste sensations. The dead always taste the same: of dust. Luke's opposition is forthright and immediate. Not only is his status as a complementary force between the appetites of the mind and stomach, the practical brain and the whimsical, under threat from this archaic resurrection of grudges now absent from the snug community. He is also opposed simply to condescension to the natural growth of the townspeople's relationships to one another through their natural sharings of appetite. In reinforcing the norms of a spartan, puritanical and violent era, Luke fears the retardation, or even suppression of appetite and the communal bonding from which it springs. Lorelai and Rory gleefully note Luke's increasing irritation, seemingly arch yet, in my view, secretly thrilling in the knowledge that their white knight will defend their estro-packed foodie pow-wows. Like the secret cowboy he is, a throwback to a genre romanticism the girls secretly thrill in, he rises. "I thought we were here to discuss *town* issues!" (1.08, "Love and War and Snow"). In this moment he concisely defines the contemporary domestic idyll Stars Hollow is, the cooking, crunchy, charmed bourgeois space all in attendance know it to be. It is a space for cooking, for estro-bonding, for mensches of the order of Jackson, and clichéd French of the order of Lorelai's employee Michel. It is a realm where leisure and idyll consumption have so long been the norm that war and patriarchy have long been erased from the collective memories of this matriarchal New England stretch of enforced oddity. Luke is effectively rejecting the town mayor's most tokenistic of attempts to assert the most tokenistic of gestures to a patriarchal, spartan history. The character of his motivations is implicitly stated in his introduction of himself as father, and to the townspeople, young and old, as his children. Yet Luke-as-Hagrid, the taciturn cowboy, understands the potential for a hypermasculine presence to identify with the matriarchy, as evidenced in his connection to the series' central relationship. A foodie, domestic male is not a figure emasculated, but rather one of privilege, spared the humiliations and injurious defeats of machodom. Luke is a gentle giant, and a hairy one at that, yet one who negotiates his testosterone in a naturally estrogen-friendly environment, and indeed, television show.

The success of *Gilmore Girls* derives, in my view, from its successful, graceful season transitions, which support the maturation of the show's relationships from that of a young family, both biologically and in the emotional terms of community, to one in middle age. As such Luke-as-asexual becomes Luke the lover. Hagrid becomes Heathcliff. Kirk, the local nebbish, enters adulthood after protracted adolescence, like Sookie, finding a partner. Rory and her mother rediscover one another as adults, just as her own mother reengages with Lorelai as a full-grown adult. Powerfully, Lorelai finally discovers the very adult anger of season five. "Nothing," clearly, is in fact the infinitesimal daily alterations to habit that accrue into the solid foundations of a new, and newly occupied, universe. This is certainly the space all, but Rory and Lorelai in particular, find themselves in by the latter seasons of the series. In the permutations of reference and engagement it becomes clear that the mother has made a major transition over the course of the series. Lorelai is, like the presence of sex within the series, suspended above the foundation realities of consumption. Now, with maturity, she is aware of consumption as an entirely complex realm, ambiguous, elusive, even interchangeable. In the fourth season a collection of interchanges suggests to the audience that Lorelai has expanded her consumer notions. Now the blessings of 21st century consumption — limitless, multi-various and inedible — stands beside her former foodie vibe and nosh. She now quotes Tsun Su at the dinner table, shares Koffi Annan diplomacy jokes with her élite-bound daughter, and seems as interested in her cell phone as she is her pastry. Is this Lorelai choosing the alternate tribe of the palmpilot-wielding alphas, a group that has always wanted to welcome her? Her marriage to Christopher, even if it is a default emotional position for her, certainly suggests Lorelai finally succumbing to the pressures of socialization. He is all she has fought against, anodyne, pleasant, and feckless. Yet it always was an acceptable social match, albeit premature. As marriage it is a social contract, and yet she cannot betray her emotions. Lorelai has absorbed Luke's lessons, through the structures of their food talks, on how the domestic, tactile and culinary may still firmly stand outside the realms of whimsy. Her ongoing love for Luke may easily be equated to her love for his diner, and the importance of that space as a venue for the structures of food talks, a space of freer exposition than her parents can ever be due to her compulsive defensiveness in their presence. What, in my view, Lorelai discovers osmotically through the presence of Rory and Lane is how unlikely transitions may be between the sensuality of food and the tactility of home spaces. Her consummation with Luke, with the food talk space of his diner, is discovered by her semi-nude parade in front of his diners. In short, a woman of breathtaking wit finds an outlet for her worldview both expanded from, and congruous with, her former foodie universe. Where once food was a mysterious passion, it is now a known lover, anthropomorphized by Luke and, in season seven, the memory of Luke as lover. Lorelai still loves to consume, yet she, and her daughter, have learned to do so with a maturity that forms a shining example to all of the show's other characters. As such, her sudden leadership in the breadth of consumption, leads to her occupying a place of increased largesse within the community. Like Sookie and Luke, the generosity of the foodie in Lorelai fulfills the needs of many. As such Lorelai's acceptance of April, her philosophical ambition for the Dragonfly Inn, and her choice of Luke and Stars Hollow, even while being socialized by the Bostonian Christopher, point to a further sublimation of sex. Food and élitist knowledge is the vehicle for generosity, and the community that inspires it its recipient.

Note

1. This entails the specific tone and content of commercials aired during the two episodes, and speaks to the manner in which sponsors would seek to represent themselves to the average *Gilmore Girls* viewer.

Works Cited

Babette's Feast. Dir. Gabriel Axel. Perf. Stéphane Audran. Panorama Film, 1987.

Big Night. Dir. Campbell Scott and Stanley Tucci. Perf. Marc Anthony, Tony Shaloub, Stanley Tucci, Minnie Driver, Isabella Rossellini. Rysher Entertainment, 1996.

Gabler, Neal. "The Tyranny of 18 to 49: American Culture Held Hostage." The Norman Lear Center. 9 April 2003. 17 May 2007 <http://www.learcenter.org/pdf/Gabler18to49.pdf>.

McLoone, Tracy. "Single White Females." *Pop Matters.* 1999–2004. 4 May 2004 <http://www.popmatters.com/tv/reviews/g/Gilmore-girls.shtml>.

Okey, Jessica, "Sex in the Media: An Influence on Adolescent Development." MS Thesis. University of Wisconsin-Stout. May 2002. 17 May 2007 <http://www.uwstout.edu/lib/thesis/2002/2002okeyj.pdf>.

Sherman-Palladino, Amy and Daniel Palladino. "Commentary on 'You Jump, I Jump, Jack.'" *Gilmore Girls, The Complete Fifth Season.* DVD. Warner Brothers. 2005.

Six Feet Under. Alan Ball. HBO. 2001–2005.

The Sopranos. David Chase. HBO. 1999–2007.

Still More Gilmore

How Online Fan Communities Remediate Gilmore Girls

Daniel Smith-Rowsey

At the end of 2006, *Time* magazine, in a showy gesture, declared "You" its hallowed Person of the Year. The cover presented a computer monitor with a mirror as its screen. The nation's newsweekly of record declared its solidarity with millions of online users and consumers over the mere "content-providers" who had given them something to use and consume. As Henry Jenkins, author of *Textual Poachers: Television Fans and Participatory Culture* and *Convergence Culture: Where Old and New Media Collide,* put it on his blog, "*Time's* cover suggests just how central the idea of participatory culture has been to popular discourse in 2006." *Time's* unusual interpellation may have represented something of a tipping point — or, in TVese, a jump-the-shark moment — of a paradigm that has been emerging at least since Roland Barthes announced the death of the author back in the 1960s. The nominal idea is that the reader's— or viewer's— interpretation of a text is just as valid, and perhaps more so, than the person(s) who created the text. In our current era of constant internet-supported remediation the meaning of art, apparently, lies with the spectator, now more than ever.

For any longtime hit television show, this remediation exists primarily through two forms, really two forums— websites for fan fiction (often called fanfic) and websites for discussion, or message boards. It is important to distinguish between these two types of sites, a distinction that little extant scholarship has observed. The prevailing tone, prejudices, and dominant ideology of the two types of communities are somewhat different, at least in the case of *Gilmore Girls* communities. Herein I use *Gilmore Girls* as a case study, and contend that while fanfic sites tend to reinforce a show's ideology, the discussion sites, perhaps counter–intuitively, tend to be more subversive. I argue that the meaning of this art has not changed overmuch in its renegotiation.

Gilmore Girls matters because TV matters and women matter. In December of 2006, *Entertainment Weekly* wrote that, unlike the bygone era of *The Mary Tyler Moore Show, Rhoda,* and *Alice,* in 2006, *The New Adventures of Old Christine* was the only sitcom centered around a female character. Without getting into major questions of genre (is it a dramedy? what is it?) *Gilmore Girls* continuously provides a very rare, privileged space where women can be funny and human without having to serve the relentlessly plot-driven needs of, say, the police procedural. In the introduction of *Gilmore Girls,* the first four credited characters are women, and that doesn't even include Lorelai's mother. The show was created and largely maintained by a woman, Amy Sherman-Palladino.

Henry Jenkins, in *Textual Poachers,* a foundational text for much of fan studies, demonstrated that he was well aware of the dangers of monolithic representations of fan communities. Even as he used the language of cultural studies to assert alternatives to authorial authority, even as he insisted on fans' complication of "dominant cultural hierarchies," he was still careful to agree with Stuart Hall, author of *Representation: Cultural Representations and Signifying Practices,* that popular culture is "characterized by 'the double movement of containment and resistance, which is always inevitably inside it'" (Jenkins, *Textual* 34). Nonetheless, in practice, Jenkins' claims about the legitimacy of fan culture have served to valorize fanfic writers as challengers to the show's dominant ideology. In the case of *Gilmore Girls,* this view needs to be complicated somewhat.

Ideology

Gilmore Girls' ideology might be summarized in a single word: precious. This word well encapsulates the following litany of defining characteristics. Through six seasons, there have been no gay relationships and no one has suddenly come out of the closet. (Michel is swishy, but we don't know him to be gay.) The show's ethnic diversity is generally limited to Michel, Lane, and Mrs. Kim, with only the latter providing nuance to the show's nominal bourgeois-bohemian-friendly tone. (Through six seasons, Gypsy and Caesar have appeared in a somewhat-marginal 18 episodes each, but were stuck in service economy jobs.) For a show that stars five fertile women (Lorelai, Rory, Lane, Paris, and Sookie), there has never been a genuine pregnancy scare — an episode where a character fretted about being pregnant. (Lorelai did wake up in Luke's bed to some concerned thoughts once, but they were dismissed soon enough. Sookie's pregnancies were quite planned.) Considering the show is premised upon an unplanned pregnancy from the 80s, perhaps that's not so odd — but lesser writers might have used that premise as polarity.

Through six seasons, no character has died. No one has been raped or killed, or been threatened with rape or murder. We've never seen a gun or even a crime on this show — Jess's vandalisms and Rory's boat theft weren't televised. Nothing supernatural has ever occurred or even been slightly suggested. The two main characters had a total of seven lovers — Lorelai had Max, Christopher, Jason, and Luke, while Rory had Dean, Jess, and Logan. Lorelai and Rory have basically been serial monogamists. If the *Seinfeld* producers supposedly had a credo of "no hugging, no learning," the *Gilmore Girls* producers might well have had a credo of "no cheap gimmicks." *Gilmore Girls* is assiduously devoted to small-town life and relationships. The show is fundamentally about tensions between mothers and daughters, without (much) recourse to stunts, or what might be called "soap opera"-type plot devices.

Arguably, the show is fundamentally about non–urban female empowerment and protecting — about Lorelai (Lauren Graham) protecting Rory (Alexis Bledel) and their way of life from the judgments of others, particularly but not exclusively her parents. Perhaps no other television show is more about the protecting of choices that were made in a year that happened about two decades before any of the events we see. On some level, this protective attitude seems to have found its way to many of the online forums.

In sum, it may be roughly claimed that the ideology of *Gilmore Girls* is both precious and protective — or, more accurately, protective of a specific kind of preciousness. This is the ideology that is most often replicated, and not complicated, on the internet.

Fanfic Sites

Online forums constitute a very particularized method of "owning" a show. Like all internet chat spaces that attract advertising dollars, they are governed by certain rules of etiquette. These include good manners and respect, as well as refraining from flaming, trolling, or pitching one's product. They are intriguingly non–gendered (in the case of *Gilmore Girls*, they are thought to be heavily female-trafficked, but that presumption can cut different ways). At the same time, they are on the internet, which means that any sort of essentialist reading of them is bound to be problematic.

In her recent essay "Archontic Literature," Abigail Derecho recognizes the importance of Barthes' declaration that intertextuality is "the condition of any text whatsoever," but distinguishes "archontic" texts as those that "generate variations that explicitly announce themselves" (65). Seeking freedom from the negative connotations of "derivative" and "appropriative," Derecho asserts "archontic" because of its shared roots with "archive," a never-ending extension of words and knowledge. She borrows the term from Derrida, who in *Archive Fever* delineated what might almost be seen as the original trauma of archives: "By incorporating the knowledge deployed in reference to it, the archive augments itself ... but in the same stroke it loses the absolute and meta-textual authority it might claim to have." Derecho hews her idea of archontic literature most closely with the ideas of Edouard Glissant, who insisted that post–colonial trauma can only be ethically managed by respecting the concept of relation, which "gives equal privilege to parts and wholes." Derecho finds that Deleuze's assertion that repetition is not merely the first time said again, but "the first time to the 'nth' power," is not merely relevant to scholarly commentary but also to fan fiction.

Gilmore Girls does not lack for archontic extensions. As of January 1, 2007 — every internet reference in this article is dated at that date — fanfiction.net houses 10,851 *Gilmore Girls* stories. Fanfiction.net sorts by category — romance, humor, drama, poetry, action/adventure, mystery, horror, parody, angst, supernatural, suspense, sci-fi, fantasy, spiritual, and tragedy. One can also sort by character — if a given canonical character is in the piece. Stories are not ranked by users, only reviewed. Fanfiction.net makes up for in quantity whatever it lacks in quality. It is the Costco of fan fiction; occasional treasures may be unearthed. One such gem, by Ozfan, from November 22, 2006, puts Rory with Luke in light of recent show events: "'I'm...' she is about to say great, that is the word she always uses. Then she decides to downgrade it to good. Then she decides to be honest. 'I think I have the Christmas blues. I don't like being home. I don't know why. It doesn't feel like home anymore.' There, she said it." Like many fanfics, this story deepens the Luke-Rory relationship beyond anything seen on the show. One might speculate that this trend may be the result of daughters looking for a father figure, or just dirty old men.

More selective sites — more specialized archives — include the "Chilton Library" at chilton.smithereen.net/chilton, which has 120 stories by 73 authors. This site is distinguished by pretending to be the official site of the school that Rory attended for the first three years of the show, the Chilton Academy (though there are many Chilton Schools in the United States, none are in Connecticut). It is somewhat user-friendly but also serves to privilege the first three seasons of the show. The home page gives you over to a new student, Rory Gilmore, with a few opening remarks: "You probably don't need my help, but then again, this place can be scary with all the gargoyles and ivy and looming stone walls." This tone, educated with slight colloquial character (e.g. "with all"), tends to characterize the best pieces.

Another selective site is blah-mah-gah.net/fanfic, where, bannered "Dante's Inferno," they provide a home for 54 authors, 145 stories, and 137 members. The site includes all the requisite photos but isn't overly distinctive. There are 394 fanfic stories at the clearing-house-style fanforum.net. "Proud & Prejudiced" is the way that the maintainers at gilmorepnp.spiralingdown-ward.com banner their site, claiming they don't mind being called elitist fic snobs. They have about 100 stories. Unlike other sites, "Proud & Prejudiced" presents Lorelai and Rory as formally dressed, perhaps giving more "class" to the surroundings. This site has a section for mature readers, labeled "Behind the Rory Curtain." One sample is "Scrabble" by mafiaprincess731, about a board game night between Luke and Lorelai, where one thing leads to another: "She lowered herself onto his large member and both let out a long moan as he filled her completely." Healthy "fantasies" about *Gilmore Girls* characters probably offer the same psychological benefits that such fantasies do in real life.

"Proud & Prejudiced" also connects to another version of itself at livejournal.com — namely community.livejournal.com/proudprejudiced. Livejournal.com has various fan fiction sites, in particular community.livejournal.com/gg_fic, but if the Chilton Library suffers from reminiscence about the past, gg_fic is perhaps too late to the party. The site only began in 2005, and has a scant 300 posts, not many of which are actual fan fiction. It should be noted that any list of web authors is not as singular as, say, a comparison of literary agencies' roll calls might be. Authors can and certainly do post to multiple sites, and may well post at one site under multiple noms de plume.

Perhaps *Gilmore Girls* fan fiction's best compromise between selectiveness and all-inclusiveness lies at gilmore–fiction.net, which is bannered as "Black & White & Read." The site claims: "We are the home of 342 authors from among our 1690 members. There have been 24947 reviews written about our 1254 stories." Its listed genres are action/adventure, angst, alternate universe, crossover, drama, general, humor, missing scene, parody, post–ep, romance, series, and vignette.

General fan fiction challenges and "ficathons" are regularly sponsored by many sites, including those named above. They do not always simply solicit stories; the site (or its members) will often ask for a specific fictional construct, for example, Jess eating at Richard and Emily Gilmore's house. (There is no need to ask for Tristin/Rory pairings; they are already so popular, they are generally known by their own category: Trory.)

The top-ranked story on Black & White & Read is called "Variation on a Theme" by an author called KinoFille. It was first published on May 27, 2005, and totals 51,294 words, not an unusual length by any means. It is an AU story, fanfic code for alternate universe. It projects a world where Lorelai married Christopher shortly after learning she was pregnant with Rory. The story describes AU Lorelai and Rory's first encounter with Stars Hollow, shortly after Rory has turned sixteen. Unlike many fanfic stories, it generally follows not only the rules of grammar but also the rules of the show's level of wit, insisting on one-liners and witty asides. The website's quote from the story, to draw in the casual reader, is: "It was just that sometimes, especially when she met someone new, she felt as if she was spending her whole life doing penance for a mistake she made on the balcony of her bedroom when she was a kid." A story like this represents the deployment of Barthes' writerly hermeneutic codes. This is the old story, revealing more of its themes in a renegotiation that the canon could not have supported. Yet it is typical of *Gilmore Girls* fan fiction in that it does not break from the show's preciousness and protectiveness as explained in the introduction.

The top-ranked and most-reviewed story on Dante's Inferno is called "Next, on *Gilmore Girls...*" by an author calling him/herself Holly Gilmore. It was first published on October 18, 2004, and totals 125,434 words. It is about a world where Lorelai and Rory actually made it to their much-planned European trip. Beginning there, it takes us through many months of alternate Gilmore life, including a far longer Jess-Rory romance, culminating in Luke and Lorelai's decision to marry after they learn that she's pregnant by him. Quite untypically, it's told in the style of a stage play, e.g., "JESS: (smirking) That's the fun part. RORY: (chuckling) Getting caught? JESS: (kissing her neck) No. The possibility of getting caught." Authors like Holly Gilmore have taken it upon themselves to gratify the fans where the show has not seen fit to do so. (Should they have spent some of that energy on their own books, where they would have had to create the images in readers' heads from scratch? Perhaps. Yet who would have read them?) This may be all the more reason they do not seriously veer from the show's worldview.

Of course research for this article has not included reading all of the more than 10,000 pieces of *Gilmore Girls* fan fiction that exist online. Yet this informal sampling, restricted to some of the higher-ranked and most-visited pieces, is striking in how little it challenges the show's basic tenets. For example, slash — fanfic code for same-sex relationships— is a category on gilmore–fiction.net, but when I sorted that way, exactly nothing came up. The only livejournal.com fanfic community to name itself as devoted to gay readings of *Gilmore Girls*, community.livejournal.com/rorytehgay, has all of two stories where any character — Rory — leans gay. tv.groups.yahoo.com/group/GilmoreGirlsSlash exists, but the site seems moribund. Heterosexual sex, on the other hand, happens all the time, but that's more of an exploration than a challenge to the show.

People in high-ranked *Gilmore Girls* fanfic don't seem to die very often. There are a few supernatural stories (mostly crossovers with other WB magic-inflected shows like *Buffy the Vampire Slayer* and *Angel*) and a few pregnancies, but they are few and far between. Obviously, this is the internet, and one can find just about anything if one looks hard enough — and if it's not there, one can just create it. Nonetheless we can tentatively postulate that as of January 1, 2007, the lion's share of online *Gilmore Girls* fan fiction is quite supportive — even protective — of the world that Amy Sherman-Palladino ostensibly created. Roberta Pearson wrote that fan fiction writers choose their shows precisely because they share some ideological affinity with the shows' worldviews. This is particularly true with *Gilmore Girls*.

Message Board Sites

Compared with fan fiction sites, there has been very little scholarship on discussion sites that do not contain fan fiction. Academics have good reasons for this. For one thing, common message board sites are even more extensive and scattered than fanfic sites. For another, they call into question the identity of the fan. Anyone can post to a topical message board, while presumably only a true fan would bother to comment on and/or write fan fiction. This is where fan studies may merge with a branch of media studies that will someday perhaps be known as internet studies. The regular posters at given message board sites are, I venture to say, less united by the pleasures of extending a fictional universe than by the pleasures of like-minded company. This may be most apparent on televisionwithoutpity.com, which unashamedly labels at least one discussion thread for each of its (more than 30) regularly reviewed shows "The Meet Market" (the *Gilmore Girls'* version is known as "Welcome to Luke's: The Meet Market"). Sure enough, the Meet Market threads do not lack for activity.

Fan fiction theorists have been quick to lay claim to the idea of "extending the middle" from narrative theorists like Peter Brooks, but have mostly ignored message board sites in their paradigms. If the ideas of Barthes and Deleuze are too often liberally applied to fan fiction, they are not applied enough to simple discussion communities. Yet these posters are also adding something crucial to the process. While the comments on fanfic sites are almost exclusively related to the fanfic pieces, the comments on message boards on most TV-show sites are generally devoted to the show itself. By this author's small sampling, fanfic posters tend to be more nurturing, while non–fanfic board posters tend to be saying whatever corrosive cleverness may get a rise out of someone. Non-fanfic board posters tend to be more deconstructive, critical, and less reverential than the commenters on fanfic sites. In the case of *Gilmore Girls*, through their snark and general pessimism, through more anarchic forms of archontic contributions, they may actually be making more of a Derridean *différance* than their peers on the fanfic sites.

The very functional, warehouse-like fanforum.com has 2,606 *Gilmore Girls* threads, many with hundreds of posts, and too many members to count. The similarly clearing-house-style Fanfiction.net, in addition to its above-mentioned fanfic, has 161 *Gilmore Girls* "communities" and 53 *Gilmore Girls* "forums" (one can't really tell the difference). Gilmoregirls.org has a very active message board — well over 200,000 posts, and still going strong. One senses a singular maintainer who did well to jump in at the outset and has kept a nice modest home. At livejournal.com, there are 35 separate communities (websites) that have "Gilmore" or "GG" (signifying the show) in their title. Community.livejournal.com/gilmore_girls has 3,552 members. Thedragonflyinn.org has a very handsome site but seems to suffer from lack of posts and members.

Some communities are on what might be called life support. Stars-hollow.org has 3,543 threads, 7,053 members, and 240,620 posts, but has now lapsed into ghost-town status. P079.ezboard.com/bgilmoregirls87533 is another site with much-diminished traffic. It's not that people have stopped talking about *Gilmore Girls*. Part of the explanation may be a relatively new feature at the corporate website. When one goes to thewb.com/shows/gilmore–girls, one can link to lounge.cwtv.com/forumdisplay.php?f=8, which is 329 pages of approximately 20 linked threads each, totaling 6,574 threads. The networks, smelling advertising dollars, have barged in on fan territory, with all the cultural capital and institutional respect they command. Sure enough, many fans have followed.

Fans "add value" and "extend the middle" of beloved TV shows especially by patronizing spoiler sites and recap sites. (If you've been living under a rock, a spoiler is a piece of information to which regular viewers/readers are not yet privy; a recap is a blow-by-blow recount of the diegetic events of a show.) Both types of sites allow internet posters to make a slight temporal reach before making their declarations in the present. On a spoiler site, people speculate about supposedly "leaked" information, representing the most material projections of fan desires about the future. On a recap site — well, on *the* recap site, televisionwithoutpity.com, always google's first destination for such a thing — fans devote their energies to deconstructing recent episodes. The banner of televisionwithoutpity.com says "spare the snark, spoil the networks," but this is probably meant ironically (or for myopic investors and advertisers), because most of the recaps are written in quite a skeptical style. As a typical example, Al Lowe, recapping the "I'd Rather Be in Philadelphia" episode from season seven, wrote, "In fact, I cried throughout this episode, though at times, as you will come upon later in this recap, the crying was out of boredom." Following the recappers' lead, the posters on the message boards are more unsparing in their criticism.

On December 31, 2006, a user named nak3dqueen asked the livejournal. com gilmore_girls community to speculate on a supposed leak about a death of a character, rumored to be funny and "not anyone close to the show." The invoking of Anna's mother occasioned some argument about who came up with a "secret-daughter" plot first, *Desperate Housewives* or *Gilmore Girls*. A user called elegantelbow said, "I bet you $1 it will be Kirk." Other speculated victims included Taylor, Mrs. Kim, Mrs. Huntzberger, and Richard (someone countered that such a plot could never be funny). In a nicely representative board message, a user named faery_fall responded to another guess, "I doubt there's a large fanbase for dog Paul Anka, but dog-deaths are sad, and ubiquitous. GG's gotta be more creative, lest I bludgen [sic] them with my rocks and small tools." Though this fan recognizes his/her power limits, some attempt at humor is the chosen outlet.

On January 1, 2007, televisionwithoutpity.com's best-attended *Gilmore Girls* thread, The Spoiler Discussion, speculated about a season eight without

Rory (not based on any actual leaked evidence — this forum's attendees don't need that, but they don't mind it when it comes). A user called domenica_marie suggested that Rory could be shipped off to a Rhodes scholarship or a job as a foreign correspondent. A user called juststandstill said the show could live without Rory because the show has been The Rory Show and The Lorelai Show since season four, and without Rory, one loses nothing of Stars Hollow, but merely Rory and Logan and Paris. A user called bellamn16 chimed in that Lorelai could be stuck with Paris, as when they both "lost Rory" at the beginning of season six. (Or perhaps, one might add, in the way Fonzie was stuck with Potsie after Richie and Ralph left.) Another user called funnyfriend said that if Rory isn't going to be in season eight, they should change the name of the series, as other shows have done. A reasonable last word on this topic — naturally surrounded by all sorts of other posts on other topics, e.g. the significance of Merchant of Venice references, and speculation on April moving to New Mexico — was from teajunkie, who said that if AB (née Alexis Bledel, the actor playing Rory, as any poster would know) is reluctant to commit to a full 22 episodes, the series could get by with her doing perhaps half of that, considering how long it had been since her character had a compelling storyline.

This piece has hardly exhausted the full internet presence of *Gilmore Girls*. (One does not exhaust internet possibilities.) For example, there are plenty of fan sites that don't have message boards, e.g. gilmoregirlsnews.com and gilmoregirlsshop.com. These sites, no doubt frequented by fans, also add cultural capital to the pre–existing ideological world of the show. The CW (formerly the WB) provides all sorts of links for merchandise. Amazon.com sells four official *Gilmore Girls* novelizations: *Like Mother, Like Daughter* by Catherine Clark, *I Love You, You Idiot* by Cathy East Dubowski, *I Do, Don't I?* by Catherine Clark, and *The Other Side of Summer* by Amy Sherman-Palladino. They all tell the show's exact stories from Rory's first-person perspective; they are not transgressive. Corporate-sponsored and corporate-friendly sites are unlikely to challenge the show's worldview.

Do Fans Affect the Show?

Network TV executives were probably not surprised by *Time*'s Person of the Year cover for 2006. After seeing the phenomenal online interest in shows like *Star Trek* and *Buffy the Vampire Slayer*, and the successful solicitation of fan input by Peter Jackson for the *Lord of the Rings* films, producers seem to have concluded that fan cultivation may be a lucrative endeavor. The last few years have seen an upsurge in online "components" for shows as well as "shout–outs" to fans; for example, *Lost* characters' web-accessible journals contain plot information otherwise unavailable to viewers, while *Everwood* named a character after its televisionwithoutpity.com recapper and a *Buffy* character was seen carrying televisionwithoutpity.com merchandise. As of autumn 2006, *Gilmore Girls* features "fan discussion pieces"—ostensible teenage girl reactions to plotlines—during the commercial breaks. As previously noted, the network sponsors a *Gilmore Girls* fan message board.

Nonetheless, none of this seems to have affected the actual diegetic world of *Gilmore Girls*. In an interview the author conducted with Pamela Ribon, who recapped *Gilmore Girls* for five years for televisionwithoutpity.com, she said, "I've still yet to see any sign that they're acknowledging what fans think. I don't think that Amy Sherman-Palladino was the kind of person who would be swayed by online strangers." Commenting on the Luke/Lorelai relationship in an interview with Amy Amatangelo of the *Boston Herald*, Lauren Graham, who plays Lorelai, recently said, "I mean, if everything had gone the way the fans wanted it to go in terms of that relationship, the show would be over, or I would just be calling Rory, like, 'What are you doing tonight?'" Graham may be intentionally misreading the fans, but her tone of casual disregard is telling.

Despite—or perhaps because of—the show's apparent indifference, hundreds of *Gilmore Girls* fan fiction writers soldier on, seemingly content not to subvert the precious, protective worldview of the show. Perhaps it is partly because Stars Hollow and the characters of Lorelai and Rory seem so immutable that online fan fiction writers do not often try to change them. The show's conservative approach to fan intervention may well have contributed to a conservative tendency among fanfic authors. It seems to be left to the posters on the discussion boards to transgress—to perform the occasional metaphoric vandalizing of Barbie dolls. And perhaps there is something essentially precious and protective—*Gilmore*-like—about fan fiction in general, and something essentially subversive about message boards.

Conclusion

We live in the "You" era—a time when media content increasingly advertises itself as more user-friendly and even user-controlled than it ever was. At the same time, online authors have demonstrated a remarkable capacity to remediate storylines from their favorite shows. *Gilmore Girls*, unlike most TV shows, presents a fictional, precious, un–soap-opera-like world and a protective, female-empowering ideology that most of its many online fans do not seek to genuinely subvert. It is as though the fans have spoken and said: people like Lorelai and Rory and places like Stars Hollow are rare enough, let us not seek to radically remake them, but only to extend and illuminate their glory. We can appreciate and thank them for their efforts, with but a moment's idle reflection of how differently their efforts might have been shaped in a world with more shows like *Gilmore Girls*—where its preciousness might not need to be protected.

Works Cited

"Aah! Rory! Is That a Girl on Your Face?" *LiveJournal.com.* 2007.1 January 2007 <http://community.livejournal.com/rorytehgay>.

Amatangelo, Amy. "The Insider: Lauren Graham." *Boston Herald.com.* 31 December 2006. 1 January 2007 <http://theedge.bostonherald.com/tvNews/view.bg?article id=174598>.

Amazon.com. 2007. 1 January 2007 <http://amazon.com>.

Bacon-Smith, Camille. *Enterprising Women: Television Fandom and the Creation of Popular Myth.* Philadelphia: University of Pennsylvania Press, 1992.

Barthes, Roland. *S/Z.* Trans. Richard Miller. New York: Noonday, 1974.

Black & White & Read: Gilmore Girls Fanfic Archive. 2007. 1 January 2007 <http://gilmore–fiction.net>.

Brooks, Peter. *Reading for the Plot: Design and Intention in Narrative.* Cambridge, Mass.: Harvard University Press, 1992.

Bury, Rhiannon. *Cyberspaces of Their Own: Female Fandoms Online.* New York: Peter Lang, 2005.

Butler, Judith. *Gender Trouble.* New York: Routledge, 1990.

Chilton Library. 2007. *Chilton Library.* 2007. 1 January 2007 <http://chilton.smith ereen.net/chilton.html>.

Dante's Inferno. 2007. *Dante's Inferno: A Fan Fiction Archive.* 1 January 2007 <http://blah-mah-gah.net/fanfic>.

De Certeau, Michel. *The Practice of Everyday Life.* Berkeley: University of California Press, 1984.

Derecho, Abigail. "Archontic Literature." *Fan Fiction and Fan Communities in the Age of the Internet.* Ed. Karen Hellekson and Kristina Busse. Jefferson, NC: McFarland, 2006. 61–78.

Fanfiction.net. 2007. 1 January 2007 <http://www.fanfiction.net>.

Fanforum.com. 2007. 1 January 2007 <http://www.fanforum.com>.

Fiske, John. *Reading the Popular.* New York: Routledge, 1989.

GilmoreGirls.org. 2007. 1 January 2007 <http://www.gilmoregirls.org>.

"Gilmore Girls Center." *EZBoard.com.* 2007. 1 January 2007 <http://P079.ezboard. com/bgilmoregirls87533>.

Hall, Stuart. "Encoding/decoding." *Culture, Media, Language: Working Papers in Cultural Studies.* Ed. Stuart Hall, Dorothy Hobson, Andrew Lowe, and Paul Willis. London: Hutchinson, 1991. 128–38.

Hellekson, Karen, and Kristina Busse, eds. *Fan Fiction and Fan Communities in the Age of the Internet.* Jefferson, NC: McFarland, 2006.

Hills, Matt. "To Boldly Go Where Others Have Gone Before: *Star Trek* and (Academic) Narratives of Progress." *Scope: An Online Journal of Film Studies* (November 2000). 1 January 2007 <http://nottingham.ac.uk/film/journal/bookrev/star-trek.htm>.

_____. *Fan Cultures.* London: Routledge, 2002.

Jenkins, Henry. *Textual Poachers: Television Fans and Participatory Culture.* New York: Routledge, 1992.

_____. "Reception Theory and Audience Research: The Mystery of the Vampire's Kiss." *Reinventing Film Studies.* Ed. Christine Gledhill and Linda Williams. London: Arnold, 2000. 165–82.

_____. *Convergence Culture.* New York: New York University Press, 2006.

_____. *Fans, Bloggers, and Gamers.* New York: New York University Press, 2006.

Lewis, Lisa A., ed. *The Adoring Audiences.* London: Routledge, 1992.

LiveJournal.com. 2007. 1 January 2007 <http://livejournal.com>.

"CW Lounge." *CW.com*. 2007. 1 January 2007 <http://lounge.cwtv.com/forumdisplay.
    php?f=8>.
McQuall, Denis. *Audience Analysis*. London: SAGE, 1997.
Pearson, Roberta, E. "Kings of Infinite Space: Cult Television Characters and Narrative
    Possibilities." *Scope: An Online Journal of Film Studies* (August 1993). 1 January 2007
    <http://nottingham.ac.uk/film/journal/articles/kings-of-infinite-space.htm>.
Porter, David. *Internet Culture*. New York: Routledge, 1997.
Proud & Prejudiced. 2007. 1 January 2007 <http://gilmorepnp.spiralingdownward.com>.
Ribon, Pamela. Email to author on December 29, 2006.
Stars Hollow. 2007. 1 January 2007 <http://stars-hollow.org>.
Television without Pity. 2007. 1 January 2007 <http://televisionwithoutpity.com>.
The Dragon Fly Inn. 2007. 1 January 2007 <http://thedragonflyinn.org>.
"*Gilmore Girls* Slash." 2007. *Yahoo.com*. 1 January 2007 <http://tv.groups.yahoo.com/
    group/GilmoreGirlsSlash>.
"Where You Lead." *LiveJournal.com*. 2007. 1 January 2007 <http://community.live
    journal.com/gilmore_girls>.
Wicks, Robert H. *Understanding Audiences: Learning to Use the Media Constructively*.
    Mahwah, N.J.: Lawrence Erlbaum, 2001.

Appendix
Episode Guide

Episodes by season, 2000–2007. Dates refer to original, initial air dates in the U.S. market. Seasons 1–6 originally aired on the WB network. Season 7 originally aired on the CW network.

Season One

1.01 "Pilot"
5 October 2000. Amy Sherman-Palladino, dir. Lesli Linka Glatter

1.02 "The Lorelais' First Day at Chilton"
12 October 2000. Amy Sherman-Palladino, dir. Arlene Sanford

1.03 "Kill Me Now"
19 October 2000. Joanne Waters, dir. Adam Nimoy

1.04 "The Deer Hunters"
26 October 2000. Jed Seidel, dir. Alan Myerson

1.05 "Cinnamon's Wake"
2 November 2000. Daniel Palladino, dir. Michael Katleman

1.06 "Rory's Birthday Parties"
9 November 2000. Amy Sherman-Palladino, dir. Sarah Pia Anderson

1.07 "Kiss and Tell"
16 November 2000. Jenji Kohan, dir. Rodman Flender

1.08 "Love and War and Snow"
14 December 2000. Joan Binder Weiss, dir. Alan Myerson

1.09 "Rory's Dance"
20 December 2000. Amy Sherman-Palladino, dir. Lesli Linka Glatter

1.10 "Forgiveness and Stuff"
21 December 2000. John Stephens, dir. Bethany Rooney

1.11 "Paris Is Burning"
11 January 2001. Joan Binder Weiss, dir. David Petrarca

1.12 "Double Date"
18 January 2001. Amy Sherman-Palladino, dir. Lev L. Spiro

1.13 "Concert Interruptus"
15 February 2001. Elaine Arata, dir. Bruce Seth Green

1.14 "That Damn Donna Reed"
22 February 2001. Daniel Palladino, Amy Sherman-Palladino, dir. Michael Katleman

1.15 "Christopher Returns"

1 March 2001. Daniel Palladino, dir. Michael Katleman

1.16 "Star-Crossed Lovers and Other Strangers"

8 March 2001. John Stephens, Linda Loiselle Guzik, dir. Lesli Linka Glatter

1.17 "The Breakup, Part 2"

15 March 2001. Amy Sherman-Palladino, dir. Nick Marck

1.18 "The Third Lorelai"

22 March 2001. Amy Sherman-Palladino, dir. Michael Katleman

1.19 "Emily in Wonderland"

26 April 2001. John Stevens, Linda Loiselle Guzik, dir. Perry Lang

1.20 "P.S. I Lo..."

3 May 2001. Elaine Arata, Joan Binder Weiss, dir. Lev L. Spiro

1.21 "Love, Daisies, and Troubadours"

10 May 2001. Daniel Palladino, dir. Amy Sherman-Palladino

Season Two

2.01 "Sadie, Sadie"

9 October 2001. Amy Sherman-Palladino, dir. Amy Sherman-Palladino

2.02 "Hammers and Veils"

9 October 2001. Amy Sherman-Palladino, dir. Michael Katleman

2.03 "Red Light on the Wedding Night"

16 October 2001. Daniel Palladino, dir. Gail Mancuso

2.04 "The Road Trip to Harvard"

23 October 2001. Daniel Palladino, dir. Jamie Babbit

2.05 "Nick & Nora/Sid & Nancy"

30 October 2001. Amy Sherman-Palladino, dir. Michael Katleman

2.06 "Presenting Lorelai Gilmore"

6 November 2001. Sheila R. Lawrence, dir. Chris Long

2.07 "Like Mother, Like Daughter"

13 November 2001. Joan Binder Weiss, dir. Dennis Erdman

2.08 "The Ins and Outs of Inns"

20 November 2001. Daniel Palladino, dir. Michael Katleman

2.09 "Run Away, Little Boy"

27 November 2001. John Stephens, dir. Danny Leiner

2.10 "The Bracebridge Dinner"

11 December 2001. Daniel Palladino, dir. Chris Long

2.11 "Secrets and Loans"

22 January 2002. Linda Loiselle Guzik, dir. Nicole Holofcener

2.12 "Richard in Stars Hollow"

29 January 2002. Frank Lombardi, dir. Steve Gomer

2.13 "A-Tisket, A-Tasket"

5 February 2002. Amy Sherman-Palladino, dir. Robert Berlinger

2.14 "It Should've Been Lorelai"

12 February 2002. Daniel Palladino, dir. Lesli Linka Glatter

2.15 "Lost and Found"

26 February 2002. Amy Sherman-Palladino, dir. Gail Mancuso

2.16 "There's the Rub"

9 April 2002. Sheila R. Lawrence, dir. Amy Sherman-Palladino

2.17 "Dead Uncles and Vegetables"

16 April 2002. Daniel Palladino, dir. Jamie Babbit

2.18 "Back in the Saddle Again"

23 April 2002. Linda Loiselle Guzik, dir. Kevin Dowling

2.19 "Teach Me Tonight"

30 April 2002. Amy Sherman-Palladino, dir. Steve Robman

2.20 "Help Wanted"

7 May 2002. Allan Heinberg, dir. Chris Long

2.21 "Lorelai's Graduation Day"

14 May 2002. Daniel Palladino, dir. Jamie Babbit

2.22 "I Can't Get Started"

21 May 2002. Amy Sherman-Palladino, John Stephens, dir. Amy Sherman-Palladino

Season Three

3.01 "Those Lazy-Hazy-Crazy Days"

24 September 2002. Amy Sherman-Palladino, dir. Amy Sherman-Palladino

3.02 "Haunted Leg"

1 October 2002. Amy Sherman-Palladino, dir. Chris Long

3.03 "Application Anxiety"

8 October 2002. Daniel Palladino, dir. Gail Mancuso

3.04 "One's Got Class and the Other One Dyes"

15 October 2002. Daniel Palladino, dir. Steve Robman

3.05 "Eight O'Clock at the Oasis"

22 October 2002. Justin Tanner, dir. Jo Ann Fogle

3.06 "Take the Deviled Eggs..."

5 November 2002. Daniel Palladino, dir. Jamie Babbit

3.07 "They Shoot Gilmores, Don't They?"

12 November 2002. Amy Sherman-Palladino, dir. Kenny Ortega

3.08 "Let the Games Begin"

19 November 2002. Amy Sherman-Palladino, dir. Steve Robman

3.09 "A Deep-Fried Korean Thanksgiving"

26 November 2002. Daniel Palladino, dir. Kenny Ortega

3.10 "That'll Do, Pig"

14 January 2003. Sheila R. Lawrence, dir. Jamie Babbit

3.11 "I Solemnly Swear"

21 January 2003. John Stephens, dir. Carla McCloskey

3.12 "Lorelai out of Water"

28 January 2003. Janet Leahy, dir. Jamie Babbit

3.13 "Dear Emily and Richard"

7 February 2003. Amy Sherman-Palladino, dir. Gail Mancuso

3.14 "Swan Song"

11 February 2003. Daniel Palladino, dir. Chris Long

3.15 "Face-Off"

18 February 2003. John Stephens, dir. Kenny Ortega

3.16 "The Big One"

25 February 2003. Amy Sherman-Palladino, dir. Jamie Babbit

3.17 "A Tale of Poes and Fire"

15 April 2003. Daniel Palladino, dir. Chris Long

3.18 "Happy Birthday, Baby"

22 April 2003. Amy Sherman-Palladino, dir. Gail Mancuso

3.19 "Keg! Max!"

29 April 2003. Daniel Palladino, dir. Chris Long

3.20 "Say Goodnight, Gracie"

6 May 2003. Amy Sherman-Palladino and Janet Leahy, dir. Jamie Babbit

3.21 "Here Comes the Son"

13 May 2003. Amy Sherman-Palladino, dir. Amy Sherman-Palladino

3.22 "Those Are Strings, Pinocchio"

20 May 2003. Daniel Palladino, dir. Jamie Babbit

Season Four

4.01 "Ballrooms and Biscotti"

23 September 2003. Amy Sherman-Palladino, dir. Amy Sherman-Palladino

4.02 "The Lorelais' First Day at Yale"

30 September 2003. Daniel Palladino, dir. Chris Long

4.03 "The Hobbit, the Sofa, and Digger Stiles"

7 October 2003. Amy Sherman-Palladino, dir. Matthew Diamond

4.04 "Chicken or Beef?"

14 October 2003. Jane Espenson, dir. Chris Long

4.05 "The Fundamental Things Apply"

21 October 2003. John Stephens, dir. Neema Barnette

4.06 "An Affair to Remember"

28 October 2003. Amy Sherman-Palladino, dir. Matthew Diamond

4.07 "The Festival of Living Art"

4 November 2003. Daniel Palladino, dir. Chris Long

4.08 "Die, Jerk"

11 November 2003. Daniel Palladino, dir. Tom Moore

4.09 "Ted Koppel's Big Night Out"

18 November 2003. Amy Sherman-Palladino, dir. Jamie Babbit

4.10 "The Nanny and the Professor"

20 January 2004. Scott Kaufer, dir. Peter Lauer

4.11 "In the Clamor and the Clangor"

27 January 2004. Sheila R. Lawrence and Janet Leahy, dir. Michael Grossman

4.12 "A Family Matter"

3 February 2004. Daniel Palladino, dir. Kenny Ortega

4.13 "Nag Hammadi Is Where They Found the Gnostic Gospels"

10 February 2004. Amy Sherman-Palladino, dir. Chris Long

4.14 "The Incredible Shrinking Lorelais"

17 February 2004. Amy Sherman-Palladino and Daniel Palladino, dir. Stephen Clancy

4.15 "Scene in a Mall"

24 February 2004. Daniel Palladino, dir. Chris Long

4.16 "The Reigning Lorelai"

2 March 2004. Jane Espenson, dir. Marita Grabiak

4.17 "Girls in Bikinis, Boys Doin' the Twist, aka Gilmore Girls Gone Wild"

13 April 2004. Amy Sherman-Palladino, dir. Jamie Babbit

4.18 "Tick, Tick, Tick, Boom!"

20 April 2004. Daniel Palladino, dir. Daniel Palladino

4.19 "Afterboom"

27 April 2004. Sheila R. Lawrence, dir. Michael Zinberg

4.20 "Luke Can See Her Face"

4 May 2004. Amy Sherman-Palladino and Daniel Palladino, dir. Matthew Diamond

4.21 "Last Week Fights, This Week Tights"

11 May 2004. Daniel Palladino, dir. Chris Long

4.22 "Raincoats and Recipes"

18 May 2004. Amy Sherman-Palladino, dir. Amy Sherman-Palladino

Season Five

5.01 "Say Goodbye to Daisy Miller"

21 September 2004. Amy Sherman-Palladino, dir. Amy Sherman-Palladino

5.02 "A Messenger, Nothing More"

28 September 2004. Daniel Palladino, dir. Daniel Palladino

5.03 "Written in the Stars"

5 October 2004. Amy Sherman-Palladino, dir. Kenny Ortega

5.04 "Tippecanoe and Taylor, Too"

12 October 2004. Bill Prady, dir. Lee Shallat-Chemel

5.05 "We Got Us a Pippi Virgin!"

19 October 2004. Daniel Palladino, dir. Stephen Clancy

5.06 "Norman Mailer, I'm Pregnant!"

26 October 2004. James Berg and Stan Zimmerman, dir. Matthew Diamond

5.07 "You Jump, I Jump, Jack"

2 November 2004. Daniel Palladino, dir. Kenny Ortega

5.08 "The Party's Over"

9 November 2004. Amy Sherman-Palladino, dir. Eric Laneuville

5.09 "Emily Says Hello"

16 November 2004. Rebecca Rand Kirschner, dir. Kenny Ortega

5.10 "But Not as Cute as Pushkin"

30 November 2004. Amy Sherman-Palladino, dir. Michael Zinberg

5.11 "Women of Questionable Morals"

25 January 2005. Daniel Palladino, dir. Matthew Diamond

5.12 "Come Home"

1 February 2005. Jessica Queller, dir. Kenny Ortega

5.13 "Wedding Bell Blues"

2 February 2005. Amy Sherman-Palladino, dir. Amy Sherman-Palladino

5.14 "Say Something"

15 February 2005. Daniel Palladino, dir. Daniel Palladino

5.15 "Jews and Chinese Food"

22 February 2005. Amy Sherman-Palladino, dir. Matthew Diamond

5.16 "So ... Good Talk"

1 March 2005. Lisa Randolph, dir. Jamie Babbit

5.17 "Pulp Friction"

8 March 2005. James Berg and Stan Zimmerman, dir. Michael Zinberg

5.18 "To Live and Let Diorama"

19 April 2005. Daniel Palladino, dir. Jackson Douglas

5.19 "But I'm a Gilmore!"

26 April 2005. Amy Sherman-Palladino, dir. Michael Zinberg

5.20 "How Many Kropogs to Cape Cod?"

3 May 2005. Bill Prady and Rebecca Rand Kirschner, dir. Jamie Babbit

5.21 "Blame Booze and Melville"

10 May 2005. Daniel Palladino, dir. Jamie Babbit

5.22 "A House Is Not a Home"

17 May 2005. Amy Sherman-Palladino, dir. Amy Sherman-Palladino

Season Six

6.01 "New and Improved Lorelai"

13 September 2005. Amy Sherman-Palladino, dir. Amy Sherman-Palladino

6.02 "Fight Face"

20 September 2005. Daniel Palladino, dir. Daniel Palladino

6.03 "The UnGraduate"

27 September 2005. David S. Roenthal, dir. Michael Zinberg

6.04 "Always a Godmother, Never a God"

4 October 2005. Rebecca Rand Kirshner, dir. Robert Berlinger

6.05 "We've Got Magic to Do"

11 October 2005. Daniel Palladino, dir. Michael Zinberg

6.06 "Welcome to the Doll House"

18 October 2005. Keith Eisner, dir. Jackson Douglas

6.07 "Twenty-One Is the Loneliest Number"

25 October 2005. Amy Sherman-Palladino, dir. Bob Berlinger

6.08 "Let Me Hear Your Balalaikas Ringing Out"

8 November 2005. Daniel Palladino, dir. Kenny Ortega

6.09 "The Prodigal Daughter Returns"

15 November 2005. Amy Sherman-Palladino, dir. Amy Sherman-Palladino

6.10 "He's Slippin' 'em Bread ... Dig?"

22 November 2005. Daniel Palladino, dir. Kenny Ortega

6.11 "The Perfect Dress"

10 January 2006. Amy Sherman-Palladino, dir. Jamie Babbit

6.12 "Just Like Gwen and Gavin"

17 January 2006. Daniel Palladino, dir. Stephen Glancy

6.13 "Friday Night's Alright for Fighting"

31 January 2006. Amy Sherman-Palladino, dir. Kenny Ortega

6.14 "You've Been Gilmored"

7 February 2006. Jordon Nardino, dir. Stephen Clancy

6.15 "A Vineyard Valentine"

14 February 2006. Daniel Palladino, dir. Daniel Palladino

6.16 "Bridesmaids Revisited"

28 February 2006. Rebecca Rand Kirshner, dir. Linda Mendoza

6.17 "I'm OK, You're OK"

4 April 2006. Keith Eisner, dir. Lee Shallat-Chemel

6.18 "The Real Paul Anka"

11 April 2006. Daniel Palladino, dir. Daniel Palladino

6.19 "I Get a Sidekick out of You"

18 April 2006. Amy Sherman-Palladino, dir. Amy Sherman-Palladino

6.20 "Super Cool Party People"

25 April 2006. David S. Rosenthal, dir. Ken Whittingham

6.21 "Driving Miss Gilmore"

2 May 2006. Daniel Palladino and Amy Sherman-Palladino, dir. Jamie Babbit

6.22 "Partings"

9 May 2006. Daniel Palladino and Amy Sherman-Palladino, dir. Amy Sherman-Palladino

Season Seven

7.01 "The Long Morrow"

26 September 2006. David S. Rosenthal, dir. Lee Shallat-Chemel

7.02 "That's What You Get Folks, for Makin' Whoopee"

3 October 2006. Rebecca Rand Kirshner, dir. Bethany Rooney

7.03 "Lorelai's First Cotillion"

10 October 2006. Rina Mimoun, dir. Lee Shallat-Chemel

7.04 "'S Wonderful, 'S Marvelous"

17 October 2006. Gayle Abrams, dir. Victor Nelli

7.05 "The Great Stink"

24 October 2006. Gina Fattore, dir. Michael Schultz

7.06 "Go, Bulldogs!"

7 November 2006. David S. Rosenthal and Rebecca Rand Kirshner, dir. Wil Shriner

7.07 "French Twist"

14 November 2006. David Babcock, dir. Lee Shallat-Chemel

7.08 "Introducing Lorelai Planetarium"

21 November 2006. Jennie Snyder, dir. Lee Shallat-Chemel

7.09 "Knit, People, Knit!"

28 November 2006. David Grae, dir. Kenny Ortega

7.10 "Merry Fisticuffs"

5 December 2006. David S. Rosenthal, dir. Jackson Douglas

7.11 "Santa's Secret Stuff"

23 December 2006. Rebecca Rand Kirshner, dir. Lee Shallat-Chemel

7.12 "To Whom It May Concern"

30 January 2007. David Babcock, dir. Jamie Babbit

7.13 "I'd Rather Be in Philadelphia"

6 February 2007. Rebecca Rand Kirshner, dir. Lee Shallat-Chemel

7.14 "Farewell, My Pet"

13 February 2007. Jennie Snyder, dir. Jamie Babbit

7.15 "I'm a Kayak, Hear Me Roar"

20 February 2007. Rebecca Rand Kirshner, dir. Lee Shallat-Chemel

7.16 "Will You Be My Lorelai Gilmore?"

27 February 2007. Gina Fattore and Gayle Abrams, dir. David Paymer

7.17 "*Gilmore Girls* Only"

6 March 2007. David Babcock, dir. Lee Shallat-Chemel

7.18 "Hay Bale Maze"

17 April 2007. Rebecca Rand Kirschner. Dir. Stephen Clancy

7.19 "It's Just Like Riding a Bike"

24 April 2007. Jennie Snyder, dir. Lee Shallat-Chemel

7.20 "Lorelai, Lorelai"

1 May 2007. David S. Rosenthal, dir.
Bethany Rooney

7.21 "Unto the Beach"

8 May 2007. David Babcock and Jennie
Snyder, dir. Lee Shallat-Chemel

7.22 "Bon Voyage"

15 May 2007. David S. Rosenthal, dir.
Lee Shallat-Chemel

Notes on Contributors

Brenda Boyle is an assistant professor of English and director of the Writing Center at Denison University. She is interested in questions of gender, especially in texts about war, and finds writing about *Gilmore Girls* refreshingly peaceful.

Ritch Calvin is a lecturer in women's studies at SUNY Stony Brook. He has written on (feminist) science fiction for *Extrapolation*, *Science Fiction Research Association Review*, and *American@*. He has an essay on Ana Castillo in the volume *(Un)Making Race, Re-Making Soul: Transformative Aesthetics and the Practice of Freedom*. He is currently working on a book on feminist theory and science fiction writers.

Lindsay Coleman is currently completing his Ph.D. with Screen Studies, the School of Culture and Communication, University of Melbourne. His work appears in *Taking South Park Seriously*, edited by Jeffrey Andrew Weinstock (SUNY Press), and *The War Body on Screen*, edited by Karen Randell and Sean Redmond (Continuum), both in 2008. In addition to being a freelance media journalist in Auckland, New Zealand, in the late 1990s, Lindsay has also acted in commercials. In the last three years he has presented on the series *Firefly*, *The Sopranos*, *Dr. Who*, *Deadwood*, and the films *Inside Man*, *The Craft*, and *Dead Poet's Society*.

Olivia Combe just graduated magna cum laude from Granville (Ohio) High School, where she was National Honor Society president, editor-in-chief of the literary magazine, vice president of the French Club, op-ed columnist for the school paper, and prom queen. She is spending her gap year in Catanduva, São Paulo, Brazil, on a Rotary International exchange program. She plans to matriculate at Oberlin College in 2008, where she will double major in modern languages and English in the hopes of living up to her aspirations of being a journalist abroad.

Anne K. Burke Erickson is a grantwriter, Arts Institute online teacher, and stagemother to some of her own girls. Her diverse publications include business writing cases, pedagogy, social services, and literature — including children's, Irish, British, and American.

Stacia M. Fleegal is a graduate of Spalding University's brief-residency MFA in Writing program. Her poetry has appeared in *Comstock Review, Asphodel, The Blue Moon Review, 3rd Muse Poetry Journal, The Furnace Review* and other journals, and in the anthology *Women. Period.: Women Writing about Menstruation* (Spinsters Ink, 2008). Her poetry chapbook, *A Fling with the Ground,* was released by Finishing Line Press (2008). In 2006, her poetry won first place in the graduate division of the Kentuckiana Metroversity Writing Competition. She is co-founder and co-editor of *Blood Lotus,* an online literary journal, a poetry editor for New Sins Press, and a coordinator in the journals department of the University of Nebraska Press.

Melanie Haupt is a doctoral candidate in the Department of English at the University of Texas at Austin. She is currently writing her dissertation on narratives of cooking and eating in diasporic Indian women's writing. She is also interested in the rhetoric of food and eating in American popular culture.

Erin K. Johns received her M.A. in English at West Virginia University. She attended the University of Pittsburgh where she received her B.A. in English. Erin is enrolled in the Ph.D. program at West Virginia University where she intends to focus her research on both American and British Modernism and its relationship to the British Romantic Sublime.

Tiffany Aldrich MacBain is an assistant professor at the University of Puget Sound, where she teaches 19th-century American literature. Her research interests include race and gender as they intersect with culture, and she is currently working on projects involving surrogate motherhood and societal anxieties surrounding contamination.

Mita Mahato is an assistant professor of English at the University of Puget Sound, where she teaches classes in writing, rhetoric, and culture and 19th-century British literature. Her primary research interests involve the impact of representations of disease on personal and cultural perceptions of the body, and her current project examines the rhetoric of cancer in new media.

Molly McCaffrey is a visiting assistant professor of creative writing at St. Andrew's College and director and managing editor of the St. Andrews College Press. She earned her M.A. in English and creative writing from Miami University and her Ph.D. from the University of Cincinnati. Her scholarly interests include contemporary American literature and ethnic American literature as well as film and television. Her fiction was recently recognized in the North Carolina State University Brenda L. Smart Fiction Contest.

Angela Ridinger-Dotterman received a M.A. from Oregon State University. She is currently a student in the doctoral program in English at the CUNY Graduate Center focusing on American women's literature.

Alicia Skipper earned an M.A. in literature from the University of North Carolina at Wilmington in 2003. Her interests include feminist theory and autobiographical writing. She is currently pursuing a Ph.D. in literature from Arizona State University where she is also a graduate teaching associate.

Kristin L. Smith is a graduate student in the English Department at West Virginia University in Morgantown. She works as a technical writer and lives with her husband, Mark, and her two-year-old son, Aidan.

Daniel Smith-Rowsey is pursuing his doctorate with the University of Nottingham in the United Kingdom. He received his M.A. in critical studies from the Department of Film and Television at the University of Southern California. His recent publications include "Whose Middle-earth Is It?," appearing in *How We Became Middle-earth*, from Walking Tree Publishers, and "Dustin Hoffman," appearing in *Star Studies: The Sixties*, from Rutgers University Press. Daniel's dissertation will probably be called "Representing Rough Rebels: Star-Actors in the Hollywood Renaissance," and his academic interests include performance, emergent genres, new media, and historicization of recent phenomena.

Faye Woods is a Ph.D. candidate in the Film and Television Studies Department at the University of Warwick. She is completing her thesis on "Popular Music, Identity and Representation in Teen Film and Television." She has presented work on *Freaks and Geeks*, *American Dreams* and the British viewing context of U.S. teen television.

Character Index

Anna Nardini 77, 106, 155, 156
April Nardini 6, 7, 76, 77, 98, 106, 155, 156, 167, 168, 191
Asher Fleming 59, 60, 61

Babette Dell 24, 42, 76, 106, 167, 169
Bobbi 40, 42

Caesar 17, 194
Christopher Hayden 13, 15, 25, 29, 36, 37, 41, 42, 43, 45, 47, 68, 69, 74–78, 85–88, 97–99, 102, 110, 116, 133, 143, 148, 153, 156, 160, 163, 165, 166, 174ff, 186, 191, 195, 197
Colin McCrae 41, 42, 111ff, 112ff

Dave Rygalski 41, 137, 139
Dean Forester 1, 12, 15, 24, 25, 33, 36, 37, 38, 41, 47, 64, 66, 69, 70, 71, 72, 73, 75, 78, 84, 88, 90, 92, 93, 94, 102, 103, 133, 136, 137, 139, 149, 151, 152, 160, 163, 168–172, 175, 177, 195
Doyle McMaster 40, 42, 60, 61

Emily Gilmore 6, 8, 13, 14, 19, 28, 29, 31, 40, 42, 43, 45, 46, 63, 67, 68, 69, 70, 71, 72, 73, 74, 76, 77, 78, 89, 90, 91, 92, 107, 115, 116, 117, 118, 119, 120, 122, 125, 127, 130, 132, 134, 143157, 159, 172, 173, 174f~ 176, 177, 182, 183, 187, 197

Finn 41, 111ff, 112ff

Gigi Hayden 76, 78, 105, 108, 156
Gypsy 17, 42, 194

Headmaster Charleston 64, 97

Jackson Belleville 6, 42, 106, 109, 123, 176, 179, 180, 181, 182, 183, 190

Jamie 58, 59, 61
Jason "Digger" Stiles 15, 25, 41, 79ff, 117–120, 160, 163, 166, 188, 195
Jess Mariano 6, 7, 15, 25, 32, 37, 38, 41, 42, 43, 46, 47, 64–67, 71, 73, 65, 102, 103, 106, 133, 134, 136, 137, 149, 151, 160, 163, 169, 170, 172, 195, 197, 198

Kirk Gleason 27, 42, 151, 167

Lane Kim 8, 17, 25, 41, 46, 65, 66, 69, 70, 76, 78, 92, 106, 112f~ 124, 125, 128, 129, 131, 132, 135–139, 140ff, 156, 157, 169, 177, 185, 186, 191, 194
Liz Danes 6, 76, 78, 106
Logan Huntzberger 15, 18, 19, 25, 30, 38, 39–42, 44, 46, 47, 48, 64, 66, 67, 73, 74, 77, 97, 102, 109, 111ff, 112ff, 134, 154, 160, 163, 168, 169, 171, 172, 195, 201
Lorelai Gilmore 1, 2, 5, 6, 8, 9, 12, 13, 15, 18, 24, 25, 26, 27, 28, 29, 30, 31, 33, 35, 36, 37, 38, 39, 40, 41, 42, 43, 44, 45, 46 , 47, 48, 49, 55, 58, 59, 63–78, 79ff, 83–94, 97–110, 111ff, 112ff, 114–126, 127–139, 140ff, 143–157, 159–169, 172, 173, 175–78, 181–191, 194, 195, 197, 198, 201, 202
Lorelai Gilmore (Richard's mother), 14, 146
Louise Grant 56, 66, 71, 136
Lucy 38, 41, 48
Luke Danes 2, 6, 7, 9, 15, 24, 25, 26, 28, 37, 41, 43, 66, 67, 68, 69, 74, 75, 76, 77, 78, 79, 88, 97, 98, 102, 103, 104, 106, 143, 146, 149, 151, 155, 156, 160, 163–169, 176, 177, 185–191, 195, 196, 201

Madeline Lynn 56, 66, 71, 136
Marty 38, 39, 41, 46, 64, 171, 172
Max Medina 15, 25, 41, 43, 70, 77, 79ff, 91, 98, 102, 103, 104, 109, 143, 160, 163–167, 182, 189, 195

Mia 68, 75, 79ff, 147
Michel Gerard 17, 78, 146, 151, 190, 194
Miss Patty 24, 70, 75, 78, 94ff, 167
Mitchum Huntzberger 30, 40, 44, 48, 73, 74
Morey Dell 106
Mrs. Kim 6, 17, 42, 49, 66, 71, 76, 92, 94ff, 112ff, 124, 125, 137, 156, 194, 200

Olivia 41, 48

Paris Geller 8, 18, 30, 40, 42, 46, 47, 48, 50, 51, 55–62, 64, 66, 71, 72, 76, 102, 131, 136, 140ff, 155, 170, 184, 194, 201
Pendleton Lott 73

Rachel 65
Richard Gilmore 6, 13, 14, 28, 29, 40, 42, 43, 44, 46, 59, 63, 65, 68, 69, 71, 72, 73, 75, 76, 77, 78, 89, 98, 99, 109, 115–119, 132, 134, 143, 152, 153, 154, 157, 166, 168, 172, 173, 174ff, 176, 177, 183, 187, 197, 200

Rory Gilmore 1, 5–9, 12, 13, 15, 18, 19, 20, 24- 28, 30, 31, 33, 35–49, 55–61, 63–77, 79ff, 83–94, 97–100, 103, 105, 106, 107, 110, 111ff, 112ff, 115–117, 120–122, 125, 127–129, 131–139, 140ff, 141ff, 143–157, 159–166, 168–173, 174ff, 175, 177, 181–191, 194, 196, 1297, 198, 201, 202
Rune 180

Sherry Tinsdale 76, 99, 133, 156, 165
Sookie St. James 6, 8, 25, 26, 33, 42, 43, 49, 65, 72, 76, 106, 109, 118, 120, 121, 123–126, 131, 136, 146, 147, 151, 176–183, 187, 189, 191, 194

Taylor Doose 134, 151, 181, 200
T.J. 76
Tristin Dugray 25, 36, 37, 41, 56, 57, 66, 169, 197

Zack 41, 42, 106, 156

General Index

Alice 7, 82, 194
Ally MacBeal 7, 84
Amanpour, Christiane 12, 14, 44, 110, 121
American Idol 2, 21ff
American Pie 58, 100–102
Angel 3, 198
Atkinson, Ti-Grace 10

Babette's Feast 179
backlash (feminist), 83, 93
The Bangles 71, 136
Baudrillard, Jean 22, 32, 34
Beck 136, 139
Beverly Hills 90210 58
Big Night 178–180
Blossom 58
Bowie, David 133, 136, 139
The Brady Bunch 5, 81, 94ff
Branch, Michelle 137
Bring It On 54
Buffy, the Vampire Slayer 2, 3, 4, 5, 7, 12, 20, 58, 131, 198, 201

capitalism 24, 26, 115
Charlotte: A Tale of Truth 53
Charmed 127
Cheers 6
Chocolat 179
Chung, Connie 50
The Clash 136
class 9, 14, 15, 19, 30, 31, 44, 73, 89, 114–116, 118, 119, 122, 125, 129, 130, 134, 135, 174ff
Clinton, Hillary 50, 75
Commander in Chief 12, 84
commodification 115
consumption 26, 74, 114, 115, 120, 121, 125, 126, 128, 129, 138, 177, 178, 183, 188–191
CSI 8, 16

Dawson's Creek 127, 131, 132, 136, 144
Dead Kennedys 139
Designing Women 8, 12
Desperate Housewives 8, 200
Dr. Quinn, Medicine Woman 7, 12
The Donna Reed Show 7, 14, 72, 81, 86, 93, 94ff, 175
Dragonfly Inn 12, 75, 78, 118, 121, 151, 152, 155, 157, 187
Drake, Nick 136

The Dukes of Hazzard 27

Echo and the Bunnymen 135
Election 55
Eliot, George 15–16
Everwood 12, 201
Everybody Loves Raymond 8

Family Friendly Programming Forum 64, 79ff, 108, 112ff, 159, 173
fanfic 2, 193–199, 202
The Feminine Mystique 81, 94ff
femininity 4, 35, 53, 54, 60, 109, 116, 140, 145, 160–165, 167–169, 172, 173
feminism 1, 2, 7, 8, 10, 11, 12, 35, 36, 40, 44, 47, 49, 76, 80, 81, 83, 84, 85, 88, 89, 91, 93, 94, 114, 125, 144, 145; postfeminism 11, 12, 13, 18, 19; second wave feminism 12, 35, 36, 82, 83, 86; third wave feminism 35, 36, 42, 48, 88
femmes couvertes 54, 62ff
Fey, Tina 52
Foo Fighters 139
Forster, E. M. 50, 62ff
Fountains of Wayne 101
Frasier 6
Friends 4, 20ff, 104, 144
Fugazi 139

gender 3, 8, 14, 37, 45, 83, 104, 114, 125, 159, 160–165, 167, 168, 173, 195
Gingrich, Kathleen 50
Gingrich, Newt 50
Girlfriends 5, 8
The Godfather 121
Goffin, Louise 19, 129
Golden Girls 8
The Graduate 100
Grandaddy 136
Gray, Macy 135

Hanisch, Carol 10

I Love Lucy 7, 81
Independence Inn 12, 20, 30, 68, 73, 74, 75, 163
Iron John 166

Jesus and Mary Chain 132
Joel, Billy 133
Judging Amy 84

King, Carole 19, 27, 128, 129, 132, 139

The La's 28, 132
Law & Order 8, 16
Leave It to Beaver 81, 94ff
Little House on the Prairie 52
Little Women 53
Lord of the Rings 123, 201
Lost 201
Love and Marriage 17

The Mary Tyler Moore Show 7, 10, 11, 12, 18, 194
masculinity 10, 101, 110, 139, 160–173, 187, 188, 190
Matchbox 20, 137
Matlock 16
matriarchy 6, 14, 143, 181, 190
Maude 8, 10
Mazzy Star 132
Mean Girls 51, 52
Mills, C. Wright 10
motherhood 4, 54, 76, 82, 89, 90, 97, 99–103, 105, 110, 123, 124, 144, 145, 150, 151, 154, 155
mothering 87, 90, 91, 93, 114, 122, 148–150, 153, 155
Mötley Crüe 136
Murphy Brown 7, 12, 13, 82, 83, 176

The New Adventures of Old Christine 7, 21ff, 194

Nico 136
98° 135

One Day at a Time 5, 11, 12, 13, 82
One Tree Hill 127
Othello 51
Over the Top 17
Oz 16

Palladino, Daniel 13, 16, 184
patriarchy 6, 13, 31, 40, 42–45, 49, 83, 85, 88, 90, 93, 98, 104, 115–120, 122, 143, 190
Phair, Liz 136
Phillips, Sam 28, 128, 132, 139
Pleasantville 176
Prince 133

Quayle, Dan 82, 83, 176

Reba 5, 7
The Return of Jezebel James 21ff
Rhoda 7, 194
Roseanne 7, 17, 84

Scream 58
Seinfeld 3, 175, 195
Seventh Heaven 16, 127
Sex and the City 2, 3, 4, 8, 104, 144
sexuality 8, 19, 36, 44, 57, 60, 61, 62, 70, 91, 100, 105, 161, 180
Shakespeare, William 4, 53, 69
Sherman-Palladino, Amy 5, 6, 9, 13, 16, 17, 18, 21ff, 49, 65, 79ff, 97, 99, 110ff, 111ff, 112ff, 133, 181, 182, 184, 187, 189, 194, 198, 201, 202
The Shins 132
The Simpsons 3, 16
Sisters 8
Skid Row 132
Smallville 127
The Smiths 135
Sonic Youth 121, 132, 136, 140ff
The Sopranos 16, 18
Sparks 132, 140ff
Star Trek 201
Stars Hollow 2, 13, 16, 17, 19, 20, 23, 24, 25, 26, 27, 28, 29, 30, 31, 32, 34, 36, 37, 58, 66, 68, 73, 74, 75, 78, 97, 100, 103, 104, 106, 107, 109, 114, 115, 121, 123, 128, 129, 157, 159, 164, 165, 167, 169–171, 175, 181, 183, 184, 188–191, 197, 201, 202
Steinem, Gloria 10

Taming of the Shrew 53
thirtysomething 87

Ugly Betty 8
Uncle Tom's Cabin 53

The Velvet Underground 136, 139
Veronica's Closet 17
Voltaire 30

Waits, Tom 135
The Waltons 5, 27
West Wing 3, 16
The Wide, Wide World 53
Wilco 132, 135

The Wild One 87, 94ff
The Wizard of Oz 16
Women's Liberation Movement 172, 173
Women's Murder Club 21ff

Xena, the Warrior Princess 2, 3
XTC 131, 132

The Yale Daily News 15, 18, 38, 60, 73
Yo La Tengo 34, 132, 135

Zack 41, 42, 106, 156